SLAVERY IN DUTCH SOUTH AFRICA

AFRICAN STUDIES SERIES   44

T0382627

OTHER BOOKS IN THE SERIES

SLAVERY IN DUTCH
SOUTH AFRICA

NIGEL WORDEN

Lecturer in History, University of Cape Town

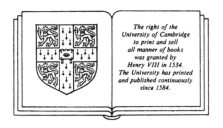

CAMBRIDGE UNIVERSITY PRESS

CAMBRIDGE

LONDON   NEW YORK   NEW ROCHELLE
MELBOURNE   SYDNEY

CAMBRIDGE UNIVERSITY PRESS
Cambridge, New York, Melbourne, Madrid, Cape Town, Singapore,
São Paulo, Delhi, Dubai, Tokyo, Mexico City

Cambridge University Press
The Edinburgh Building, Cambridge CB2 8RU, UK

Published in the United States of America by Cambridge University Press, New York

www.cambridge.org
Information on this title: www.cambridge.org/9780521152662

First published 1985
Reprinted 1987
First paperback printing 2010

A catalogue record for this publication is available from the British Library

Library of Congress Catalogue Card Number: 84–12721

ISBN 978-0-521-25875-3 Hardback
ISBN 978-0-521-15266-2 Paperback

To the memory of my father
CHARLES NORMAN WORDEN

Contents

Illustrations

Map

Figures

Tables

Tables

Acknowledgements

Research for this study has been carried out over a period of six years and in three countries, and I am indebted to a large number of people and institutions for the help which they have given me during that time.

Support for research was provided by Jesus College, Cambridge, and the Social Science Research Council in London. Amongst fellow researchers whose interest has helped me, I am especially grateful to Roger Beck, Margaret Kinsman, Susan Newton-King, Mary Rayner, Robert Ross and Robert Shell. Valuable comments on my work were given by Hermann Giliomee, Shula Marks and Jim Armstrong. Hans Heese, Leon Hattingh and the staff at the Instituut vir Historiese Navorsing at the University of the Western Cape permitted me to join their computer *opgaaf* project upon which some of the findings in this study are based, and Robert Ross and Pieter van Duin of the University of Leiden gave me access to their collection of census return figures. Colin Webb and Christopher Saunders permitted me to test out some of my material by teaching at the University of Cape Town, as well as providing me with a base in South Africa which has now become more permanent. Most of all, John Iliffe of St John's College, Cambridge, has guided me with care and patience from the time when he first evoked my interest in South Africa by his undergraduate classes, through my period of doctoral research to the end of this project, and I am exceptionally grateful to him.

I have been fortunate to have found Caroline Kingdon in Cape Town, who converted my illegible scribble into clear text with exceptional patience and efficiency, and Ken Behr, cartographer in the Department of Geography, University of Cape Town, who produced the map and figures. Finally I am indebted to all those who supported me personally at various stages of my research: James Patrick, David Lowe, Marica Frank, Nora Smith, Janine de Villiers and the staff of the Department of History at the University of Cape Town, especially Marie Maud whose tragic death in 1981 cast the greatest shadow over my work. Most of all, my thanks to my parents, Vena and John Bates, who have encouraged, aided and supported me in everything.

Cape Town
December 1983

Abbreviations

AR	Algemene Rijksarchief, The Hague
CA	Cape (Government) Archives, Cape Town
PRO	Public Records Office, London
Rxds	Rixdollars
SAL	South African Library, Cape Town
VOC	Verenigde Oostindische Compagnie (Dutch East India Company)

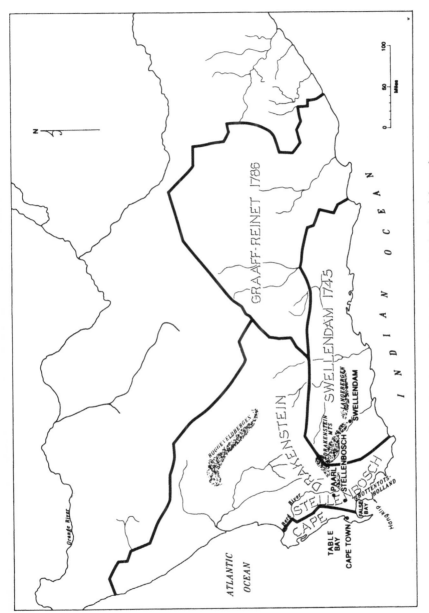

Cape colony showing administrative districts in the eighteenth century

1

The study of Cape slavery

The study of slavery has undergone a transformation in the past three decades as a result of the prolific output of writing by historians, as well as sociologists, economists and anthropologists. Much of the impetus behind these developments came from the United States, where the Civil Rights movement of the 1950s and 1960s drew attention to the historical plight of American Negroes and the upsurge of Afro-American studies in the 1960s began to probe the institution of slavery which had first brought them to the New World. Slave historians had much prejudice to overcome. Writing in 1952, Kenneth Stampp referred to the slow beginnings of a reaction against the prevailing bias, 'It may only be a sign of the effeteness of the new generation of scholars, but there is a tendency among them to recognize that it is at least conceivable that a colleague on the other side of the Mason and Dixon line could write something significant about slavery.'[1]

Thirty years later analysis of North American slavery has gone far beyond the levels of sophistication which Stampp could have imagined. Seminal and often controversial works opened up new approaches of study, such as that of Elkins on resistance and passivity, the examination of the contribution of slaves to the dynamics of Deep South society by Blassingame, Genovese and others, the calculation of profitability using econometric techniques by Fogel and Engerman and perhaps most significantly the assessment of class structure and paternalism of slaveowners by Genovese.[2] Moreover, the impact of this work gradually came to be felt in a comparative context. Comparison with other slave systems was explicit in the work of Elkins, Genovese and Davis, which raised problems in the techniques of comparative history, notably the applicability of models for one economic and social system to another.[3] The plantation systems of the New World provide one obvious group for comparative analysis, and Cooper's pioneering study of plantation slavery in East Africa has direct parallels with them.[4] Study of slave societies which were based on very different premises, such as those of the classical Mediterranean or African and Asian indigenous systems, has also benefited from increasing interest in slavery as a system of labour and exploitation. One recent comparative work extends its scope far beyond

1

European colonial slavery to include medieval Korea and the ancient world amongst other societies.[5] Study of African slavery has also benefited by the work of anthropologists and has stressed the interaction between the external slave trade and the developments within the continent of slavery as a means of production.[6]

This is a study of the slavery that existed in South Africa during its earliest period of colonial rule; the Cape colony under the control of the Dutch East India Company, the Verenigde Oostindische Compagnie (VOC) from 1652 to 1795. Justification is needed for adding yet another case study to the long list which has emerged in the last twenty years. This is made on two counts. First, the state of writing about slavery at the Cape is almost equivalent to that which existed in the United States at the time of Stampp's comments in 1952. The emphasis in recent developments of South African historiography has been on industrialisation and its impact at the end of the nineteenth century, and only now is research into earlier periods of Cape colonial history beginning to develop beyond a parochial and often apologist stage. Secondly, slavery in Dutch South Africa was similar in many ways to those of other colonial societies. It was closely integrated into a colonial economic and mercantilist system whose driving force lay elsewhere – in the Netherlands and the VOC centre of power in the East Indies – and in which slaves were used as units of coerced labour with an overwhelmingly economic function. Yet there were also significant differences. Cape slavery thus has a part to play in highlighting the mechanics of slavery in a comparative framework.

Many of the assumptions made about slavery in South Africa need to be challenged in the light of recent research into the VOC period. The traditional belief that the economy of the Cape colony before the nineteenth century was stagnant and pre-capitalistic has led to the view that slavery was relatively mild in comparison with the export-orientated staple plantations of North America and the Caribbean. The assumed low levels of profitability of Cape farming and the isolation of the colony from external market forces led to the belief that Cape slaves were not intensively exploited as a labour force and were primarily domestic servants, treated with care and a high degree of paternal kindliness, which contrasted with the violence of the coercive plantation systems that existed in other slave societies. Some of these opinions seem to serve ideological purposes rather than historical truth, the implication being that early South Africa lacked the racial tensions and rigidity of North America. Their influence has been perpetuated by a recent comparative study of South Africa and North America which utilises the only available secondary works on the subject.[7]

Now, however, many of the fundamental beliefs about early Cape economy and society are beginning to be challenged. Essays in two edited collections on the pre-industrial Cape published in 1979 and 1980 marked the start of the process, emphasising the levels of interaction amongst the Cape population and the degree of social transformation that had taken place by the end of the VOC period.[8] Close analysis of land and census records are producing new

2

insights into demographic trends and the spatial distribution of property ownership.[9] The nature of the economy is being completely re-assessed. It is now clear that the early Cape was not an isolated economic system but was integrated into the wider structure of the VOC's mercantilist empire, with a level of capitalist farming which responded closely to market forces.[10] Analysis of legal records has also stressed the role of the VOC administration in maintaining the hegemony of a wealthy elite of slaveowners.[11]

Many of these developments have important consequences for the study of Cape slavery. Ten years ago the only comprehensive accounts of the subject were a descriptive and largely anecdotal work written before any of the developments in slave studies described above, and an account of the process of emancipation in the nineteenth century which was based entirely on British archive and printed material.[12] Several monographs dealt with specific aspects of slavery, but it was not until 1973 that the value of applying some of the insights of comparative slave studies was realised in an article which pointed out that Cape slavery was by no means as 'mild' as prevailing orthodoxy had suggested.[13] Examination of the impact of slavery was included in the debate which developed around the origins of class formation and racial attitudes in South Africa, although with more emphasis on the pastoral frontier than the main area of slave use in the western Cape.[14] The first systematic account of slavery in the VOC period by Armstrong appeared in the 1979 collection, although it is of necessity brief and shows only a fraction of his extensive archival research.[15] Elphick and Shell have systematically examined manumission records and the role of Free Blacks, Böeseken and Hattingh have used records of sale in the period before c. 1720 to analyse early profitability and Ross has produced a major study of slave resistance based on judicial records.[16] Other work, notably by Shell and Rayner, is in progress.[17]

This study is an attempt to draw together some of these new developments based on my own research into rural slavery under VOC rule and to set Cape slavery in a comparative context.[18] From a small garrison, refreshment station and trading post established in 1652, the VOC settlement grew into an extensive colony by the time of its takeover by the British in 1795, in which arable agriculture, wine production and pastoral farming were major occupations and Cape Town was a sizeable port and trading centre. In this process of growth and diversification, slavery played an important part. As the basis of the arable labour system, it underpinned the development of a major sector of the economy, and was also used in Cape Town, although to a lesser extent in the pastoral regions further inland. The proportion of slaves in the total population and the incidence of slaveholding was high in comparison with other colonial slave societies of the period. The levels of profitability obtained by some colonists from their slaves were akin to those calculated for the plantation systems of the New World. The process of capital accumulation in the colony owed much to the ownership and exploitation of slave labour.

On the other hand, the Cape slave system possessed some unusual features. The small scale of most slaveholding units and the extremely diverse ethnic origin of slaves from a range of African and Asian societies, together with the limited development of a locally born slave population, meant that the potential for a clearly identifiable slave culture or unity was restricted, especially in the rural areas. 'The world the slaves made' at the Cape did not offer the same degree of refuge from the full impact of the master and his control system that it did in many New World societies. Moreover, close contacts between master and slaves did not lead automatically to the paternalistic relationship which comparative slave studies might lead one to expect. The isolation of many farmsteads in a society in which male slaves greatly outnumbered male colonists led to a level of control and coercion which at local levels could be violent and extreme. The lack of differentiated labour functions in an economy which inhibited the development of specialised slave skills, limited the scope for a hierarchical system of work routine and incentives. The slave response to this situation was varied, but involved a high level of individual resistance, although lack of unity or concentration of forces on farmsteads prevented any attempt at rebellion during the VOC period.

There were, however, variations in the character and the forces shaping Cape slavery in differing sectors of its economy. Although the majority of slaves were concentrated in the arable rural districts of the western Cape, a significant proportion also worked in Cape Town. In the town slaves were used for services rather than for production and there was a greater degree of social mobility including some access to manumission. A degree of independent slave culture existed, especially in the adoption of Islam. Although the basic instruments of control existed as much in Cape Town as in the hinterland, there were variations in the nature of slavery which resulted from the differences of the urban economic system and its social structure.

The most significant feature of Cape slavery was that it shaped much of the society of early colonial South Africa. The shortage of slaves led to the incorporation of Khoikhoi and San labourers into the economy. They entered into a social structure already conditioned by the slave system and, although nominally free, became subject to similar means of coercion and control which were later to be applied in a modified form to Bantu-speaking labourers. The widespread use of slave labour meant that there was little development of a settler labouring class, and no indentured labour system of the kind that developed in colonial New England or the West Indies in their early stages of European settlement. The *knechts*, VOC employees who were hired out to farmers on contract, were few in number and were mainly used as slave overseers and teachers rather than as manual labourers. Although institutionalised racism did not emerge until later in South Africa's history after contact with peoples of the interior and the growth of industrialisation, society in the areas dominated by slavery at the beginning of the nineteenth century was already polarised along racial lines in the rural regions and was moving in that direction in the city. The processes of the later period by which racial divides became entrenched still further coincided with the distinctions that had emerged within the slave society of the Dutch Cape.

A final word should be said about sources. The administrative and financial concerns of the VOC led to the collection of detailed annual census records, as well as inventories and deeds of sale which would be the envy of historians of other colonial societies of the period. Many of these have been preserved, although records are much fuller for the eighteenth than the seventeenth century. The census returns for Cape Town and its immediate hinterland after 1773 and the records of the Fiscaal's office, responsible for the registration of slave sales and minor criminal offences in Cape Town, are however missing.[19] Moreover, the Cape entirely lacks any personal diaries or records of slaveowners apart from official estate inventories and accounts, and there are no writings by slaves themselves. Re-creation of the social conditions in which slaves lived and worked is thus not easy. The main sources of such information are accounts of travellers to the colony and the extensively preserved criminal records of the local landdrosts and the central Council of Justice. It is only in the evidence given either as accused or as witnesses that the voices of slaves may be heard, if obscured by the intervention of the clerks who summarised the evidence in their own words. By their nature, criminal records reflect a rather unrepresentative view of society.[20] Nevertheless, much of the evidence obtained from these sources was given incidentally by slaves or others who mentioned aspects of their lives which were not central to the case in question. They thus provide a means of scratching below the surface into the lives and experiences of an under-privileged group of people who left no written records of their own. Many of the cases also reveal points of tension which emphasise some of the dynamics of Cape slave society. Analysis of that society may thus bring the Dutch Cape into the wider framework of comparative slave studies and contribute to the changing historiography of early South Africa.

2

The creation and growth of a slave society

The introduction of slavery to the Cape was the result of the policy of the Dutch East India Company. Although a few domestic slaves were used by the Dutch in the first years of the settlement at Table Bay, the widespread use of slave labour for cultivation had not been envisaged by the Company's directors, the Heren XVII, when they gave instructions for the establishment of a 'place of refreshment' there.[1] From the start, however, Van Riebeeck complained in his despatches at the inability of the small garrison to produce sufficient fruit, vegetables and grain to feed itself as well as to supply passing ships, and suggested the importation of 'some industrious Chinese', or slaves obtained from the south-east African coast.[2] It was the proposal to establish permanent burgher farmers in the region which gave the impetus to the idea of using slaves as the main source of labour. In April 1655, three years after his arrival, Van Riebeeck wrote in his despatch to the Heren XVII favouring the idea of burgher farming that,

> to place them the sooner on their legs, a good many slaves would be necessary for them which could, as before stated, be easily fetched from Madagascar or even India and given out upon credit until the settlers are in a condition to pay for them ... we shall at all events send to Madagascar for some slaves for the use of the settlers – as well as of the Company.[3]

The first shipments of slaves for private ownership were landed in 1658; one brought by the Company from the Guinea Coast, and another of Angolan slaves captured from the Portuguese.[4] Some were forwarded to Batavia and others kept in Company service at the Castle garrison in Cape Town, but at least forty were distributed amongst the burghers. The first year of agrarian slave labour was a disaster; many slaves died of disease and inability to adapt to the rigours of a Cape winter, and more deserted into the interior. Only a few months after the landings a group of burghers brought many of the slaves they had been given on credit back to the Castle, starting that it would be easier to do without them, and asking for remission of their debts of purchase.[5] By the time Van Riebeeck left in 1662, there were only twenty-three privately owned slaves in the colony.[6] It was not until the 1670s that there were further major imports; by 1677 there were eighty-one slave males and twenty-two females in burgher possession, and the figures rose steadily during the last two decades of the century as the rural economy of the settlement expanded. By 1700, there was a total of 838 slaves, of whom 668 were adult males and fifty-four were children.[7]

The first twenty-five years of slave labour use at the Cape were thus beset with difficulty. Nevertheless, despite problems of desertion, by January 1680 the Council of Policy was determined to increase slave numbers and to ensure the continuation of the slave system.[8] Indentured Company servants, *knechts*, were also used by the farmers, especially in the first decades, and there were sixty-two under contract in 1700, but the distinction between slave and hired labourer was clearly established from the start, and there was no blurring of status of the kind that some historians have described in early colonial North America.[9] Slavery was introduced to support burgher agriculture and its growth was to be closely associated with the development of the rural economy in the following 140 years of Dutch Company rule.

The support of the VOC for Van Riebeeck's proposals was of major significance in the creation of a slave society. The immediate causes of the importation of slaves were the manpower shortage at the garrison and the difficulty of cultivating the required amount of produce in adverse geographical conditions by Company employees, which had led to the introduction of burgher farming.[10] Yet the choice of slavery as the labour system on which settler agriculture was to be based was caused by other factors.

One reason was the apparent lack of any viable alternative labour source which would fit in with the Company's strategy for the settlement. There were major impediments to using indigenous labour as hired labourers or as slaves. There was no means at first of enforcing Khoikhoi to work for the colonist farmers without enslavement; they had an abundance of grazing land and cattle, an intact social organisation, and could have easily evaded attempts at coercion by the Company and settlers by moving further inland. Although Van Riebeeck, in frustration at the inability to secure regular trade with the Peninsular Khoi and disputes over land and cattle (which both groups viewed as having been stolen from the other), did propose a scheme of enslaving them in 1654, the Heren XVII did not approve of such a move; enslavement of indigenous peoples was forbidden by the VOC.[11]

As the colony expanded and Khoikhoi polities disintegrated, indigenous labour was used on the farms, both as serfs and wage labourers. During the first decades, however, the VOC was determined to attempt to maintain amicable relations with the Khoikhoi to ensure regular supplies of meat from their herds. It was also concerned to limit contacts between the settlement and the hinterland; extension of control over an area outside the immediate confines of the Castle and gardens was not planned. In Java, the Moluccas and Ceylon, Company rule had been extended to protect profitable trading routes and supply areas on the initiatives of local officials, although attempts were made to rule through local chiefs and kings and colonisation was not encouraged.[12] It was not intended that the Cape should follow the same pattern, since there was no possibility of profitable trading goods to offset the costs of administration. Numerous instructions and decrees issued in the Netherlands and at the Cape attempted to limit trading contacts between the burghers and the Khoikhoi as part of the strategy of the Company to maintain the isolation of the settlement from the hinterland.[13]

Another alternative to slavery was to encourage emigration from Europe of men who would act as indentured labourers on the newly established farms of the Cape. Here also there were conflicts with Company policy. The establishment of settler farms was a concession by the VOC in an attempt to maintain the economic viability of the refreshment station, but it did not want to encourage large-scale emigration and the first farmers were Company servants released from their contracts of service.[14] Although during the 1680s there was a larger number of immigrants, including the Huguenot refugees of 1688–9, during the first decade numbers were deliberately limited. Some *knechts* did act as contractual labour, but the experience of the first couple of years of the settlement seemed to indicate that labour undertaken by Company servants alone would be unsatisfactory. Moreover, the expense of hiring labour on a contractual wage basis would handicap the struggling early farming community.[15]

It seemed clear therefore to Van Riebeeck that labour would have to be sought elsewhere. His suggestion of using Chinese labour reflected the use that was made of Chinese immigrant labourers in Batavia, whose value as industrious workers would be appreciated by the VOC.[16] There were plans to send insolvent Chinese workers to the Cape, although the Heren XVII raised the problem of the cost of their passage and it was recognised that most of them would wish to return to the East or establish themselves as traders rather than remain a subservient labour force in the colony.[17] Indeed, some Chinese traders did come to Cape Town in the VOC period but not as slaves.

The use of slaves thus seemed to comply more readily with the policies of the VOC than any other potential labour system. Another important factor was the experience which the Dutch had of slave trading and slave labour in their colonial system. Just as the importation of Negro slaves into New England was largely the result of the English experience in the West Indies and the channels of trade between the two regions, so the introduction and use of slaves at the Cape was closely associated with the Dutch slave trade from West Africa and the experience of slavery in the VOC empire in Asia.[18] The first slaves brought to the Cape were obtained from West Africa with the backing of the VOC's sister company, the Dutch West India Company, which was heavily involved in the trans-Atlantic slave trade, although rivalry between them prevented further regular use of that source of supply.[19] In the East Indies, the VOC had contact with indigenous Asian slave systems, and slaves were used by the Company in Batavia for public works as well as on some of the spice-producing islands. Indigenous slave supply systems, such as that centred on Sulawesi (the Celebes), were utilised by the VOC who developed the slaving links established by the Portuguese. There was thus already in Batavia a slave legal code, and under Coen slavery was extended on many of the islands of the Indonesian archipelago.[20] Van Riebeeck was well aware of the implications and advantages of using slave labour and was following Batavian precedent; slavery at the Cape was established within an already existing legal framework since the Cape came under Batavian authority.

The early introduction of slavery in the colony was thus the result of a decision of the VOC, influenced by its experiences and policies in the East Indies and its desire to retain control over a limited area of agrarian settlement at the Cape. This was of major significance to the development of Cape slave society. Slavery was not established because it was felt to be particularly suited to the kind of economy or society which the Company envisaged at the Cape. Yet its identity with burgher agriculture was developed from the start. As the colony expanded to produce a settlement which deviated considerably from the purely commercial orientation envisaged by its founders, slavery also spread. It became the mainstay of arable farming in the western districts, played a significant role in the functioning of Cape Town as a centre of exchange and was used to a lesser extent for domestic and pastoral labour in the remoter northern and eastern regions. In many of these occupations, comparative study indicates that slavery was not a characteristic form of labour; for example, grain production was rarely associated with slavery in other colonial settlements.[21] Company policy and the legislative structures which it introduced nevertheless made it a virtually universal labour system amongst Cape arable producers. The early precedent of using slaves in extensive agriculture was thus of primary importance.

The Company had indicated that it regarded slavery as necessary in order to produce the required surplus production by giving slaves on credit to the first burghers. It continued to express this belief after the expansion of farming and with the growth of a sizeable immigrant community. The initial period of difficulty in the early years of the colony was gradually overcome, as methods of extensive cultivation were adopted, further land grants made and wine began to be produced.[22] All of these developments were dependent on the use of slave labour, and after the placing of the arable economy on a firm basis in the 1680s, slave numbers rose steadily, as Figure 1 shows. In 1690 there were 350 privately owned slaves altogether; by the end of VOC rule in 1795 the figure recorded in official census returns was 16,839 although this doubtless underestimated the actual total.[23] In addition, and not included in Figure 1, the Company itself owned a number of slaves throughout the period, varying from over 300 during the later seventeenth century to between 400 and 600 in the eighteenth century.[24] The vast majority of the Company slaves worked in Cape Town, although some were based on Company outposts and used in rural labour, especially during the seventeenth century, and others were occasionally hired out to burghers.[25]

The increase in slave numbers was closely associated with the growth of the burgher population and particularly the expansion of arable agriculture. As

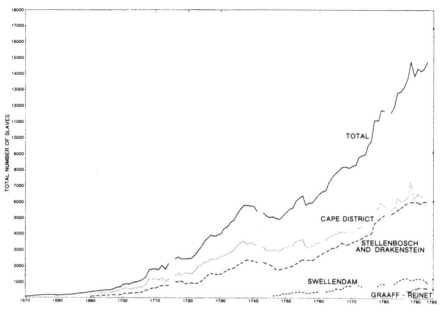

1 Total number of slaves per district recorded in census returns, 1670–1795

Sources: Annual census returns available in Algemene Rijksarchief, The Hague (VOC series) and Cape (Government) Archives, Cape Town (J series)

Mentzel, an observant visitor to the Cape, stated of the 1730s, 'the expansion of the colony demands an ever increasing number of slaves. Every farmer requires many more slaves than members of his own household to grow his crops and develop his land.'[26] The expansion of Cape Town also led to an increasing number of urban slaves. The growth of the burgher population in the course of the eighteenth century was rapid, caused by low marriage ages, high fertility and low mortality rates as well as some continued increase by the granting of burgher rights.[27] Nevertheless, from the end of the first decade of the eighteenth century the number of privately owned slaves outnumbered that of the burgher population in the colony. By December 1713, there were 209 more slaves than burghers and although the total size of each group grew at comparable levels, burghers never again obtained ascendancy of number during the VOC period, as Table 2.1 shows.

Although the ratio of slaves to freemen in the private sector was very much less than that in plantation societies such as the British West Indian sugar islands or the Zanzibari clove plantations, where ratios of 10:1 or 5:1 were normal, the Cape figures do compare favourably with several other notable slave societies.[28] According to a sociological study of slavery in the Roman Empire 'only a handful of human societies can properly be called "slave

Table 2.1 *Slave and burgher numbers, 1692–1793*

Year	Number of slaves	Number of burghers	Slave percentage of freemen numbers
1692	337	799	42.2
1701	891	1,265	70.4
1711	1,771	1,756	100.8
1723	2,922	2,245	130.2
1733	4,709	3,074	153.2
1743	5,361	3,972	135.0
1753	6,045	5,419	111.6
1763	7,211	6,750	106.8
1773	8,902	8,465	117.0
1783	11,950	11,040	108.2
1793	14,747	13,830	106.6

Sources: Census returns, CA J 183 (1692) and Beyers 1967, pp. 339–49. The figure for slaves in 1773 has been altered from 9,902 to 8,902, a copying mistake made by the Cape Town official transcribing the original rolls, AR VOC 4121, Cape census returns, 1773

societies", if by slave society we mean a society in which slaves play an important part in production and form a high proportion (say 20%) of the total population'.[29] Comparisons of the Cape with other societies that qualify as 'slave societies' under this definition are enlightening. Estimates made for the slave systems of the classical world, notably Roman Italy or classical Athens, vary enormously, but the average percentage given for slaves in the total population of Italy in the imperial period, whose economy was more akin to the Cape than the New World plantation systems, is between 30% and 40%.[30] Total population figures for the Cape are lacking because of the absence of any precise enumeration of the Khoikhoi and San during the eighteenth century; it is known that Khoikhoi and San numbers fell dramatically during that period, but Barrow's estimate of 5,000 'in the white district' in 1798 was certainly too low.[31] Guelke has estimated a total of about 20,000 Khoikhoi and 3,000 San 'in areas controlled by Europeans' by 1780, which would have formed almost exactly half of the total population and given the slaves a percentage of about 26%.[32] This includes, however, the eastern pastoral districts of the colony where slaves were very much less numerous than Khoikhoi. The first reliable estimate for the western agrarian areas which includes figures for Khoikhoi labourers is the 1806 Stellenbosch and Drakenstein district tax roll, which listed 4,952 burghers, 3,922 Khoikhoi and 9,002 slaves; slaves thus forming 50.35% of the total.[33] Demographically, therefore, the Cape seems to have contained as high a proportion of slaves in the eighteenth century as Italy under the Roman Empire. Moreover, in certain areas of the colony where slaves were especially concentrated, such as the Stellenbosch farming district, there were periods at which the ratio of slaves to free whites rose to almost 2:1 (slaves formed 63% of the total of slaves and burghers in 1739, for example).[34] The situation was thus not very far removed from eighteenth-century South Carolina, which was described in 1737 as looking 'more like a negro country than a country settled by white people' at a time when the ratio of slaves to freemen was about 2:1.[35]

The uneven distribution of slaves at the Cape is normally explained by the distinction between the labour demands, and the suitability of slaves to meet them, of the urban, arable and pastoral sectors of the colony. The majority of slaves worked in the wealthier arable farming regions of the south-west, especially in the hinterland of Cape Town itself, whilst the large areas of land brought within the confines of the colony in the course of the eighteenth century were inhabited chiefly by pastoral farmers who had less need for slaves and less ability to afford them. They relied primarily on the indigenous Khoikhoi, San, and, to a lesser extent, the Xhosa. Much of the debate over the impetus behind the 'frontier' expansion is based on the ability of colonists to afford slave labour and hence find a place in the arable sector of the south-west, where the use of a slave system pre-empted the opportunities for free white labour.

Clearly there was a major distinction between the labour market of the western districts, dominated by slaves, and that of the frontier areas where the Khoikhoi and San were more frequently used. But the pattern of distribution was not that simple. Within the immediate hinterland of Cape Town and the mixed arable and pastoral districts of Stellenbosch and Drakenstein there were geographical distinctions in the density of the slave population, and only gradually did slaveholding become the practice of the greater majority of the farming burgher population. Table 2.2 indicates the percentage of farming burghers – those making census returns which included livestock or crops – who owned at least one slave, by year and district during the eighteenth century. From these figures it is clear that only in the immediate rural hinterland of Cape Town, in the Cape district, was slaveholding virtually universal amongst farmers throughout the eighteenth century. By 1723, when it had reached 97.2% in that region, less than half of the farmers of Stellenbosch and only 56.0% of those in Drakenstein had slaves. Nevertheless, comparison with the southern United States as late as 1860, where the highest proportion of slaveholding families in South Carolina and Mississippi was only about one-half, shows that the western rural Cape had an exceptionally high level of slave ownership.[36]

During the course of the century a gradual geographical spread of slaveholding took place; by 1731 it had reached its highest level of incidence in Stellenbosch district, which thereafter remained at a fairly stable level, and the following decade saw an equal spread in Drakenstein, reaching a peak in 1752. The increase between 1741 and 1752 in Drakenstein is explained by the creation of the new district of Swellendam in 1745, which included areas of Drakenstein occupied by pastoralists less likely to own slaves than the arable farmers who remained within Drakenstein boundaries. The figures for

Table 2.2 *Percentage of farming burghers with at least one slave*[37]

	1705	1723	1731	1741	1752	1762	1773	1782
Cape district	85.5	97.2	98.2	100	98.5	97.4	96.5	?
Stellenbosch	59.3	48.0	74.1	64.1	67.5	67.0	69.3	74.5
Drakenstein	39.1	56.0	53.0	71.3	81.3	79.4	72.1	67.0
Swellendam	–	–	–	–	46.7	48.3	51.4	?

Sources: Figures calculated from census returns; AR VOC 4052 (1705), VOC 4091 (1723), VOC 4115 (1731), VOC 4147 (1741), VOC 4187 (1752), VOC 4228 (1762), VOC 4276 (1773), CA J. 213 (Stellenbosch and Drakenstein, 1782). Complete records for the Cape district and Swellendam in 1782 are not available

Swellendam confirm this; the eastern limits of the colony until the creation of Graaff-Reinet in 1786 consisted almost entirely of pastoralists and the slaveholding frequency was considerably lower than the more westerly regions. The Landdrost of Swellendam complained frequently at the lack of slaves in his district, and Swellengrebel commented on the virtual absence of them in remoter regions such as the Sneeuberg and Camdebo.[38] Both Stellenbosch and Drakenstein districts incorporated pastoral land on the northern frontier in the course of the century, which explains the lower incidence of slaveholding than in the entirely arable Cape district. Even in this pastoral belt, however, slaveholding was by no means negligible, and about half of the farmers in Swellendam owned some slaves.

A clear indication of the concentration of slaves in the rural peripheries of Cape Town with a gradual spread from that centre is provided by the totals of slaves for each administrative district, and the percentage of freemen and slaves in each region of the colony. Figure 2 indicates the comparisons between districts for selected years, and the contrast between the geographical distribution of slaves and freemen. Throughout the period 1688 to 1793, the percentage of total slaves in Cape district exceeded that of total freemen, whereas this was only true of Stellenbosch after 1743, in Drakenstein in the final year of 1793, and never in Swellendam or Graaff-Reinet. This indicates a process by which the proportion of slaves in the colony as a whole gradually increased in each district over time at a speed relative to its distance from the Cape Town hinterland. The proportion of freemen reached a peak in each district and then dropped thereafter, the peak year being earlier the nearer the district was to Cape Town. Thus a year in which the proportion of the whole colony's slave and free population reached an equal level was only evident in the Cape district in the very early stages of its development before 1688, in Stellenbosch in the 1730s, Drakenstein in the 1780s and never in the remoter districts of Swellendam and Graaff-Reinet. A process is revealed of gradual changing of balance of the free population from the original settled area to the

13

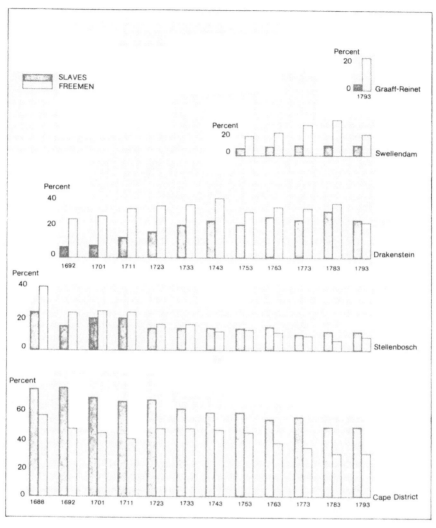

2 Percentage distribution of slaves and freemen in Cape colony per district, 1688–1793

Sources: Census return figures, CA LM 30, p. 1 and p. 10, Precis of Cape Archives Annual Returns (1688 and 1692); Beyers 1967, pp. 339–49

remoter regions as the colony expanded in the course of the period. Amongst the slave group, however, this process was much less marked; in Cape district the percentage of slaves did fall but less dramatically than that of the burghers, whilst in Stellenbosch it remained stable after 1723. In Drakenstein, the percentage of slaves was still rising throughout most of the century, whilst in Swellendam there was a more constant but lower slave level. These figures indicate that the geographical spread of the slave population was very much slower than that of the free, and that the demographic emphasis of the slave group was still heavily in the older established areas. In terms of the use of slaves, Drakenstein, and to a lesser extent, Stellenbosch, were still developing areas of the colony at a time when the regions of white expansion had moved much further to the east. Well into the nineteenth century, despite some spread of slaveholding further from the Cape district core, the concentration of the colony's slave population was still in the old established areas.[39]

This was also true of Cape Town itself. Although slaves had been introduced to serve the needs of the farming community in the colony they were also used in the town, both by the Company and by burghers. The number of slaves in Cape Town can only be approximately determined from the census records since no distinction was made between farmers and urban residents in the Cape district returns. Nevertheless, most slaves owned by masters who made no returns for rural produce may be assumed to have lived in Cape Town. During the seventeenth century the number of privately owned 'non-rural' slaves was very low but by the eighteenth century there was a significant perceptible urban slave population. As Table 2.3 indicates, the number of such slaves steadily increased, as did their proportion in the slave population of the whole colony. No census records for the Cape district under VOC rule survive after the 1770s, but it may be assumed that the growth of urban slave numbers increased in the final quarter of the century, a period when Cape Town was flourishing as a port and market centre; by 1806, when the first accurate total may be determined, there were 9,297 slaves in the city.[40] Estimates of the incidence of slaveholding amongst urban burghers cannot be made, since the records do not include a full profile of the city's population, but it is apparent that a number of town-dwellers, especially those identified by their names as Free Blacks, were not slaveowners. The nature of the economic and social structure of the city led to differing uses and features of slavery than in the rural districts. Nevertheless, the town played an important part in the development of Cape slave society.

In terms of numbers and geographical distribution, the colony under Dutch East India Company rule was thus continually dependent upon slavery as a system of labour. The creation of a slave society was also marked by the attitudes of the slaveowning class which emerged within it. There is a notable lack of written material by Cape burghers revealing their concepts of slavery but some important developments can be traced. The vast majority of the immigrant farmers at the Cape had little direct experience of slavery before their arrival, although some were ex-Company servants who would have seen

15

Table 2.3 *Number and percentage in total colony of non-rural Cape district slaves, 1705–73*

	Number of slaves		
Year	Cape district (non-rural)	Total colony	Percentage of non-rural slaves in colony
1705	142	1,057	13.4
1723	468	2,922	16.0
1731	790	4,303	18.4
1741	1,036	5,436	19.1
1752	1,203	5,622	21.4
1762	1,635	6,683	24.5
1773	2,123	8,902	23.8

Sources: Census returns, AR VOC 4052 (1705), VOC 4091 (1723), VOC 4115 (1731), VOC 4147 (1741), VOC 4187 (1752), VOC 4228 (1762), VOC 4276 (1773). The figure for total slaves in the colony in 1773 has been altered from 9,902 to 8,902, a copying mistake made by the Cape Town official transcribing the original rolls

slaves in the East Indies. As in the New World European settler societies, however, they adapted themselves to their position as slaveowners.

At the Cape this was done swiftly. The circumstances under which slavery was introduced and the backing given to it by the VOC meant that it was perceived as an institution ordained by ruling authority and accepted as such. It had not emerged gradually in response to the demands of the colonists themselves. The first settlers accepted slaves in much the same way as they did land and seed. Even after slavery became well established, owners saw it as a system of labour maintained and supported by the government which controlled imports of new slaves, established a legislative code of control and guaranteed the rights of property in slaves and the authority of masters over them.[41] This was the result of the political structure of the colony by which the Company regulated trade and internal administration. It meant that the concepts of slavery which were developed in Batavian law as a result of the VOC's experiences in the East Indies were transferred intact to the Cape.

Thus settlers of primarily northern European origin adapted to the legal order of slavery which had been developed elsewhere. By 1717, the emergence of a slaveholding mentality in the colony was revealed by the answers given by members of the Council of Policy to a question from the Heren XVII asking whether slaves should continue to be imported or whether immigration of European labourers should be encouraged.[42] Their responses marked the level to which attitudes to slavery had become entrenched. The major concern, characteristically, was with costs, and the answers given by almost all members stressed the economic argument that it was considerably cheaper to obtain and keep slaves than white labourers; a response that doubtless convinced the

Heren XVII. Yet other issues were also apparent which reflect the growth of an identifiable slaveowning class at the Cape. The government was especially concerned at the difficulty of controlling immigrant labourers and artisans, since 'the majority accustom themselves to a life of dissipation, so that they are of no service to the inhabitants, are a burden to the Company and gradually become vagabonds'.[43] The advantage of slaves was clearly expressed by H. van der Meer Pietersoon;

> We need not even mention the great difference in obedience and subjection in the relations between slave and master and between freeborn servant and master... would there not be reason to fear that these labourers would always be the master, would one servant if ordered to do so by his master, dare to punish and bind the other, if the latter had displeased his master? I do not think so; the slaves do this, however, when ordered to do so, always remembering who they are, in the hope that by means of good service they may one day earn their freedom. There are thousands of examples of this.[44]

Closely linked to the power that masters had over their slaves was the belief that manual labour was not fitting for whites in the colony:

> it must be remembered that here, as well as throughout the whole of India [the East Indies], Europeans are not, as befits their position, as industrious in carrying out their trades as in the land of their birth. No matter how poor a person is, he will not accustom himself to perform the work of slaves, as he thinks in this way to distinguish himself from a slave.[45]

Not only was slavery a more economically viable system than free immigrant labour, but it was also entrenched by social attitudes and coercive structures that had already developed in the colony.

There was one exception to this view; D.M. Pasques de Chavonnes believed that if further importation of slaves were prohibited, and 'people were gradually to accustom themselves to employ Europeans, or Dutchmen born in this country, as farm labourers, etc., I am certain that it would be of advantage to the Company, the country and its inhabitants'. Not only would the problem of slave escape, the fear of rebellion and the necessity of punishment be removed, but money paid as wages would be spent within the colony, creating a larger internal market.[46] Whilst many of De Chavonnes' arguments later proved to be valid – fear of the slave population was a major problem and much capital was tied up in slaves which was lost at their death – this idea had little appeal in the early eighteenth century. Slaveholding was too well established to be removed. After the ending of VOC rule, commentators on the Cape economy again noted the problem caused by slavery. W.S. van Ryneveld, for example, stressed the advantages that would have occurred 'if slavery had been interdicted at the first settling of this Colony... Yet, the business is done. Slavery exists and is now even indispensable.'[47]

The point was that by the beginning of the eighteenth century slavery had become the basis of the economic and social position of a large proportion of the settler community. This was made inevitable by the establishment of extensive arable agriculture based on slave labour and the subsequent widespread incidence of slaveholding. As the colony expanded and diversified, slavery continued to play a key function both in its economy and in the social attitudes of its inhabitants. In the south-western districts a group of farmers described as a 'landed gentry' by several recent historians based their wealth on slave production whose local power led to a remarkably closed slave system.[48] Meanwhile slave labour was becoming important elsewhere, especially in Cape Town during the eighteenth century. The critical issue is the way in which an institution established by the VOC developed in the context of local economic and social circumstances to produce a complex slave society.

3

Slave labour and the Cape economy

The primary factor affecting the numbers and distribution of the slave population was the demand for their labour in the differing sectors of the economy. This was especially evident in the regions of arable agriculture. The Cape agrarian system differed from that of many other colonial slave societies. Although the original design of the VOC had been to establish a small settlement in Table Valley, by the eighteenth century the Cape had become a colony with a rapidly growing settler population. The Cape farmers were there to stay, unlike the VOC employees, or the Dutch in Indonesia and Ceylon. Some grain and Constantia wines were exported, mainly to Batavia, and the Cape was certainly not a stagnant economy with no external market for its goods. There emerged a significant link between some rural producers and the market of Cape Town with its resident settler population, Company garrison and crews of passing ships. A level of commercial farming helped to produce a prosperous elite of arable farmers especially by the eighteenth century.[1] Yet there did not develop a monoculture plantation system supplying a metropolitan market and owned by absentee landlords as a means of profitable investment, such as the West Indian sugar islands or the Brazilian coffee estates, nor the large-scale cash crop economy of the Zanzibari clove plantations or the cotton belt of the southern States. The Cape slave economy bore closer parallels to the early colonial settlements of North America, such as Virginia or Maryland, before the development of export staple crops, where slaves were used in small-scale non-plantation agriculture.[2]

The products of Cape agriculture, primarily grain, wine and cattle and sheep, and the nature of the rural economy more closely resembled Europe than colonial systems; as originally intended by the VOC, crops were primarily farmed by and marketed to a locally based population. Yet there were several significant differences between the rural production system at the Cape and that of eighteenth-century northern Europe which the slave system itself helped to bring about. After an initial abortive attempt at intensive agricultural methods under Van Riebeeck, the Cape cereal producers developed extensive farming techniques. This was partly the result of a climate and soil fertility which required larger acreages to produce sufficient yields, more akin to the Mediterranean regions than to the Netherlands, and was also made easy by the rapid process of land alienation from the indigenous Khoikhoi groups.[3] Moreover, relatively large land areas for farming units were more suited to a slave production system than small-scale plots on the Dutch model. In the similar physical terrain of classical Italy where grain and wine were also produced, the replacement of peasant farming by slave labour led to the amalgamation of farms into larger estates.[4] The presence of the slave system at the Cape thus prevented more intensive white settlement. By 1751, the Stellenbosch and Drakenstein local authorities were lamenting the problems of land overcrowding and the lack of pastures; in 1775, good land for arable farming in these districts was said to be entirely occupied or exhausted.[5] Whilst the normal farm unit at the Cape held very many fewer slaves than the large-scale plantation economies of the New World, the domination of a slave production system was one factor inhibiting the emergence of single plot smallholdings.

Despite considerable variations in the sizes of farms, there was a common pattern of labour and little change in farming methods after the initial period of adjustment to local geographical conditions. Cape agriculture was extensive in its land use but the labour demand of each farm was intensive, especially at peak periods of the farm production cycle. Although specialisation did emerge within the arable sector, it remained true for most of the VOC period that many farms were mixed; producing grain or wine (and sometimes both) and keeping livestock and oxen, often on grazing lands separate from the main farm.[6] The slaves thus usually performed a variety of tasks throughout the year, and on most farms work was more varied than on the monoculture plantations of the New World. This was especially true of the smaller farms with only a handful of slaves. There was thus considerable diversification of labour and less specialisation.

Farm work was above all seasonal. With the exception of the purely pastoral farms, where labour demands were relatively constant throughout the year (although there was a need for greater care during the lambing and calving periods in May and June), most slaves were concentrated on similar activities at each point of the agrarian cycle, since both grain and wine cultivation had highly seasonal labour demands. This caused problems for the farmers, who complained when obliged to undertake militia service at peak labour periods.[7]

The production of grain – primarily wheat, but some barley and rye was also grown for animal fodder – required a heavy concentration of labour in the sowing and ploughing period and during harvesting and threshing. The former normally took place at the Cape between May and July, and involved the preparation of the soil from April with manuring on most farms where there was a plentiful supply from the livestock, and then ploughing by oxen-drawn ploughs.[8] According to Kolb, 'Oxen are more steady and keep the line better than horses', but most writers commented on the inefficiency of the heavy ploughs used at the Cape.[9] Van Ryneveld pointed out that heavy ploughs were necessary, however, since 'the ground is hard and either hilly or clayish; – so that the utensils imported, viz., spades, pickaxes, ploughs, ploughshares that are used in other countries, are not strong enough for, and of course no use to this Colony'.[10] The ploughing period on the Cape grain farm thus required a concentration of particularly heavy field labour during the southern hemisphere's autumn season when rains and cold could make outdoor work unpleasant. By 1787, some farmers were sowing seed both before and after ploughing.[11] There was then little further work required in the grain fields, apart from keeping birds away from the growing seeds, a task normally performed by the slave children, and occasional weeding of the fields between furrows.

At the end of the year, between December and February or March, when the weather was hottest and again liable to be very uncomfortable, came the threshing and harvesting period.[12] Again, the labour involved was heavy in both nature and demand. The grain had to be quickly harvested between the period of its ripening and before the onset of the strong south-eastern winds which could flatten a field of ripe corn. The grain was cut with sickles, and was a back-breaking task, although Mentzel commented that since 'the reapers dislike bending too low when cutting the grain, the stubble remains a foot high on the field'.[13] Slave women were also often involved in reaping, and it was at this time of year that many of the farmers hired extra slave or Khoikhoi labour. Slave children were also occupied in 'following the reapers and gathering the wheat into piles, ready for tying into sheaves'. Mentzel describes this period of activity on the grain farm at this time as one in which, 'while the children in our German fatherland are looking forward to a Christmas-box, the African children on the other hand, usually weep for they have to rise very early and work in the fields the whole day'.[14] The work routine of the day is described as beginning at dawn and continuing until the heat became too intense and the grain would fall out of the husks as it was reaped. Between midday and about 4.0 p.m. in the afternoon was a period of rest, and then work resumed until dusk at about 8.0 p.m. in the fields. This was a task which had to be performed swiftly, as sheaves were not to be left lying for long in the fields.[15] After dark, the grain sheaves were brought to the threshing floors by wagon from the fields, and laid out at night ready for threshing the next day.

Work at threshing also occupied many slaves. The grain was trampled on a circular threshing floor by horses; oxen rarely being used because they dropped too much dung. At daybreak, slaves had to spread the sheaves on the floor, which were then trampled by horses for between two and three hours, led and driven at a steady trot by slaves with small whips. These were skilled tasks, and the inaccurate positioning of the sheaves or loss of control over the horses could ruin the grain. By afternoon, the sheaves were well trodden-out, and the slaves then had to separate the grain from the straw by winnowing with sieves. Often the straw had to be collected for hay fodder, and the grain then collected, bound into sacks and loaded into either wagons or a barn on the farmstead. This was a period of heavy work with crude utensils and

1 'The process of threshing' from *Gleanings in Africa* (Anon.).
Reproduced by permission of the Cape Archives

methods, involving the whole slave labour force and often additional hired slaves.[16] An anonymous engraving (Illustration 1) of the process during the late eighteenth century indicates the variety of activities and number of slaves involved, although it was unlikely that the horse-trampling and winnowing processes would have been carried out at the same time of the day.

On the wine farm, there was a similar cycle of labour according to the season, but it dovetailed with grain production demands so that mixed farmers could utilise their slaves to maximum advantage throughout the year. Between July and September, after the ploughing and weeding period on a mixed grain farm, the vines had to be pruned and cut and the soil fertilised; new vinestocks were planted during July and August.[17] In October and November weeds were pulled out, stocks propped, and the soil regularly hoed. Some of this was relatively skilled work; pruning in particular was a task which required knowledge and supervision. During January and February when the grapes were growing, slaves were employed at keeping birds and stray animals out of the vineyards.[18] The main period of activity on the wine farm came immediately after the grain harvest season, when the grapes were picked and pressed for wine-making. Grape-picking was another task which occupied the whole labour force from late February to the end of March.[19] The pressing was also carried out by slaves, who according to a description by Thunberg, a Swedish botanist who visited several wine farms in the 1770s:

> gather the grapes and put them in a large vessel . . . the sides of which are bored full of holes. [When the grapes are] heaped up to the brim, three or four slaves, after having previously washed their feet very clean in a tub of water standing at

the side, get into the vessel that contains the fruit, and holding themselves fast by a rope fixed to the ceiling, trample upon the grapes and squeeze out the fruit as long as they are able.[20]

Many slaves were then occupied with the process of distilling and fermentation and the pouring of the wine into vats, which could continue until late into the evening. Red wine was to be left for 'four meals' duration before being put into vats, and care had to be taken to remove the pips, stalks and leaves by hand.[21] Before the pressing season, during the lull in field labour requirements in September to November, the vats were cleaned, according to Mentzel by scalding with peach-leaves and boiling water and a process of sulphuration.[22] This could be highly unpleasant work, and on some farms where the quality of the wine was critical to its marketing slaves were made to crawl inside the vats to scrape the residue from the walls.

The kinds of labour performed by slaves on the arable farms of the Cape was therefore varied, but followed a regular seasonal pattern which was not dependent upon the scale of output of the farm. Periods such as the ploughing, harvesting and wine-pressing seasons clearly involved a heavier and more consistent labour exertion than at other times. In addition to these seasonal tasks were a wide variety of labours which the slaves undertook throughout the year. Almost all arable farms had some livestock, and slaves often acted as shepherds or cattleherds; the lack of fencing made this especially important, even when herds were small in size.[23] It appears that the keeping of livestock was a task normally given to the older slaves who were of less use in the heavy demands of field labour. Some slaves were specifically described in the sources as 'shepherds' and spent their whole time with the cattle and sheep herds, often on pastures away from the main farm. Such slaves, where their ages were given, were on average older than those described as merely 'labourers' or 'field-hands'; in a list of slaves sold at auctions in Stellenbosch dating from 1820, the mean age of the twelve 'herdsmen' listed was forty-eight years, whilst that of the other male slaves was only thirty-two years, and this difference of age seems also to have been true of the preceding century.[24] Sometimes slaves who normally worked in the fields of a mixed farm assisted in the herding of cattle and sheep for brief periods, especially on the larger farms where livestock were transferred from one pasture to another. Other routine tasks which were performed by farm slaves included collecting fuel and driving wagons, as well as domestic work in the farmhouse.[25] There is also evidence that on some farms vegetables were grown for sale as well as for consumption on the farmstead, and by the 1780s peas and beans were the main crop in the Bokkeveld region.[26]

Assessment of the demand for slave labour within the rural economy must thus take account of the differing requirements of each type of farming, as well as the variations in scale of output on individual farms and the broad trends of development over time in each district of the colony. The major sources for such an analysis are the annual census returns (*opgaaf*) which list for each farm the burgher family, slave and *knecht* numbers as well as livestock

23

holdings and crop output. There are, however, gaps in this material, most notably for the core Cape district after 1773, and more seriously severe distortions caused by deliberate under-representation on the part of farmers who were taxed on the amount of grain they declared.[27] The number of livestock was often rounded off to the nearest hundred and in the remoter districts, especially by the middle of the eighteenth century, many farmers made no returns at all. A further problem is the calculation of slave numbers required for each crop. Precise estimates of labour demand are therefore impossible. Nevertheless, with the aid of some contemporary comments, some broad trends can be identified.

All writers were agreed that the work of arable farms, producing wine, grain and often with a few animals, was more suited to slave labour than the cattle or sheep ranches. Grain was the staple product of the colony. Some regions became centres of large-scale grain farms, producing for export and internal marketing, such as Tijgerberg and the Swartland, but most arable farmers grew at least some grain for their own consumption and the feeding of their labour force. Although this was often excluded from the *opgaaf* returns in the VOC period, concern at the grain shortage that developed after the British takeover in 1795 led to a general survey of all the farms of the colony and a more accurate census at the end of 1797/8. This showed that 85.8% of all the arable farmers in Drakenstein and Stellenbosch districts had some grain.[28] In the Cape district a census in 1799/1800 revealed that 67.7% of arable farmers were grain producers.[29]

A reasonably full account of the demands of a large grain farmer for labour is given by the answer of the knowledgeable and influential Van Ryneveld to questions posed by Macartney in 1797:

> a common cultivator of grain, who is supposed to get an annual crop of 800 muids of corn and 400 muids of barley, wants for his labour 30 slaves... when he wants to sow and to finish properly his work, must properly have six to eight ploughs agoing at a time, each of them drawn by ten to twelve oxen, and attended by three slaves.

The need to harvest rapidly before the onset of the south-eastern winds destroyed the corn standing in the fields also required 'a double number of hands to get the corn speedily cut down and gathered'.[30] Mentzel observed that grain cultivation at the Cape required more labour than in Europe and that at least three men were needed for every plough drawn by six to twelve oxen, 'one to lead the team, another to drive it on, and a third to guide the plough'.[31] An earlier estimate is given in a list of average expenses of grain producers presented to the Burgerraad in 1744 by petitioners in the Cape district who were farmers. In order to produce 300 *mudden* of wheat for sale, it was considered necessary to have fifteen slaves, 'to work 3 ploughs, 2 harrows and as cattle herders'. Another estimate in the same petition, based on the number of ploughs owned, concluded that thirteen slaves were needed on a farm with three ploughs.[32] Since, however, these estimates were concerned to stress the high costs which grain farmers faced in an attempt to persuade the Company to raise its purchasing prices, there is cause to be suspicious of them. Barrow calculated at the end of the eighteenth century that an 'ordinary corn-boor', producing 300 *mudden* of wheat and 100 *mudden* of barley, would need to keep only six slaves.[33] Such figures accord roughly with the requirements of Roman grain producers under similar conditions.[34]

The 1744 calculations significantly included the cost of hiring slaves for the sowing and harvesting periods. As indicated, grain farming was a highly seasonal activity, which when carried out on an exclusive basis in any region required a large labour force for short periods only. For this reason in most societies grain farming was rarely associated with slave labour, which lacked seasonal flexibility.[35] In order to own sufficient slaves to be able to sow and harvest, the grain farmer had to keep and purchase a number of slaves whose labour at other times of the year was under-utilised. This problem was dealt with in differing ways. Some of the largest grain producers, most of whom were situated in the Tijgerberg and Swartland regions of the Cape district, did keep a slave force adequate to cover their heavy period demands, and hired slaves out to work in Cape Town, or used them in their own forges and repair sheds during the rest of the year. Thus some of the larger exclusive grain farmers, primarily based in the Cape district, and with a higher average annual yield per farm than for the whole of the colony, kept a slave labour force which was larger than grain monoculturists elsewhere, and this is one factor explaining the higher concentration of slaves near to Cape Town.

The hiring of labour by grain farmers to cover the demands of their peak periods was a more common solution, especially by less wealthy colonists. Slaves owned either by townsmen in Cape Town or by neighbouring wine farmers whose peak labour periods did not coincide with those of grain producers were used, whilst according to Mentzel, 'those farmers who live further inland engage Hottentots, give them enough to eat, and agree on wages for the entire harvest period, or a little longer until the grain has been threshed'.[36] Although there are no complete estate records of such farms, there are indications of hiring practices. Jan Jacob Necker, a large grain farmer in the Tijgerberg, hired six Khoikhoi for ten days and eight for eleven days in 1789 to help gather his harvest and in the 1797/8 grain survey, several farmers referred to grain that they had used with which to pay hired Khoikhoi labourers.[37] Use of Khoikhoi labour had the advantage that payment could be on a limited time basis, and that hired labourers could return to their own societies after their services were no longer required. But slaves were also often used as hired labour.

Seasonal variation in the demand for labour must also have been a considerable problem for a wine farmer with slaves of his own. As in grain farming, the peak periods of labour during the grape gathering and pressing required large numbers of slaves since it was 'in general, for want of proper tools and contrivances performed in a more simple manner than it is in Europe'.[38] Thus wine farming required a relatively high number of slaves.

25

Johannes Colijn, owner of a Constantia estate, one of the largest wine farmers in the colony, estimated in 1789 that he needed fifty-two slaves to produce annually eighty leaguers of wine.[39] Such an estimate, however, was by no means typical, and, like the 1744 grain farmers, Colijn was attempting to convince the Company of his high costs in order to obtain an increase on the price it paid for his wine. Barrow records that 'one of the most respectable wine boors' held only fifteen slaves, but sold 100 leaguers of wine each year.[40] Certainly Constantia wine was of a superior quality and therefore required a higher concentration of labour than wine farms further inland, and this was another factor boosting slave numbers in the Cape district. Like the Tijgerberg grain farmers, Constantia wine producers had closer links with the Cape Town and foreign markets and a considerably larger scale of investment and enterprise than other farmers in the colony.[41]

Some wine farmers, like the grain cultivators, hired slave or Khoikhoi labour for the peak periods of labour activity. Johann Buttner, who lived during the earlier part of the eighteenth century, stated that although many of the hired Khoikhoi workers were paid off and returned 'back to their lands and kraals' after the grain harvest, 'some of the others however stay behind for two more months, February and March, to cut the grapes and to help to press them for wine making'.[42] Some wine farmers may presumably have hired slaves from grain producers, since the peak periods in each crop culture did not overlap. Yet the impression given by the extant sources is that by the middle of the eighteenth century at least, hired labour was used more by grain farmers than by wine cultivators. Concern at the shortage of grain in the 1790s led to attempts to curtail the widespread practice of grain producers paying for slaves hired from wine farmers in kind.[43]

It would appear that wine farmers tended to own sufficient slaves to cover their full labour demands, although earlier in the century some relied on Khoikhoi hired labour, whilst grain producers more often supplemented their own slaveholding with hired slaves or Khoikhoi at peak periods. The heaviest concentration of slaves might thus be expected in the wine-growing regions. A general survey of the incidence of slavery in agrarian societies throughout the world showed a positive correlation of slaveownership with viticulture and fruit production, but not in grain-producing economies.[44] Wine farming may have required a more constant seasonal labour supply than grain production, but a more likely factor favouring slave labour was that slaves could be concentrated in a smaller area, and were thus easier to manage and control in a vineyard or pressing area than on extensive grain fields. Furthermore, the greater prosperity of wine farmers than the average grain farmer enabled them to be able to afford to keep slaves who were under-utilised at some parts of the year.

A sizeable proportion of Cape arable farmers made census returns showing production of both wine and grain. The most reliable census of 1797/8 shows that 40.1% of the arable farmers in Stellenbosch district and 31.9% of those in Drakenstein produced some grain and wine, but the proportion of mixed farmers in the first half of the century was higher.[45] The development of specialisation in the rural sector as it expanded in the second half of the century meant that more farmers grew grain or wine exclusively. Most of the mixed farmers tended to be producers on a more modest scale than the specialist wine or grain cultivators.

Mixed farming permitted an optimum use of the slave labour force on the wide variety of labour tasks required throughout the year.[46] The scale of enterprise could vary considerably from a small farm with only a handful of slaves to a moderate-sized unit producing primarily for the market. Moreover, some of the largest wine farms also produced grain to cover their own needs, and the grain fields were worked by part of their slave labour force. The most intensive use of slave labour related to crop output may therefore be expected on the mixed farms, despite variations in their scale of enterprise.

Whilst the use of slave labour at the Cape was concentrated in the areas of arable farming, slaves also worked for masters who recorded only the keeping of sheep and cattle in the census returns. The growth of pastoralism was the most dramatic development in the rural economy of the colony in the eighteenth century. The percentage of pastoralists in Stellenbosch and Drakenstein grew notably as the lands to the north and east of the arable centre of each area were gradually occupied by cattle and sheep owners; the new districts of Swellendam and Graaff-Reinet were represented in the returns as exclusively pastoralist regions. Only the core Cape district maintained a majority of arable producers amongst its farming population.

In the combined analysis of ten census rolls for the districts of Stellenbosch and Drakenstein taken between 1688 and 1783, the percentage of pastoralists who were slaveowners was only 46.25%, a figure which compares with 66.7% for all farmers in the sample and 90.3% for arable producers.[47] Some of those pastoralists who did own slaves kept only a handful for domestic work. As already indicated, slaves did work as shepherds and cattle herds on mixed farms in the western districts. On the purely pastoral farms of the interior, however, they were used very much less although there were some slave herders, drivers and shepherds and slave women were involved in domestic labour and in producing tallow and butter for the market.[48] Control over slaves in isolated frontier districts was, however, very difficult. Moreover, the greater availability of Khoikhoi and San labour in these regions, whose skills at livestock-keeping were highly developed, reduced the need for slaves. Often in the western districts, the existence of large flocks of sheep and cattle owned by exclusive pastoralists, which became more prevalent in Stellenbosch and Drakenstein as the century progressed, reduced the dependence of this sector of the farming population on slavery.

Correlations between slave numbers and crop output or livestock returns in the census returns confirm these general comments on the levels of dependence on slaves in differing sectors of the rural economy. Census inaccuracies and individual variables such as the death of slaves, the time lag between new purchases or annual fluctuations in crop yields make such calculations very approximate. In general, however, analysis of census returns for each decade of the period between 1688 and 1773 showed that correlations between the number of adult slave males (those used primarily for field labour) and output figures were highest amongst mixed farmers, slightly less amongst those who reported only wine or grain produce and very low amongst exclusive pastoralists. The highest level of correlation was amongst the forty-three Cape district mixed farmers in 1731.[49] In Stellenbosch and Drakenstein, the differences between arable farmers varied from decade to decade, and showed little consistency. Wine farmers tended to have higher correlations than those growing grain, but the differences were marginal.[50]

Of greater significance were variations between districts and over time which may be related to the broad trends of development within the rural economy. In the earliest decades, the uncertain development of grain farming meant that output was less directly linked to slave numbers, and wine production did not become significant until the 1680s.[51] It was not until the beginning of the eighteenth century that levels of correlation rose. Throughout the remaining period, the correlation was higher in the core Cape district than elsewhere, and was notably lower in Drakenstein.[52] This further reflects the dependence upon slavery in proportion to the distance from Cape Town. Table 3.1 shows that mean size of slaveholding followed a similar geographical pattern, but that there was an increase in all districts over time.

The processes of change and development within the agricultural sector of the Cape under Company rule are only beginning to be studied by historians. The traditional picture is one of stagnation, caused by Company restrictions on export and trading and the problems of over-production and a limited market. There is a need, however, to seriously qualify this view. It is true that at the Cape there was no labour-intensive crop for export marketing equivalent to those of the New World or Indian Ocean plantation systems. Nor was there a dramatic change in the balance of the economy such as the expansion and subsequent collapse of wine production that took place in the nineteenth century.[53] Yet certain trends within the VOC rural economy were of significance.

The most rapidly expanding sector in terms of farming numbers was pastoralism; the move away from the area of arable cultivation by many settlers was the beginning of the celebrated South African trekking process, and the incentives of the meat market, the availability of land and the limited geographical and economic potential for arable production led to a rapid growth of exclusive livestock herding.[54] The pastoral growth was thus most notable in the remoter areas of the colony, especially in the north and east of the Stellenbosch and Drakenstein districts, part of which later formed the new districts of Swellendam and Graaff-Reinet which were almost entirely pastoral in the VOC period. Although some pastoralists were also found in the western districts, by the end of the century they formed a greater percentage of the total farming population of each district in inverse proportion to proximity to Cape Town; 49.2% of Drakenstein in 1797/8, 35.8% of

Table 3.1 *Mean holdings of adult male slaves by districts and farming types, 1705–1799/1800*

Year	Cape district			Stellenbosch			Drakenstein			Swellendam
	All farmers	Arable	Pastoral	All farmers	Arable	Pastoral	All farmers	Arable	Pastoral	All farmers (pastoralists)
1705	6.85	8.35	2.27	2.47	2.62	0.25	0.88	1.00	0.08	–
1723	11.49	15.86	4.34	3.80	6.14	0.40	2.89	3.59	0.45	–
1731	12.88	14.68	5.66	6.17	7.38	1.20	3.80	4.87	1.56	–
1741	19.34	22.07	7.26	6.29	8.45	2.64	3.93	5.51	2.11	–
1752	11.31	12.65	5.36	5.09	7.02	1.52	3.50	4.57	1.65	1.65
1762	11.41	14.17	5.50	6.76	9.98	1.84	3.65	6.00	1.93	1.78
1773	11.68	12.89	7.06	5.41	8.33	2.16	3.65	6.51	1.89	1.84
1797/8	–	–	–	6.58	9.01	2.25	4.84	7.84	1.71	–
1799/1800	15.75	16.50	11.96	–	–	–	–	–	–	–

Sources: Census returns, AR VOC 4052 (1705), VOC 4091 (1723), VOC 4115 (1731), VOC 4147 (1741), VOC 4187 (1752), VOC 4228 (1762), VOC 4276 (1773), CA J 224 (1797/8), J 37 (1799/1800)

29

Table 3.2 *Mean number of vines and reaped 'mudden' of grain per farmer including each crop in census returns*

Year	Mean number of vines			Mean *mudden* of grain reaped		
	Cape	Stellenbosch	Drakenstein	Cape	Stellenbosch	Drakenstein
1723	20,129	10,914	11,768	194	68	54
1752	26,406	18,745	13,027	187	98	118
1773	39,574	42,510	29,929	138	17	105

Sources: Census returns, AR VOC 4091 (1723), VOC 4186 (1752), VOC 4276 (1773)

Stellenbosch in the same census, and only 16.4% of the Cape district in 1800.[55] This variation in the proportion of pastoralist farmers accounts for some of the distinction in slaveholding averages between the districts. When the pastoralists are isolated from the other farmers, the mean slaveholding figures are notably higher in the Cape district than elsewhere, and are roughly comparable in Stellenbosch and Drakenstein for each year. Those pastoralists who remained in the central Cape district tended to have larger herds than farmers further inland, which may have been the result of proximity to the Cape Town market. Also significant was the greater use of Khoikhoi labour than slaves by animal herders of the interior.

Within the arable sector of the farming community there was a difference throughout the century between the average outputs per farm of each district which accounts at least partially for variations in slaveholding size. Table 3.2 indicates the mean number of vines and *mudden* of grain reaped by farmers who included each crop in their census returns at four separate decades. These figures indicate that the highest mean number of vines and grain yields were in the Cape district although there was a decline in the average reported grain yields and the mean male slaveholding size was therefore high in comparison to the rest of the colony.[56] In Stellenbosch, the boom crop of the arable sector was the growing of vines, although most farmers grew some grain for home consumption, even if they did not include it in their census returns. In the middle of the century the mean vine holding was still less than in the Cape district but, by 1773, the Stellenbosch region held the highest mean in the colony, whilst the Cape district fell slightly behind. The mean male slaveholding figures reflect this growth of output in wine farming, although there was a lower slaveholding average than in the Cape district. Drakenstein, as the region amongst the western districts which was expanding from a relatively new area of arable farming in the beginning of the century, with the exception of some of the Huguenot wine farms of the Franschhoek valley established earlier, steered a middle course, and maintained both wine and grain production, but on a lesser average scale than either the large grain farms of the Cape district or the specialised wine-growing areas of

Stellenbosch. Not only were its mean slaveholdings lower than those of the other two districts, but the dispersal around the mean was also considerably less.

An indication of the distribution of adult male slaveholding size, which is concealed by a single mean figure, is given in Table 3.3. In terms of the distribution shown, only the Cape district had a majority of slaveholdings with over ten adult males; in both Stellenbosch and Drakenstein, the largest number of slaveholding units were of minimal size. There are signs of the growth of a group of arable farmers in the course of the eighteenth century with a higher land and slaveholding ownership than the average at the start of the period, although still with only medium assets.[57] The trend in slaveownership by numbers of slaves was one of very gradual increase rather than sudden accumulation of large holdings. Slaveholding thus continued to be widespread, at least amongst the arable sector, but as contemporary estimates had indicated, it was limited in size, with units of over twenty adult male slaves still being rare by the end of the century. The process of division of slaveholdings by the inheritance laws inhibited large-scale slave accumulation in normal circumstances, and the limitations of capital accumulation prevented the creation of a small minority of very large landowners. A steady progression towards a group of moderately prosperous arable farmers, especially in the Cape district, with between ten and twenty adult male slaves, was the major trend of development.

Table 3.1 and Table 3.3 both reveal that this process of gradual increase in slaveholding size was not continuous throughout the century, but that average slaveholdings fell slightly in all districts during the 1740s and 1750s, a period when the total number of slaves in the colony fell. Moreover, at no stage after the middle of the century did Cape farmers approach the degree of correlation between output and slave numbers achieved in the earlier part of the period, especially in the 1730s and earlier 1740s.[58]

This may be attributed to a shortage of slaves in the colony. Despite a temporary shortage of labour in the 1710s, and a request from farmers to be allowed to apprentice the offspring of Khoikhoi women and slaves, there appears to have been no major problem of labour supply until the 1740s, and slave numbers kept pace with agrarian expansion.[59] In the 1740s, however, a crisis emerged. The total number of slaves in the colony fell, mainly due to a rise in the mortality rate, in all three districts, beginning in 1738/9, and continuing to the end of the following decade. Yet at the same time, both the arable and pastoral sectors of all three districts were increasing the level of output. In most sectors, this increase was part of a steady growth, which continued throughout the 1730s and into the first few years of the 1740s. Indeed it has been suggested on the basis of the first results of studies of the Cape economy by the Leiden group, that the 1740s may have been the one period in the eighteenth century when wheat farmers were overproducing.[60] This combination of an increase in output and a decline in slave numbers led to severe shortages of labour, which may have been the major cause of a

Table 3.3 *Percentage distribution of holdings of adult male slaves by district, 1705–1799/1800*

				Slave numbers					
	Cape district			Stellenbosch			Drakenstein		
Year	1–9	10–19	20+	1–9	10–19	20+	1–9	10–19	20+
1705	85.8	10.7	3.5	84.2	15.8	0	97.5	2.5	0
1723	61.5	25.0	13.5	77.1	12.5	10.4	94.2	4.8	1.0
1731	53.3	27.6	19.1	70.8	16.9	12.3	88.3	10.4	1.3
1741	45.3	31.1	23.6	73.2	15.5	11.3	87.6	10.0	2.4
1752	55.0	24.8	20.2	83.7	11.9	4.4	92.1	6.4	1.5
1762	56.0	31.4	12.6	76.3	15.0	8.7	90.5	9.1	0.4
1773	53.0	31.8	15.2	83.3	12.1	4.6	87.3	12.1	0.6
1797/8	–	–	–	70.6	20.7	8.7	76.0	19.5	4.5
1799/1800	31.8	41.6	26.6	–	–	–	–	–	–

Sources: Census returns, AR VOC 4052 (1705), VOC 4091 (1723), VOC 4115 (1731), VOC 4147 (1741), VOC 4187 (1752), VOC 4228 (1762), VOC 4276 (1773), CA J 224 (1797/8), J 37 (1799/1800)

depression in the rural economy which set in towards the end of the 1740s and continued into the 1750s. Certainly this was the impression given by a petition of complaint from the major farmers of the Cape district to the Burgerraad in 1744: 'The large number of slave deaths, which in the past two or three years has increased by the thousand, over and above the escape of the same . . . and without whom agriculture cannot be carried on, causes considerable hardship to the farmer at this time more than ever before.'[61] The farmers of Stellenbosch complained as early as 1740 that the loss of slaves was causing them severe labour shortages, and by 1744, many grain producers stated that they were forced to limit the size of their crops because of the lack of labour and the high cost of obtaining hired slave labour during the harvest period.[62] It may have been that the labour shortage hit Stellenbosch earlier than the Cape district, which was able to rely on purchases or hire of slaves from the town for the earliest years of the 1740s. By 1744, however, both regions were equally adversely affected.

The crisis of the 1740s provided a setback to the move towards the maximum potential use of slaves in the arable sector from which the western districts never recovered completely. Figures for the boom period of the 1780s are lacking, and the inaccuracies of the census returns by that date would probably have rendered them of little value. By the end of the century, correlation between slave numbers and output figures was at a low level.[63] The period of the first British Occupation and the last years of Company rule saw another crisis of labour supply. Throughout the 1790s there were increasingly strident complaints of labour shortages; in May 1793, for example, Stellenbosch farmers complained to the Landdrost that they were unable to plough or to gather the grape harvest because of a lack of slaves.[64] By 1798, just after the ending of VOC rule, a petition signed by most of the leading farmers in the colony was presented to the Burgher Senate, complaining that 'The incontestible Scarcity of Slaves is actually risen to its utmost . . . and yet slaves cannot be dispensed with in this Settlement.'[65] In November of the previous year, the Senate had informed Governor Macartney that the scarcity of slaves in the colony meant that 'the grain and wine farmers are not in a condition to be able to expand their holdings whilst the majority of young men who wish to set up in agriculture are held back in their intentions since there is no opportunity . . . to purchase the necessary number of slaves.'[66] The problem of labour shortage in the colony continued until the nineteenth century, and although it was considerably exacerbated by the abolition of the slave trade in 1808, the foundations of the scarcity were laid in the last years of the VOC period.[67]

Clearly the demand for slaves at the Cape was relatively inelastic. Slight fluctuations in the supply system or changes in demand could have an effect on slave prices and cause a noticeable labour shortage. As the evidence above suggests, there were periods in the eighteenth century when such a shortage became acute. A number of cases are recorded of farmers who captured escaped slaves, and kept them working on their own lands before handing them over to the authorities because they were short of labourers.[68] As so often in time of shortage, some farmers blamed hoarders and speculators for the lack of slaves available.[69] It may certainly have been true that some of the wealthier colonists kept more slaves than they needed for their own labour use; Van Ryneveld complained at the beginning of the nineteenth century that slaves should be used only for necessary agricultural labour rather than for 'luxury', although his comment may have been aimed at the urban slaveowner more than his rural counterpart.[70] Some farmers would, however, have been able to delay the effects of a general labour shortage if they had been able to afford to purchase slaves before the onset of the crisis, or if they had access to supply lines; those living in the Cape district who could more easily draw on the market in Cape Town were evidently at an advantage. There is some sign that wealthier farmers were accumulating slaves in excess of their minimal labour demands in the later 1780s after the agrarian boom of that decade; the Council of Policy expressed concern in 1786 at the extent to which profits from agriculture were being absorbed by slave purchases.[71] Clearly factors of market conditions, price and slave supply had a major effect on the degree to which slaveownership was meeting the demands of the rural sector.

A general picture thus emerges of an expanding rural economy, both geographically and in terms of individual farm output size, which was heavily dependent upon slave labour in its arable sector, and in which slaveholding units gradually grew in size as the century progressed with variations caused by the nature of crops produced and geographical proximity to Cape Town. However, units remained small in size in comparison to the plantation societies of other colonial regions or the latifundia of ancient Rome. As such, they were particulary vulnerable to variations in supply and demand, and the move towards an ideal distribution according to labour demand was disrupted at several stages in the century when labour was in short supply.

There is one important qualification to be made to this analysis of the rural economy which marks the Cape as an unusual slave society. Although the labour conditions and social structure of the colony were clearly conditioned by the slave system, slaves were not the only kinds of labourers used. There was little use of 'poor white' labour alongside the slaves, as in the ancient Roman grain farms, although, as in the early development of the West Indies, some whites did work in the fields on the earliest farms in the seventeenth century, and during the labour shortage of 1713.[72] The main source of non-slave labour was the indigenous Khoikhoi. Despite the Company's initial ban on the use of Khoikhoi labourers, and Mentzel's assertion that slaves were necessary 'since the hottentots will not work', the absorption of Khoikhoi traditional grazing lands by the colonists and the gradual erosion of their social systems which followed, drew a large number of Khoikhoi labourers into the labour market of the colonists.[73]

That Khoikhoi were frequently used as hired labourers has already been indicated during the peak labour demand periods of ploughing, threshing and grape harvesting. In the eastern districts, Khoikhoi labour was a major source

Table 3.4 *Types of labour employed by Stellenbosch and Drakenstein farmers in 1806*

Types of labour	Number of farmers	Percentage
Khoikhoi and slaves	518	54.2
Slaves only	381	39.8
Khoikhoi only	57	6.0
Total	956	100.0

Source: Stellenbosch census return 1806, CA J 233

of supply to pastoralists, and virtually replaced slavery in some areas; the use of Khoikhoi and San labourers explains the low correlations of slaveownership and output of pastoral farmers in all regions of the colony. In the Graaff-Reinet district in the final decades of the century, Khoikhoi labourers were undertaking all the demands of the farm, not only in livestock-herding but also in ploughing and reaping, and were permanently attached to the farm owner.[74]

In the western districts no precise figures are maintained of Khoikhoi labourers for the eighteenth century and they were not included in the census returns. Some estimates have been made which indicate that there were a large number employed by the farmers and the first census to record them, the 1806 survey of Stellenbosch and Drakenstein, listed 3,922 Khoikhoi labourers and 9,002 slaves; Khoikhoi thus forming 30.3% of the total labour force in these western districts.[75] Other evidence – primarily the court records – show that Khoikhoi were often permanently attached to the arable farms of the west, especially in Stellenbosch and Drakenstein, where they lived and worked alongside the slaves performing tasks that were little differentiated from them. Hendrik Cloete stated in 1789 to the Council of Policy that he employed permanently twenty Khoikhoi labourers on his wine estate, Constantia, since he had lost many slaves by death and could not obtain replacements.[76] As Table 3.4 indicates, the majority of farmers with labourers in Stellenbosch and Drakenstein in 1806 employed both slaves and Khoikhoi and a small percentage – mainly pastoralists – used Khoikhoi labour exclusively. Only 39.8% used slave labour to the exclusion of Khoikhoi.

These figures may indicate a higher percentage use of Khoikhoi than was normal in the eighteenth century, since by 1806 the shortage of slave labour supply had become acute. Nevertheless, the permanent as well as hired use of Khoikhoi labour must have reduced the absolute dependence of many farmers on slaves for labour, and was responsible for the relatively low levels of correlation between slaveholding size and output levels amongst some categories of farmers. This seems to have been especially true for Stellenbosch and Drakenstein; regions in which, for much of the eighteenth century, some relics of Khoikhoi indigenous social formations survived, and from which seasonal contracted labour was more easily accessible. Le Vaillant, writing of his travels to the Cape in the early 1780s, commented that 'For twelve leagues round the Cape the colonists do not employ Hottentots, rather buying Negro slaves who are not so lazy, and whom they can more safely trust.'[77] Ignoring for the moment Le Vaillant's reasoning, it seems evident that the Khoi were less used in the Cape district than further inland, and slave–output correlations for that area are correspondingly higher. It also appears that the permanent employment of Khoikhoi labour by arable farmers increased in the second half of the century, possibly induced by the falling slave supplies and the influx of Khoikhoi to the western areas with the loss of grazing lands to colonists further north and east. By the 1790s, Stellenbosch and Drakenstein farmers were complaining that the use of Khoikhoi by the Company in commandos and in Cape Town was seriously limiting their labour supply.[78]

A further indication of the importance of Khoikhoi labour to the farmers of the western districts was the emergence in 1775 of the indenture system for the offspring of male slaves and Khoikhoi females; the *bastaard hottentots*. They were legally indentured until the age of twenty-five years, and could provide a notable working force of young males for some farmers.[79] Other methods of obtaining labour by farmers could be more ruthless. The raiding of the Khoikhoi and San for children drew many non-slaves into the labour structure against their will. Precise levels remain unknown, although a list of indentured *bosjeman hottentot* children in the Stellenbosch district cites 255 such cases, owned by 145 separate farmers between 1776 and 1800. Aged between one and sixteen years, many were indentured until eighteen years; some until fifteen years and others until the age of twenty-four years.[80]

Although this *inboek* system was mainly carried out in the remoter frontier pastoral regions, it is clear that by the end of the eighteenth century a large number of non-slave labourers was working on the farms of the western Cape.[81] Nevertheless, the fact that the arable economy was still firmly based on slavery meant that those Khoikhoi and *bastaard hottentot* labourers who did live and work on the farms were absorbed into a coercive labour structure and system of living which reduced them to only nominal freedom. This was to have an immense impact on the social structure of the farmsteads and on the formation of racial attitudes within the community.

The urban sector of the Cape economy was also dependent on the use of slave labour. Under the VOC Cape Town served as the centre of the Company's administration and its garrison, as well as the sole port of the colony and an increasingly important market centre for exchange with links to the rural sector.[82] Analysis of the precise role of slavery in the occupational structure of the settlement is less easy than for the hinterland since the census returns did not record details of the possessions or occupations of urban slaveowners, but some indications may be obtained from other records and especially the accounts of visitors to the city.

Almost a third of the slaves working in Cape Town in the middle of the eighteenth century were owned by the VOC itself.[83] Housed in the Slave

Lodge at the entrance to the gardens as well as in other Company buildings, they were vital to the functioning of the VOC within the city and colony.[84] The large majority of them undertook the manual labour of building, porterage, working in the docks and fetching wood fuel from the surrounding countryside.[85] Some were employed in the Castle garrison, warehouses and other administrative departments. Mentzel recorded that 'six to ten slaves attend the patients by night and day' and served the food in the Company hospital whilst others dug the graves of those who had died there.[86] The Company gardens were worked by slaves who Valentyn claimed also acted as 'spies' and reported anybody who tried to pick the plants, although they were open to bribery.[87] Female slaves worked as domestics in Company buildings and as servants to the officials, although some may also have been used in building construction.[88] In addition, some slaves worked with craftsmen such as carpenters, coopers and potters and developed skills of their own.[89] Others acted together with *bandieten* (political exiles from Batavia) as *Caffers*, working under the Fiscaal and officials of the Council of Justice to carry out punishments and to keep order in the streets, a role which earned them much unpopularity with the local population.[90] In case of fire in the town, all Company slaves were required to work the fire engines and water buckets.[91]

The majority of urban slaves, at least by the end of the seventeenth century, were privately owned. The increase in the size of the population of Cape Town was not intended when the settlement was established but was the inevitable result of the growth of the settler population and the opportunities for retailing and exchange in the town which its role as a port and market centre provided. As a result, the number of slaves owned by Cape Town burghers steadily increased as Table 2.3 (page 16) shows, and by the 1760s they formed almost a quarter of the total slave population in the colony.

One of the main functions of privately owned urban slaves was domestic labour. Thunberg described how, 'in the houses of the wealthy, every one of the company has a slave behind his chair to wait upon him. The slave has frequently a large palm leaf in his hand by way of a fan to drive away the flies, which are as troublesome here as they are in Sweden.[92] De Jong, writing at the end of the eighteenth century stated that 'except for the least substantial burghers, there are many houses, large and small, where ten or twelve (slaves) are to be found.[93] Joachim van Dessin, a wealthy Cape Town inhabitant in the mid-eighteenth century, had eight adult and five child slaves to carry out the work of the household.[94] Their tasks included cooking, cleaning and acting as personal maids and servants to their master and his family. An important duty was the collection of water, carried in buckets yoked over the shoulders (Illustration 2). Slave children were also used as companions to the children of the family.

It appears from analysis of non-rural slave numbers in the Cape district that many households in Cape Town had considerably fewer than ten. In 1752, for example, the mean number of slaves owned by the non-rural masters was 5.3, a figure which reduces to 4.3 if children are excluded.[95] Table 3.5 indicates the

2 Greenmarket Square, Cape Town, 1764. Reproduced by permission of
the Cape Archives

distribution of adult slave numbers per household for three separate decades
during the eighteenth century. Although there was an increasing percentage of
households with over ten slaves and the figure may have been much higher by
the end of the century, it is apparent that up to the 1770s the large majority of
Cape Town households had less than five adult slaves and approximately a
quarter of them had only one. The average number of slaves owned by a Cape
Town resident appears to have been less than that of the rural slaveowners,
and the distribution pattern was very similar to that identified amongst slaves
in the VOC settlement at Colombo at the end of the seventeenth century.[96]

Some of the work undertaken by the Company slaves was increasingly
supplemented by the labour of the privately owned slaves. Mentzel stated that
even the Governor, although entitled to the use of Company slaves had his
own, 'since the Company's slaves were of little use'.[97] By the 1780s, Hendrik
Swellengrebel wrote that Company slaves were inefficiently used in the
transport of produce and that farmers and traders were better served by slaves
hired from private individuals.[98] Certainly many urban slaveowners profited
by the hiring out of their slaves; in the 1730s the rate was 4 Rxds per
month.[99] Brick-making, carpentry and work as tailors were the most common
and profitable activities of hired slaves.[100] They were also used as coachmen,
porters and to unload cargoes from ships in Table Bay.

The slaves themselves could sometimes profit from their activities. One
common means of obtaining earnings was by selling wood which they
gathered in the vicinity. The attempts of the Company to control tree-felling

38

Table 3.5 *Distribution of adult slaves amongst non-rural Cape district households, 1723–73*

Year	Number of slave-owning households	Number and percentage (bracketed) of adult slaves			
		1	2–5	6–9	10 +
1723	113	30 (26.5)	57 (50.5)	19 (16.8)	7 (6.2)
1752	223	58 (26.0)	105 (47.1)	41 (18.4)	19 (8.5)
1773	366	89 (24.3)	167 (45.6)	56 (15.3)	54 (14.8)

Sources: Census returns, AR VOC 4091 (1723), VOC 4187 (1752), VOC 4276 (1773)

by forbidding it in Table Valley and later around the False Bay region is an indication of the growing size of the town and its demand on the local environment, and it made the task of wood collection increasingly burdensome.[101] Some urban slaves exchanged food with escaped slaves living around Table Mountain in return for felled timber which they were then able to sell in the town.[102] Fruit and vegetables grown on plots in Table Valley were also hawked in Cape Town by slaves, as shown on the right of Illustration 2. Thunberg, describing his arrival in Table Bay in 1772, commented that 'we were hardly come to anchor before a crowd of black slaves and Chinese came in their small boats to sell and barter for clothes and other goods, fresh meat, vegetables and fruit, all of which our crew were eager to procure'.[103] The mention of slaves with boats also reveals that some of them may have been fishermen, an occupation that was widespread amongst the Free Blacks of the town.[104].

Both Company and privately owned slaves thus formed an important part of the labour force of Cape Town in its role as an administrative and market centre. Their roles were, however, more related to the provision of services than to production as in the arable hinterland, although there were some skilled slave craftsmen. There was a high proportion of personal domestic slaves who played little role in the functioning of the economy. Cape Town was not entirely dependent on slavery as were other areas of the western Cape. The institution had been established to maintain the production of foodstuffs and it was the rural economy which provided the basis for its continuation. Slaves formed only one sector within the labouring community of the city. Other inhabitants, especially Free Blacks, Chinese traders, the *bandieten* as well as the burghers, provided a more complex occupational structure than that of the farmsteads. Nevertheless, the importance of slavery in the town was considerable and there are signs that it expanded its urban functions in the course of the VOC period.

Despite some regional and chronological variations, slavery was thus an essential part of the labour force within the colony, vital to the functioning of its economy. It served both in the development of rural production, in the exchange economy of the city and as domestic labour. The continuation of this structure was dependent upon the maintenance of supplies to meet the demands of an expanding economic system, either by import or by natural demographic increase. It is to these aspects of the slave supply system that we now turn.

4

Slave trading

The expansion of the rural and urban economies of the Cape led to consistent demands for slaves in the colony. Although slaves had been introduced as a result of the trading activities of the VOC in the East, there was no well-established source of slaves, and imports to the Cape were organised in a very haphazard fashion. Moreover, colonists were forbidden to engage in trading outside the colony themselves and also competed with the Company's need for slaves of its own. The problem was partially solved by local slave births, although there was never a self-reproducing slave population. One source of slaves within the colony was the high number of internal sales caused by the unusual system of partible inheritance which existed under Roman Dutch law. Such methods were only partial, however, and problems of slave supplies were an important factor in the complaints of labour shortage made by colonists especially in the rural areas, and account for the increasing use of Khoikhoi and other forms of labour in the eighteenth century.

The VOC was never as involved in the slave trade to the same extent as its partner in the west, the Dutch West India Company, which not only supplied its plantation slave colony in Surinam during the eighteenth century, but also, together with private Dutch shipping companies, played an important intermediary role in the trans-Atlantic trade.[1] The impetus to provide slaves for the Dutch colonies in the East was lacking. In Indonesia and Ceylon the VOC either utilised local labour resources or drew on already existing indigenous supply systems, such as the trade centred on Makasar.[2] Nevertheless, the Company at the Cape did spend a great deal of time, energy and cost trying to ship slaves to Cape Town both for its own use on the Company works and outposts and for the burghers. Voyages were sporadic, however, and many of them unsuccessful. Links were established as early as 1654 between the Cape and Madagascar and provided the major source of slaves shipped by the Company, especially in the seventeenth century, but competition with other European powers and Arabs, difficulties of ensuring regular supplies from local rulers and even piracy made the operation hazardous.[3] Excluded from Dahomey and Guinea by the Dutch West India Company after initial imports from these areas, the VOC frequently considered alternative regions. A settlement temporarily established at Delagoa Bay from 1721 to 1730 produced fewer slaves than hoped, however, and plans of sending slaving ships to Ceylon in 1742 came to nothing, although there was a more successful attempt to open up routes along the East African coast and Zanzibar in the later 1770s. Yet even this was brought to an end by the outbreak of war with England.[4] The Company also experienced problems of high slave mortality on board, despite the relative shortness of the middle passage, as well as occasional mutinies and uprisings by its slave cargo. Armstrong's careful calculations show that only about 4,300 slaves were brought to the Cape by Company-sponsored voyages throughout the whole period.[5]

The Company thus had considerable difficulty in meeting its own requirements and little incentive to offer many slaves to the colonists. After the initial provision of slaves imported by the Company on credit to the first burghers in the 1650s, 'it but very seldom happened that a few of them were disposed of to the inhabitants'.[6] Moreover, the Company refused to allow the burghers to trade for slaves. In 1719, shortly after the Council of Policy affirmation of the future of Cape slavery, there was a proposal that 'een vrijen vaart' to Madagascar and the east coast of Africa be made, backed by burgher capital, for a supply of slaves for the Cape farmers, but twelve years later the Burgerraad reported that nothing had been done. Those burghers who knew the area were now dead or too old to travel and the presence of the French in Mauritius made any such venture dangerous.[7] By the time of the Burgher Memorial of 1779, there were complaints that the banning of slave trading by Cape inhabitants gave all the profits to foreigners. A request made in 1783 that ships should be provided to enable 'free slave trading to Madagascar, Zanzibar, etc.' was turned down. There are indications of some illegal private trading by employees on Company voyages although the scope was limited.[8]

Thus despite initial slave supplies by the VOC, for the greater part of the Dutch period the Cape burghers received little help from regular Company imports of slaves. There were two other means of obtaining slaves from outside the colony, although the Company maintained an ambivalent attitude towards both of them. The first was the landing of slaves by foreign traders who stopped at the Cape and were prepared to sell some of their cargo before proceeding to their main destination. According to Thunberg, who was at the Cape in the 1770s, most such sales to private persons were from Dutch and French ships returning from the East Indies, 'seldom of the English and never of the Swedish'.[9] A later account of slavery given in a report made in 1831 stated that a principal source of supply in the Company period was 'the occasional visits of Portuguese Traders in their voyages from Mozambique and Madagascar'.[10] Clearly such a supply system was highly irregular in frequency and dependent upon the ability or inclination of individual captains to sell some of their cargo. Direct trading rivalry with the Dutch may have made English captains reluctant to sell slaves at the Cape in the 1770s and French ships were more frequent visitors in that decade, but before the mid-

1750s the English were the major foreign users of Table Bay and must have supplied some.[11] English interlopers in the slave trade of the East India Company called at the Cape in the 1720s and sold slaves privately, and such actions may well have occurred at other times.[12] De Mist cited French slavers from Mozambique and Madagascar as the main source of slaves in the later part of the eighteenth century.[13] It was only after 1780 that Portuguese ships began to visit the Cape on a regular basis, and then normally only a handful each year, but since almost all of them were involved in the Mozambique to Rio slave trade they were potentially good suppliers.[14]

There are no complete records of such sales by foreign slavers. Company permission was generally required, and duty paid to the Fiscaal, but the loss of the Fiscaal records has removed the evidence of such transactions. A similar problem is encountered when examining the second major means of obtaining imported slaves by the colonists: purchase from individuals on VOC ships travelling from Batavia to the Netherlands. The status of slaves owned by Company officials and employees who were taken back to Holland was uncertain; legally they were entitled to freedom once they set foot on Dutch soil, but in practice there was much confusion, and the Council of Policy at the Cape was forced to ask for clarification on the matter in 1790.[15] Permission was granted on a regular basis for Cape inhabitants or officials to take their slaves with them when travelling back to Europe, provided they paid in advance the cost of their passages for both the outward and return journeys. Many travellers from the East took advantage of the stopover in Cape Town to sell some slaves, an indication of the higher prices that could be obtained in the colony than in Batavia itself. There were obviously limits to the number that could be taken from Batavia on board, and the Company tried to restrict the amount of goods that passengers could carry as part of its general policy to control private trade.[16] Purchases by the Cape colonists from such individuals were therefore limited in number.

Evidence from the seventeenth-century records preserved in the Cape Town Deeds Office show that there were between three and twelve clearly identifiable cases of slave sales to individuals at the Cape from personnel or passengers on returning ships from Batavia each year, including some which were made by captains or skippers on behalf of masters still living in the East Indies.[17] Records of sale (*transporten*) in the eighteenth century are less well preserved, but those in the Council of Justice files show that this annual total was maintained, and in some years rose to twenty.[18] This is a minimal figure; there were many cases which were not officially recorded or have since been lost, and others where the nomenclature *van Batavia* or the name of a ship after the vendor was not included. The Slot ter Hoge, which sailed from Batavia in 1783, had twenty slaves on board destined for sale at the Cape, and was only one of the 137 ships that left Batavia between 1780 and 1790, although the fact that the slaves on board staged a mutiny might indicate that the number was higher than average.[19] Departures direct from Batavia, which were probably the ships with most private slaves on board, averaged between

128 and 141 a decade between 1740 and 1790; earlier there were more ships (a total of 260 in the 1720s) but of lesser tonnage. Their arrival at the Cape was not spread evenly throughout the year, however; to avoid the Mauritius cyclones and the Cape winter storms, most dropped anchor in Table Bay between December and April; in winter they had to use Saldanha, and later False Bay. The Cape summer would thus have been the peak period for slave purchases by private individuals in Cape Town and coincided with the season of heaviest labour demand by grain and wine farmers.[20]

In 1767, the Council of the Indies in Batavia forbade the carrying of eastern slaves to the Cape, 'either for sale or on order', on pain of confiscation; a response to the fear of uncontrollable eastern slaves in the colony expressed by the Council of Policy, but also a measure to attempt to cut down the extent of private trading outside Company control.[21] The order had little effect, however; in 1776, the Batavian Council urged the officials at stations to which slaves were brought, especially Ternate, Makasar, Timor, Banjermassing and Sumatra, to search ships carefully to ensure that Cape-bound slaves did not leave port, and the ban was repeated, with fines for abuse, in 1784 and 1792.[22] Strict checks were also maintained in Cape Town, and the Council occasionally returned slaves from the East who were caught on landing.[23] The fact that the captain and major officers of the Slot ter Hoge were all carrying eastern slaves for sale at the Cape in 1783 indicates that its effect may have been minimal and there are surviving copies of sale deeds of eastern slaves brought to the Cape after the prohibition.[24] The Council of Policy complained, in 1790, that the ban on imports from the East meant that its supply of *Caffers* was dwindling and more were requested from Batavia.[25] The whole question is indicative of the ambivalent attitude of the VOC to the haphazard imports of slaves for sale to the burghers of the Cape.

It was only in the last two decades of the eighteenth century that more precise estimates of the needs of the private burghers for slaves were made and note taken by the Company of the numbers landed and the means by which they were sold. This reflects the increasingly strident demands being made by the farmers for labour, with the expansion of arable production and urban growth as well as the inflation of slave prices which made the Company aware that it was losing out on a potentially profitable business. In 1786, the Council of Policy noted the problems of slave shortages and uneven distribution and estimated that between 200 and 300 would be required for sale to the colonists annually. It was realised that purchase from foreign ships or individuals was sapping the colony of wealth and specie, and decided that the Company should import slaves itself for sale and foreign traders be more strictly controlled.[26] The previous year, the Company had bought 194 slaves from the Portuguese ship L'Estrella and sold 177 of them in public auction at a profit of 38%, as well as seventy-five from the French brig La Télémague which were sold at 52.6% profit, although some of the burghers had defaulted on payments.[27] The Council of Policy expressed concern, however, at the export of specie or grain to foreign traders, and there were indications that it was beginning to assert itself in the provision of slaves for private owners.[28] In January 1786, the Governor and Council refused to permit the captain of a Portuguese slaving vessel to sell any of his slaves, and only granted permission for them to be brought to land for a few days on condition that they were closely watched, fearing that their sale would be 'a great handicap... to the slave trade which has been carried out on several voyages with great success for the Honourable Company'.[29] There were no signs, however, that the Company did have any greater success at supplying the burghers with slaves than in previous decades although control over foreign traders was continued.[30]

The continuing problems of slave supply caused by Company controls over both the import of slaves from the East and over foreign traders led to renewed demands by the burghers for the opening of a free trade system for slaves to the Frijkenius and Nederburg Commission in 1792. The commissioners conceded finally the right for such a trade, but nothing had come of it by the time of the British takeover in 1795. Characteristically, their concern was as much to eliminate the competition of foreign and private traders from Batavia as to aid the Cape labour market.[31]

Precise estimates of the scale of slave imports into the colony are difficult to make because of the fragmentary nature of the surviving evidence and the degree of disorganisation in sales to the private burghers which the Company permitted. A rare indication of complete lists of slave imports is a surviving note of import duties paid to the Fiscaal for the four months March to June of 1792.[32] This was a slack period for shipping at the Cape, but nevertheless 115 slaves were landed by private individuals, sixty-seven by one burgher alone. A large cargo of 113 slaves was imported from a Portuguese vessel, and a further landing of twelve from another of the same nationality, making a total of 240 slaves. It is not known how many of these were subsequently sold to the Company and what proportion was left over for the burghers. Nor is it known how typical this sample is. Estimates have been made of an average of about 600 slaves a year being brought into the colony in the Company period in the late 1780s and the 1790s. This was 4.2% of the total slave population of the Cape in 1790, a figure which compares with an import level into Jamaica in 1790 of approximately 3.2% of the total slave population.[33] However, the Cape import levels varied enormously from one year to another. In general, the Company placed its own interests in slave supplies well above those of the colonists, especially in the later eighteenth century when there were complaints that only old and frequently punished slaves were made available and the problems bequeathed by the VOC to the British at the end of the century of slave shortages were considerable.[34]

Since all slaves were brought into Cape Town, their accessibility to farmers living in the hinterland was restricted. Certainly the vast majority of the individual sales from Dutch ships in Table Bay were to burghers living in the town. Rural inhabitants were given more notice of the arrival of slave cargoes for sale from foreign ships when the Company stood to profit by re-sale of such acquisitions; in 1785, notice was sent round to the Landdrosts of Stellenbosch and Swellendam advertising the event, but this appears to have been exceptional.[35] Auction was the accepted means of sale of landed cargoes of slaves at Cape Town, and access to them by the farming population was dependent upon distance from Cape Town, or the means of designating others to act on their behalf. Powers of attorney for slave purchases were sometimes given by farmers of the remoter pastoral regions of Graaff-Reinet.[36] The potential for profitable slave dealing by Cape Town inhabitants was thus considerable.[37] There was also greater potential for residents in Cape Town to obtain slaves smuggled ashore from visiting ships; although there is no direct evidence that this happened extensively, evasions of the ban on eastern slave imports and investigations carried out after the abolition of the slave trade in 1808 reveal that it was possible.[38]

There were thus limitations to the extent of slave trading from external sources at the Cape, and access to those slaves who were imported was easier for Cape Town residents and those in its immediate hinterland. Nevertheless, analysis of slaves in the Stellenbosch district inventories during the eighteenth century shown in Table 4.1 reveal that locally born slaves remained in a minority throughout the period, and when children are excluded the percentage of imported slaves is considerably higher.

Although these figures cannot provide a complete profile of slave origins, some evident points emerge from them. Most notably, rural imported slaves were certainly not restricted to those of African origin – Madagascar and Mozambique – but included a significant proportion from India and Indonesia.[39] There is thus little justification for the frequent assertion that only 'Negro' slaves were suited for field work, whilst eastern slaves were mainly urban craftsmen, although it is possibly true that the proportion of Indonesian slaves was higher in Cape Town than in the hinterland, and that fewer eastern slaves were used in the frontier pastoral districts.[40] Certainly some urban inventories which indicate slave occupations show that whilst slaves from Mozambique and Madagascar may have formed a significant percentage of urban slaves, most artisans were from Asia.[41]

Trends in the Stellenbosch figures correspond quite closely to the patterns of slave imports, which suggests that the Stellenbosch farmers did have reasonably well-established links with the Cape market, either directly or after a process of internal sales in the colony. Slaves from Mozambique, for example, primarily brought by Portuguese traders, acquired a significantly higher proportion of the total in the 1790s after the influx of Portuguese sales in the late 1780s and 1790s, whilst the percentages for Indonesian and Indian slaves fell throughout the eighteenth century, and especially after the ban on eastern imports, much of the leeway being made up by African imported and Cape-born slaves. The drop in the proportion of Indonesian slaves – primarily imported by private individuals returning from Batavia – before the ban of 1767, may indicate that the growth of the demand in Cape Town filtered off a number of these individual transactions and

Table 4.1 *Percentage distribution of slaves by origin recorded in Stellenbosch district inventories*

| Years | | Cape-born | Madagascar | Mozambique | India | | | | Unknown/Others |
					Bengal	Malabar	Ceylon	Indonesia	
1722–39	M	10.3	13.0	3.4	8.6	11.2	10.3	27.6	4.3
N = 58	F	0	0.9	0	3.4	0.9	0	0	0
	C	5.2	0.9	0	0	0	0	0	0
1740–59	M	12.0	6.5	4.7	13.0	14.8	0.9	21.3	6.5
N = 108	F	7.4	0.9	0.9	0.9	0	0	0.9	0
	C	9.3	0	0	0	0	0	0	0
1760–9	M	23.6	8.3	2.7	5.5	16.6	0	16.6	0
N = 144	F	20.8	1.4	0	0	0	0	0	0
	C	4.2	0	0	0	0	0	0	0
1770–89	M	13.4	10.0	3.8	8.9	9.6	0	12.6	1.1
N = 739	F	14.7	0.8	0.9	0.3	1.1	0	0.5	0
	C	22.0	0.1	0	0	0	0	0	0
1790–9	M	16.0	12.1	14.9	5.6	6.7	0.9	6.9	0
N = 461	F	11.0	1.3	0.9	0.65	0.65	0	1.7	0
	C	21.0	0	0.4	0	0	0	0	0

M Adult males
F Adult females
C Children
N Total sample
Sources: CA 1/STB 18/32–18/35, Stellenbosch district estate inventories, 1722–1804

47

reduced a previous supply route to the farms, although Indonesian slaves brought by foreign traders in the earlier years may also account for the higher percentages in the 1720s and 1730s. A surprising factor is the relatively high proportion of Indians – either from Bengal or from the west coast of Malabar. The latter was a frequent source for Dutch traders, and Bengali slaves may have been predominantly brought to the Cape by British traders in the first half of the eighteenth century.[42] In some cases, however, slaves with names of Indian origin could have been brought to the Cape from Batavia, after undergoing a series of sales from their birthplace through southern Asia, and slave names do not always indicate the region of departure for the Cape.[43] Although the growth of the Cape-born slave population reduced the level of dependence of Cape farmers on slave imports by the 1760s, it is clear that the variables of the import slave supply system had a notable impact on the labour force of the western Cape farmsteads.

The question remains how slaves came from Cape Town to the farms and what mechanisms of internal supply existed in the colony. Rural estate records occasionally indicate sales of slaves, or money owing by farmers on such sales, directly from private individuals from Batavia temporarily stopping in Cape Town, or on behalf of owners still resident in Batavia.[44] Some farmers, especially those in the Cape district, also had houses in Cape Town and could obtain slaves there which were then sent to work in the country.[45] However, such indications in estate records are relatively rare. The surviving *transporten* recorded by the Council of Justice in the eighteenth century indicate that many Cape Town inhabitants acted as middlemen in the supply of imported slaves to the rural areas.[46] This situation gave a good opportunity for them to engage in slave speculation, and those with sufficient capital could hoard slaves purchased at reasonable prices and wait until demand rose or the potential for selling them inland at profit was presented. Evidence from the more complete records of the seventeenth century show that this was certainly a common practice then and a number of Company officials and burghers resold slaves at profit within a short period.[47] During the first British Occupation period, Cape farmers complained that the 'censorable conduct' of some inhabitants led them to 'keep more slaves than their vocation or household requires', and such hoarding of slaves gave a good opportunity for profiteering when market conditions were right.[48]

Apart from sales of imported slaves from Cape Town up-country as part of the external supply network to the farms, there was no equivalent at the Cape to the extensive inter-regional trade of, for example, nineteenth-century Brazil or the American 'selling states' which depended upon slave breeding for the continuation of supplies to other areas when the external trade was removed or diminished.[49] There was no region of slave 'surplus' created by self-reproduction and demand was sufficient throughout the period to inhibit extensive sales from one region to another, although there could be some short-term movements such as sales to Cape Town after the urban epidemics or during the temporary agricultural slump of the 1740s.[50] In general, however, there was little cause for many slave sales when they were purchased for labour use rather than speculation.[51] Despite fluctuations in the economy there was no major shift in production scale or emphasis which brought a significant number of slaves onto the market.

There were, of course, individual exceptions to this general pattern. The threat of sale could always be used by a master who wished to keep his slave in control, on the principle that the devil of a master you know is better than a stranger, and as Mentzel suggested, 'the most sensible course to take up with a slave whom correction does not improve is to send him to the auction and dispose of him at any price'.[52] Notes were occasionally made in inventories for auctions that a slave was a known runaway, or liable to crime, but often the vendor attempted to hide the fact which would reduce the price. In one case in 1760, the purchaser of a new slave in a Tijgerberg auction was only told by the *knecht* after the sale that his acquisition had been sold because he had murdered another slave in Swellendam.[53] Sometimes slaves convicted of crimes in the Company courts placed their masters under the obligation to pay costs for the trial, and were sold to the Company to cover the debt, whilst others were publicly sold as part of their punishment.[54] In cases where masters were found guilty of crimes, slaves could be sold with the provision that they were not to be purchased by their previous owner or members of his family.[55]

Such individual and personal factors did not significantly affect the overall scale of the Cape slave market. Moreover, sales once made could sometimes be retracted later or the price reduced if the slave could be proved to have been handicapped in a way not revealed at the sale; in one case when a female was discovered to be without a uvula, in another when the purchased slave was suspected of insanity.[56] Slaves could also be bought on approval and returned after a year if the new owner was unsatisfied at the return of the sale price and a hiring fee; alternatively, a condition could be made that if the vendor needed his slave back, he must be returned.[57] Such cases were, however, exceptional responses to the exigencies of particular sales.

Individual sales on the internal market at the Cape thus seem to have been limited in number. Yet the Cape lacked a self-reproducing slave labour force and was not supplied with a steady import trade of sufficient scale to cope with the growing demand of the farmers. This picture of a limited market was, however, modified in one very significant manner and by a means not found in American or Caribbean slave societies. The Roman Dutch laws of inheritance, which enforced partible inheritance and gave women equal rights of share in an estate, led to frequent auctions of whole estates, land and property with a significant and wide redistribution of moveable assets, including especially the slaves.[58] It was at the sales by auction of such dissolved estates that newly established farmers or those expanding their production could most easily obtain slaves as well as farm equipment and livestock.

The redistribution of slaves from the estate of a deceased wealthier farmer was not usually a problem. Many of the notable and propertied Cape farmers made wills in which the distribution of their slaves amongst the children was specified.[59] In such cases slave units were split but were at least kept within the family circle and never brought to the public market. Sometimes particularly favoured slaves – normally females or children – could choose with which heir they wanted to live and be owned by.[60] A Drakenstein farmer in 1745 solved the problem of splitting his twenty-two slaves between his only son and his step-son by declaring in his will that they should be divided out, with the exception of three named slaves who were assigned to the son, 'so that each of the two aforementioned heirs shall have the same number, they must choose by means of drawing lots who shall take the first slave, and then in turn each shall name one and take [the slave] for himself'.[61] Sometimes it was decreed by will that all slaves should be left to the children of the benefactor and never sold out of the family.[62]

Family inheritance was thus one means by which the wealthier farmers obtained slaves. In the vast majority of cases at the Cape, however, no will was made, or minors were left on whose behalf slaves had to be sold and the money thus obtained kept in trusteeship for them by the Orphan Chamber. In such an event the complete estate was valued, and then put up for public auction. By this relatively frequent occurrence – which in rural areas took place on the farm itself and not inaccessibly in Cape Town – many farmers were able to purchase slaves on the internal market. The public *vendutie* was indeed a notable feature of Cape rural life and a major social occasion and sometimes lasted several days; 'a public sale of any importance', wrote Thompson, a traveller to South Africa in 1827, 'usually collects a number of the inhabitants together, as much with the view of meeting company as making a bargain'.[63]

Nevertheless, many slaves were sold at such public auctions. The legitimate heirs of the estate were awarded their due proportion of the total sum fetched by the auction, once all debts and costs from the estate had been paid. They were also entitled to bid for the goods and to have any purchases made deducted from their total inheritance. Similarly those who were owed money by the deceased could also offset purchases against the debt. This meant that many of the slave sales at auctions were to existing members of the family, and often to the surviving spouse with half of the estate to his or her credit. If the estate was not especially wealthy, however, and particularly if the land was not owned by the deceased but was on loan from the Company and there were many heirs, it often happened that no single heir could afford one slave from his portion. On such occasions the slaves were sold to other colonists who appeared at the auction. Analysis of auction records of intestate rural estates during the eighteenth century shows that despite individual variations, between 60 and 70% of all slaves auctioned were sold to outsiders.[64] Many purchasers were farmers who travelled to district auctions when they were trying to build up a labour force; the data is incomplete, but certainly the number of young or newly married farmers at auctions was high. Estate auctions therefore provided the most readily available source of slaves in rural districts, and supplemented external supplies to Cape Town. The effects of such ordeals on the slaves may well be imagined. They were 'led forth like so many Horses or Cows and made to throw out their Arms and Legs etc. to show they were perfect after which they were consigned to the best bidder'.[65]

Death was the most usual cause of estate auctions, but there were occasionally other reasons. Estates could be liquidated when burghers were sentenced by the courts to exile or compulsory sale, or, more frequently, when declared bankrupt. In the latter case creditors frequently obtained the slaves of the estate, although a certain proportion were sold publicly by auction.

Newton-King's research into the political economy of the Graaff-Reinet district reveals that 'the system of inheritance ... made for a high degree of involvement in the market'.[66] Certainly estate auctions caused by the inheritance laws were a major means of obtaining slaves, especially in the remoter rural slaveowning community. This was, however, offset by the problems of the external supply system, and the rising demand of the growing burgher population for labour. Furthermore, the slaves sold at estate auctions, having already served under at least one master, were no longer at prime age or condition for labour, especially those who had been imported into the colony. The Cape slave market for many farmers was thus primarily a 'second-hand' one and the supply system only went a part of the way to meeting the labour demands of the colony as a whole.

5

Slave demography

One source of slaves which was not dependent on external supply or internal sale was by birth of children to slave women at the Cape. Such children were automatically enslaved.[1] According to Mentzel, usually a reliable observer, who lived in the colony in the 1730s and published his account in 1785, 'the labour requirements are, nowadays, fully met through the natural increase among the slaves'.[2] It is certainly true that an increasing proportion of the slaves was locally born but the Cape, like most colonies at this period, did not achieve a completely self-reproducing slave population and remained dependent upon external sources. A more reliable indication is the comment of Van Ryneveld in 1797 that although sole reliance on the natural reproduction of slaves would be desirable, 'as they would then be not only fitter for every kind of work, but also, of course, more attached to the country... experience shows us that this is not attainable'.[3] Unlike the free burgher population which grew markedly throughout the Company period, slave numbers fluctuated despite an overall upward trend as Figure 1 (page 10) shows.[4] At certain points the levels of natural reproduction as well as importation were not keeping pace with slave mortality.

As in many slave societies, there was a marked imbalance in the sexual ratio of the Cape slave population. Table 5.1 shows that only in the final decade of the VOC period did the number of females in the adult slave population exceed 25%. By contrast the proportion of women amongst the burghers remained remarkably consistent during the eighteenth century at about 40%. Furthermore, the number of burgher children exceeded the number of adults from the 1720s onwards; a sign of the high burgher birth rate and the rapidly growing settler population. Amongst the slaves, by contrast, children formed less than 15% of the total until the 1790s.

This imbalance of age and sex is itself an indication that the slave population was not self-reproducing and that its composition was distorted by the importation of adult males who were best suited for the labour demands of the colony. The inventories of Stellenbosch and Drakenstein farms in the eighteenth century, which give the birthplace of slaves, show that a much higher proportion of female slaves than males was born at the Cape.[5] This

Table 5.1 *Numbers of men, women and children in burgher and slave
populations, 1687–1793*

	Burghers			Slaves		
Year	Men	Women	Children	Men	Women	Children
1687	254	88	231	230	44	36
1691	378	145	313	285	57	44
1701	418	242	605	702	109	80
1711	545	337	874	1,232	290	249
1723	679	433	1,133	2,224	408	290
1733	793	547	1,684	3,384	711	614
1743	1,075	700	2,197	3,804	815	742
1753	1,478	1,026	2,915	4,137	1,031	877
1763	1,862	1,278	3,610	5,072	1,214	929
1773	2,300	1,578	4,587	6,102	1,707	1,093
1783	3,158	2,042	5,840	7,808	2,533	1,609
1793	4,032	2,730	7,068	9,046	3,590	2,111

Sources: Census returns, MacCrone 1937, p. 59 (1687 and 1691); Beyers 1967, pp. 339–49
(1701–93). The figure for adult male slaves in 1773 has been altered from 7,102 to 6,102, a copying
mistake made by the Cape Town official transcribing the original rolls, AR VOC 4121, Cape
census returns, 1773

indicates an imbalance of sexes in slave imports. Traders preferred male
slaves; higher prices were normally paid for males in Madagascar than for
females, and Company trading expeditions returned to the Cape with cargoes
of which males formed between 60 and 75%.[6] Most of these were destined for
Company use, but the preference of farmers for males is also shown by a
comment of a private trader in 1798, three years after the ending of VOC rule,
that a ratio of five males to every female should be imported as 'an adequate
proportion' for the colony as a whole.[7]

It thus appears that the number of slave women in the colony was too low to
produce a locally born male slave force of sufficient size to meet the demands
of the expanding economy, although there are signs from the census figures
that the proportion of females and children was slowly increasing towards the
end of the VOC period. Moreover, there were differences in the demographic
composition of the slave population between the rural and urban sectors. In
the arable areas, the ratio of females to males was considerably lower than the
average for the whole colony, especially in the farming region of Cape district,
where only 16.1% of the adult slaves owned by farmers in 1752 were female.[8]
Analysis of the census returns from the farmers of the Stellenbosch and
Drakenstein districts at different decades in the eighteenth century showed
that of the 2,448 slaveholders included in the whole survey, 925 (37.8%) owned
no female slaves at all.[9] Table 5.2 indicates the variations of this percentage

Table 5.2 *Number and percentage of Stellenbosch and Drakenstein farming slaveowners with no adult female slaves, 1705–82*

Year	Total number of slaveowners	Number and percentage (bracketed) of slaveowners with no adult female slaves
1705	53	78 (67.9)
1723	152	81 (53.2)
1731	228	109 (47.8)
1741	281	119 (40.3)
1752	295	124 (42.0)
1761	377	141 (37.4)
1773	462	122 (26.4)
1782	600	151 (25.1)
Total	2,448	925 (37.8)

Sources: Census returns, AR VOC 4052 (1705), CAJ 185 (1723), J 188 (1731), J 194 (1741), J 197 (1752), J 201 (1761), J 207 (1773), J 213 (1782)

over time; although the proportion of farms with no female slaves fell in the course of the century, there was still 25% of such slaveholding units by the 1780s. Even in eighteenth-century Jamaica, or nineteenth-century Cuba, both intensive slave plantation economies with high demands for male labour, the imbalance of sexual ratio was not as high as in the rural Cape during this period. Mentzel's assertion that, 'it pays farmers to keep an equal number of male and female slaves and by their natural increase to cope with the growing needs of the farm and avoid the necessity of buying additional slaves' thus bore no correspondence to the actual situation.[10]

In Cape Town, whilst males still formed the majority of the slaves, the proportion of females in the adult population was higher than the average for the whole colony, as Table 5.3 shows. This reflects the greater demand for females for domestic labour in the town than in the area of arable farm labour. There was also a slightly higher proportion of females in the purely pastoral districts of Swellendam and Graaff-Reinet than in the mixed arable and pastoral districts by the end of the eighteenth century. In 1787, for example (the year after the creation of Graaff-Reinet), 28.7% of the adult slave population of Swellendam and 37.0% of that in Graaff-Reinet was female; in the same year 22.8% of the adult slaves in Stellenbosch and 24.5% of those in Drakenstein were female.[11] The use of non-slave male labour in the pastoral districts and the utility of female slaves for domestic labour created a rather different demographic balance in these remoter districts.

In some areas, especially in Cape Town, there was thus a potential for higher numbers of slave births. Estimates of fertility levels for Cape slaves

Table 5.3 *Number and percentage of females in adult slave population of non-rural Cape district and of total colony, 1705–73*

	Cape district (non-rural)			Total colony		
Year	Total adults	Female adults	Percentage of female adults	Total adults	Female adults	Percentage of female adults
1705	125	31	24.8	942	138	14.6
1723	396	107	27.0	2,632	408	15.5
1731	633	208	32.9	3,789	649	17.1
1741	825	254	30.8	4,690	819	17.5
1752	963	269	27.9	4,790	956	19.9
1762	1,411	334	23.7	6,065	1,183	19.5
1773	1,776	488	27.5	7,809	1,707	21.9

Sources: Census returns, AR VOC 4052 (1705), VOC 4091 (1723), VOC 4115 (1731), VOC 4147 (1741), VOC 4187 (1752), VOC 4228 (1762), VOC 4276 (1773). The figure for total adult slaves in the colony for 1773 has been altered from 8,809 to 7,809, a copying mistake made by the Cape Town official transcribing the original rolls

cannot, however, be made with anything like the same degree of accuracy as those for some other slave societies where plantation and census records indicate slave ages and birth rates. Nevertheless, some indications can be obtained. A very approximate indication of the growth of the locally born slave group is provided by the totals of slave children, since few children were imported. Table 5.4 shows the totals and percentage increase per decade of slave children in the whole colony during the eighteenth century.

Although the trend was upwards, the rate of increase can be seen to have been highly irregular. Moreover, the number of children is not an indication of birth rates, since infant mortality, as in all pre-industrial populations and especially slave groups, was high. Armstrong has calculated that the number of slave children per adult female slave for the whole colony remained relatively stable at between 0.7 and 0.9; this contrasts strikingly with estimates of between 2.5 and 3.2 children per adult female in the burgher population.[12] Nevertheless, these figures include women who were past the child-bearing age and ignore both mortality levels and the age at which slaves were considered to be adults for census purposes: probably fourteen for girls and sixteen for boys.[13] Comparative slave studies indicate that there were also likely to be distinctions in the fertility rates of locally born and imported slave women at the Cape.

In the absence of systematic information on slave births or the origin of slave mothers for the whole colony, some indication of comparative fertility levels may be obtained from the inventories of rural estates in Stellenbosch and Drakenstein. Of the forty-two slave women in the inventories of the 1770s who are recorded together with their own children, thirty (71.4%) were born in the Cape; a percentage which closely matches the proportion of locally born

Table 5.4 *Number and percentage increase per decade of slave children, 1702–92*

Year	Number of slave children	Percentage increase of slave children per decade
1702	77	
1712	242	214.3
1722	267	10.3
1732	521	95.1
1742	744	42.8
1752	830	11.6
1762	818	− 1.4
1772	1,068	30.6
1782	1,622	51.9
1792	1,861	14.7

Sources: Census returns, AR VOC 4047 (1702), VOC 4068 (1712), VOC 4088 (1722), VOC 4118 (1732), VOC 4152 (1742), VOC 4186 (1752), VOC 4228 (1762), VOC 4272 (1772), VOC 4302, f. 311–314 (1782), VOC 4358, f. 194–196 (1792). I am grateful to Robert Ross and Pieter van Duin for access to their compilation of census return totals

females in the sample as a whole. What may be of significance is that the average number of children for the Cape mothers was 2.7, whilst that for the foreign-born mothers only 1.4.[14] No definite conclusion may be drawn from this, since children may have been sold or have grown into adults by the time the estate inventory was drawn up, but it is possible that the Cape followed the pattern of societies such as Jamaica and Cuba where the locally born slave women were more fertile than African imported slaves.[15] Clearly slaves who were brought up and reached puberty in the colony were likely to produce more children than those brought to the Cape from outside who were often already into their potential reproductive cycle at an older age. Factors of social adaptation to a new environment must also have played a role. As Table 5.5 indicates, the percentage of slave girls (the vast majority of whom were Cape-born) in the slave population of the whole colony was maintained at a relatively stable level. These potential future Cape-born mothers, with a fertility rate higher than imported women, thus maintained a constant proportion of the slave population, although they did not markedly increase in percentage terms.

The precise levels of fertility per female cannot, however, be calculated since age distribution and mortality levels of the slaves were not recorded in the VOC period. A rare figure of Cape slave births is given in the South African Almanac for Swellendam district in 1832, when 133 slaves were born from a total of 767 adult females; assuming that no female slave gave birth twice in that year, this means that at least one out of every six slave women was

Table 5.5 *Number and percentage of slave girls in the total slave population of Cape colony, 1705–93*

Year	Number of slave girls	Total number of slaves	Percentage of slave girls
1705	56	1,057	5.29
1721	118	2,485	4.75
1731	249	4,303	5.78
1741	376	5,436	6.91
1752	358	5,622	6.37
1763	421	7,215	5.84
1773	529	8,902	5.94
1783	805	11,950	6.74
1793	979	14,747	6.64

Sources: Census returns, AR VOC 4052 (1705), VOC 4087 (1721), VOC 4115 (1731), VOC 4147 (1741), VOC 4186 (1752), VOC 4232 (1763), VOC 4276 (1773), VOC 4302, f. 275–278 (1783), VOC OI Comite 134, f. 77–79 (1793). I am grateful to Robert Ross and Pieter van Duin for access to their compilation of census return totals

pregnant.[16] However, the differing circumstances of the nineteenth century, after the slave trade was abolished, minimise the utility of this figure for the VOC period. Only impressionistic conclusions can therefore be made. We know from Mentzel's comments that the value of encouraging slave-breeding was recognised at the Cape; certainly in Cape Town masters encouraged the cohabitation of female slaves and whites, since, 'the cost of upkeep of the slave is reduced through the presents she receives from the man, and her children are the property of her master since children of female slaves are themselves slaves'.[17] In the arable districts the lack of females was a problem; Sparrman records a conversation with the *knecht* of a farm near Paarl, who stated that, 'The chief of my master's income from this farm derives from the breeding of horses. Could he keep female slaves here, he would get still more by the propagation of the human species'.[18] In a society where slave prices were high and supplies limited, it is to be expected that many masters would have encouraged their female slaves to breed. Certainly the Company imposed no limitations on its own slaves, and the Company Slave Lodge in Cape Town was the best-known brothel in the colony. Female slaves in both town and countryside were always subject to sexual abuse from their master or his sons. More significant were sexual relationships with other slaves.

There was no formal marriage ceremony for slaves until the reforms of 1824, and even then, slave marriages were limited in number, being 'incompatible with slavery'.[19] Nevertheless, slaves did often form what they regarded as permanent unions, and referred to themselves as *man* and *vrouw* in legal testimonies, although there was no protection against adultery or separate sale unless specified in wills.[20] Martin Melck, who owned one of the largest farms in the western Cape with over 100 slaves, kept separate living quarters for his 'married' slaves. He appears to have been very conscious of the need to control the birthrate of his slaves, keeping males and females who were not 'married' in separate sleeping places.[21] Contact with female slaves was clearly easier in Cape Town than on the more isolated farmsteads of the country districts. In some cases, however, *man* and *vrouw* could be living on separate farms, 'belonging to different masters but frequently cohabit together, by permission of their owners, in which case the children always become the property of him who is the owner of the female slave'.[22] An ex-slave woman described to a Cape Town newspaper in 1910 how, 'she had a husband who worked on another farm, but that they were not legally married'.[23]

To a certain extent, such contacts minimised the disadvantages of uneven or limited distribution of female slaves in rural areas, although the lack of stable family units severely undermined the equilibrium of the Cape slave population and had major implications for slave cultural and psychological response. The imbalance of the slave sexual ratio caused slave women to be in high demand, male slaves complained at the lack of females, and conflicts between males over women were constant points of tension.[24] Moreover, since any child produced by a female slave was also a slave from birth, children with Khoikhoi fathers also added to the slave population. Considerable concern was caused to farmers by the frequency of births to Khoikhoi women of children with slave fathers, who grew up on the farms where their mothers worked but were not enslaved; only in 1775 were such *bastaard hottentots* indentured to farmers until the age of twenty-five. A total of 397 were recorded at the Stellenbosch landdrostdy between December 1775 and April 1798, belonging to 172 separate masters.[25] Sexual contact between slave women and Khoikhoi males may have been less prevalent but certainly also took place.

It would thus seem that, if the master so chose, the opportunity could arise for slave females to reproduce at a fairly high level. Occasional indications from the legal records show that this could be so; many slave women in their later teens, twenties and thirties were noted as being pregnant. On the farm of a Stellenbosch widow in 1784, for example, there were six female slaves, of which three were pregnant and four had a total of nine children still living with them.[26] An idea of the possible fertility rate of women living under conditions of subservience on the farmsteads is indicated by the *bastaard hottentot* lists; one Khoikhoi mother, Kaatje, had eight children, all with the same slave father, over the space of seventeen years who were all still alive in 1776. In 1798 a case was recorded of a slave man and Khoikhoi woman who had thirteen children in the twenty-seven years they had been living together. Even excluding possible children who had died in childbirth or in infancy, this gives a rate of one birth every two years; a figure which compares well with the fertility rates of white women at the Cape and certainly of slave women in other societies.[27]

Such cases were, however, evidently exceptional. Moreover, there were notable checks on the natural fertility rates of slave women. Van Ryneveld added to his comments on the failure of the slave population to reproduce itself that, 'Procreation in proportion to number is amazingly small ... for the small number of fertile women slaves there is a very large number of them who either are entirely sterile or do not bring forth more than one or two children during their whole lives.' He ascribed this to 'the continual labour, a circumstance very prejudicial to procreation', as well as to 'their loose life, in having carnally to do with many men' which existed at the Slave Lodge in Cape Town.[28] The effects of field labour on women in the farming areas was significant. Slave women were employed for long hours during the peak labour periods of sowing, harvesting and grape-gathering and this may have affected their child-bearing intervals. The practice of using young slave women as wet-nurses for burgher children also reduced the chances of conception.[29] Poor diet and housing conditions may have weakened the strength of slaves and reduced their capacity for breeding or for surviving childbirth. Some cases are recorded of miscarriage or stillbirths after the maltreatment of slave mothers.[30]

Further, studies of other slave societies have revealed the possibility of deliberately induced abortion. Percival, whose sympathies did not lie with the slaves, claimed that many Khoikhoi women 'deprived themselves before marriage of the power of procreation' to 'prevent themselves from having the mortification of beholding their unfortunate offspring born to slavery and wretchedness', and there are occasional mentions of possible deliberate abortions by slaves for similar reasons. In one case, a slave woman drank brandy mixed with soot and then ate a snakeskin in an attempt to kill herself and the baby she had been carrying for four months.[31]

The spread of venereal disease, especially from the Slave Lodge, was a cause for comment by many travellers to the Cape, and must also have lowered the fertility rates of the urban slave population and spread to the hinterland. Deaths from venereal disease, or punishment of slaves who had contracted it were not uncommon, and by 1803 the government had become so alarmed at its spread that a decree was issued to attempt to limit it, which was blamed on the Khoikhoi women in Cape Town.[32] There is a further possibility that imported slaves from malarial areas may have had reduced fertility as a result of their malarial immunity.

There were thus many variables on the levels of fertility of rural Cape slaves. The incentive of masters to profit by the breeding of their slaves, the imbalance of sexual ratios which meant that male slaves and Khoikhoi were often ready partners, and the use of slave women as concubines by their master or his offspring, could lead to a high fertility rate. Yet, as in most slave societies, the maltreatment, poor living conditions, degrees of infertility and stillbirth or abortion, had a notable effect on some women.

The most critical factor determining the fertility levels of the slave population was its age distribution. There are, however, no systematic records of slave ages during the eighteenth century, and the overall view must be very impressionistic. An analysis of the ages recorded of those slaves who were accused or who acted as witnesses in the records of the Council of Justice showed that of 248 female slaves whose ages are noted between 1750 and 1778, 160 (64.6%) were between puberty and twenty-five.[33] This seems to indicate that a high proportion of the female slave population was of child-bearing age. Nevertheless, court records are not representative; young females could have been more often involved as witnesses in the many cases of assaults by male slaves caused by jealousy over women, and it was easier for the clerks of the court to estimate their ages more precisely.

Certainly younger and therefore healthier slaves with a longer life expectancy were more highly valued. Although purchasers often did not have much choice in the matter, younger labour of optimum use was evidently preferred; in 1678, the Council of Policy declared that slaves 'under 16' were preferred for imports, 'a time of life which experience and the English have taught us to be the best; for those which are older take to fretting . . . and soon die; whereas the young are light-hearted and frolicsome and thus preserve their health better'.[34] Yet older slaves were not unknown. Even as early as 1705, there is record of a male slave who 'did not know his age, but who had grey hair', and who ran away from his master because he was poorly clothed and fed and because the 'master's wife and children constantly scolded and mocked him for his age'.[35] Older slaves could be employed as cattle herds or shepherds and wills and inventories frequently made special provision for slaves who were too old to work.[36] Sometimes, however, they were not so fortunate; a memorial to Governor Somerset by two of 'the only surviving old slaves of the later Governor Tulbagh' who were both ninety years old and 'incapacitated from earning an honest livelihood', complained that they had been forced to leave their home and 'far from having the means or prospect of sheltering their old and decrepit bodies elsewhere, they see nothing before them but misery and starvation' unless charity from the Reformed Church be extended to them.[37]

The main determinant of life expectancy was, of course, the mortality rate; fertility and mortality are closely related in the demography of any population. However, slave mortality rates are no easier to calculate for the Cape under VOC rule than fertility levels. The only reasonably complete record maintained of slave deaths in the VOC period is of the Company slaves, where the annual mortality rates seem to have been very high, rising in some years to between 20% and 30% of the total number of Company slaves.[38] The high incidence of death in the Slave Lodge was nearly always cited as the motive behind the equipping of a new slaving expedition to Madagascar.[39] A rare indication of the mortality rate on an eighteenth-century farm was the complaint in 1789 of Hendrik Cloete, the owner of the large wine estate Constantia in the Cape district, that he had lost by death twenty-five slaves, 'both adult and children', since he purchased the estate in 1778. The Cape district *opgaaf* rolls for this period do not survive, but the deed of sale indicated that Cloete purchased sixteen slaves with the estate, and in the first available census, that of 1800, he had built up his slaveholding to a total of sixty-seven.[40] It would thus seem that Cloete lost at least half of his slaves by death in a period of eleven years, or approximately 4 to 5% per annum.

Barrow estimated that the mortality rate of privately owned slaves in the Cape district between 1790 and 1797 was an annual average of 3%, which although higher than that for the whites, was 'less perhaps than in any other country where slavery is tolerated'.[41] According to Van Zyl, the annual death rate between 1797 and 1822 for the rural western districts was only between 2 and 3% for males and was lower for females, although analysis of the 1826 *opgaaf* roll for Stellenbosch and Drakenstein indicates a rate of 8.04% and this excludes the many cases of infant mortality.[42] Certainly, as Barrow stated, the poorer diet and harder labour of rural slaves led to a higher death rate than in Cape Town. Malnutrition would have particularly increased child mortality levels.[43] Yet such figures compare favourably with slave societies in the New World; the climate and disease environment of the Cape was less lethal to both whites and slaves than that of, for example, the West Indies.[44]

There were variations in the mortality levels of the slaves. As in the West Indies, there were considerably higher rates of death amongst newly landed slaves than those who were 'seasoned' and had been living in the colony for several years or their whole lives; the Company records include frequent complaints of high mortality of newly landed slaves.[45] Infant mortality was high, and in at least one case the practice of using a slave woman to suckle the children of her master led to the neglect and subsequent death of her own children.[46]

The most significant variable in the mortality rate, however, was the incidence of disease. Barrow agreed that there was 'little real unhealthiness in the climate' at the Cape, although stressed that slaves 'who labour from morning to night in the field' or who gathered wood on the mountains, 'are subject to bilious fevers of which they seldom recover', and Van Ryneveld stated that, 'a very considerable number of slaves are lost by continual disorders, especially by bile and putrid fevers to which they are very subject', possibly a reference to typhus.[47] Smallpox was the disease worst feared at the Cape and there were three major outbreaks in 1713, 1755 and 1767. Smallpox was believed to have been brought into the colony from abroad; Percival records that many 'Dutch ladies' in Cape Town would have married British officers during the first British Occupation, 'but that the fear of going to Europe and catching small-pox deterred them'.[48] Certainly precautions were taken with ships docking in Table Bay, and those with suspected cases of smallpox on board were quarantined or forbidden to land; in 1776, imported slaves from such a ship were placed on Robben Island for several months before being brought over to the mainland, and in 1803, vaccine was used on board a Portuguese slaving ship with success, which led the Governor and Council of the Cape to recommend the use of vaccination in the colony to prevent 'the devastation which it [smallpox] brought about amongst the colonists at several periods in the preceding century'.[49]

61

That the smallpox outbreaks which hit the Cape 'every thirty, forty or fifty years' were catastrophic was the impression given by several contemporary writers.[50] Ross's analysis of the three main outbreaks suggests, however, that only that of 1713 had an effect on the slaves of the rural hinterland, the other two being confined to Cape Town, and that even in 1713, its impact was not as disastrous as Mentzel and others believed.[51] Precise mortality figures are unknown; although the slave population of the Cape district did slump in 1713, it continued to rise in Stellenbosch and Drakenstein but at a lesser rate of increase than in the previous two years. Ross suggests that levels were possibly maintained by purchases from Cape Town. The slight decline in 1755 in the rural district may have been caused by sales to disease-stricken Cape Town; sales from country to town appear to have been higher in that decade than any other.[52] The 1767 outbreak was more prevalent in the town when the mortality rates of Company slaves increased dramatically, although the Landdrost of Stellenbosch reported that he was unable to investigate a case of suspected bestiality by a slave on a farm in his district because of the outbreak of smallpox in that area.[53] The total slave figures for Stellenbosch and Drakenstein seem, however, to have been little affected in that year.

Smallpox, however dramatic in its sudden appearance, was not the only disease prevalent at the Cape. Although the landdrosts were supposed to investigate all slave deaths, their reports were normally only concerned with cases of wounding and even post mortems conducted by surgeons rarely indicated the nature of diseases. Often the only verdict was death as a result of 'fever'. The Cape was spared the kinds of tropical diseases which caused high slave mortality in Dutch Surinam, although malaria was not unknown, and 'fever' may also have referred to such diseases as measles or whooping cough. In 1756, a case of leprosy was recorded on a Drakenstein farm and measures were taken to control it.[54] Venereal disease, gastro-enteritis and the common cold were also often cited in reports, the latter especially amongst imported slaves who presumably had not built up the immunities held by the white and locally born population.

A major mortality crisis amongst the rural slaves took place in the 1740s which may have been closely linked to the depression of the economy in that decade.[55] This appears to have been caused, at least in part, by an epidemic of gastro-enteritis but possibly there was an outbreak of measles in 1743–4, as several such cases were investigated by the Landdrost of Stellenbosch and his surgeon.[56] Farmers complained that the death of many of their slaves had led to a severe labour shortage as well as a ruinous loss of capital, and the holder of the milling contract, Pieter Wion, incurred heavy losses since slave mortality had reduced the amount of grain brought to his mill.[57] A decree of 1747 declared a day of prayer in all the churches of the colony to atone for the sins of the inhabitants which had led 'Almighty God . . . to visit upon us for some period of time the heavy burden of a great number of deaths amongst our slaves.'[58] The heavy impact of such mortality may have been caused by the deaths of a large number of older slaves who had entered the colony in the boom period of the first two decades of the century and had reached their life expectancy levels, although this cannot be proved.

Slave sickness was a constant problem for their owners. Wion complained again in 1752 that he was unable to fulfil the terms of his contract to supply meat to Stellenbosch because 'my slaves are all sick'.[59] There is little evidence of many slaveowners giving consistent medical attention to their slaves, although the Company hospital did admit some private slaves from Cape Town and the immediately surrounding area, and Johannes Colijn, owner of the De Hoop op Constantia wine estate, included an estimate of 60 Rxds per annum to pay for a surgeon to 'tend the slaves'.[60] Such a large-scale enterprise with over sixty slaves was, however, exceptional. Most medical treatment for slaves was on an *ad hoc* basis, using local remedies and herbs, often with as much danger of hastening death as preventing it.

There is no doubt that slaves were more likely to succumb to disease and sickness than their owners because of the inadequacies of their diet and the circumstances of their employment. The comment of the Burgher Senate in 1798, just after the ending of VOC rule, that the shortage of labour would lead to a reduction in the levels of corn sown and reaped, 'rather than losing by the death of one single slave the whole profits of the harvest', indicates the importance of the variable of labour demand on slave mortality.[61] As Barrow stressed, the circumstances of slave labour were not conducive to low mortality.[62] Deaths of slaves caught trying to escape, by maltreatment, accident at work and by suicide were also aspects of the mortality rate that did not affect the free population. It may be impossible to give precise mortality level figures from the Cape material, but certainly slaveowners had to constantly battle to maintain slave numbers against a rate of slave death that at times rose to critical proportions and was notably higher than that of the colonist population.

A final aspect of Cape slave demography to consider is the effect of manumission on the total numbers of slaves. Recent studies of manumission levels have suggested that they were very low in the rural areas, if somewhat higher in Cape Town, and the free black population as a result was minimal in size.[63] Moreover, the tendency of Company practice to demand another slave in the place of one manumitted tended to reinforce rather than to break down the pattern of slavery and to maintain slave numbers, although most rural slaves were emancipated by wills without such a condition. In general, manumission in the eighteenth century had little overall effect on slave numbers.

Thus despite some variations according to area, and an increase in locally born slaves over time, the combination of high mortality rates and a low proportion of females meant that the Cape slave population had to be constantly supplemented with imports if it was to meet the demands of the expanding economy. These problems of supply, and the diverse origins of slaves which resulted were to have significant implications for the economic and social characteristics of Cape slavery.

6

Prices and profits

Despite the complaints of labour shortages by farmers and the problems of the supply system, slavery continued to be the basis of the production system of the colony throughout the VOC period, especially in the arable western districts. As Janssens, Governor of the Cape during the Batavian period, pointed out in 1804, although abolition of slavery might have been morally desirable,

> it would destroy all property and plunge the colony into misery (perhaps for good)...the whole industry of this country is based on the existence of slaves....Those who possess many slaves can easily be recognised by the condition of their farms; everything looks better and more prosperous than with those who have to work with scanty means.[1]

This association of slavery with prosperity reflects a common position in slave societies; those who had the capital assets or the political influence to own slaves were the wealthiest and economically most powerful members of the community. Yet there has been considerable debate, both amongst contemporaries at the time of abolition, and by recent historians, on the precise levels of profitability which slave production gave. Certainly slave labour must have been profitable to have existed at all, but the calculated rate of returns of slave labour must be compared with other forms of labour or options of capital investment. As Genovese has pointed out slavery was not only continued in New World plantation societies because of its economic profitability but because it represented political interests and social status to the slaveowning class. There were elements of slave production that were economically irrational and which placed slaveowners at a disadvantage in comparison to other labour systems; the size of the labour force was fixed, capital outlay on slave purchase was high and lost by slave mortality, and there were limitations to the development of agrarian innovations.[2]

The calculation of a rate of return on slave labour does not therefore explain fully the rationale behind the use of slavery as a production system. There are also major problems in deriving such a figure which the sophistications of American econometricians have not been able to overcome.[3] In an urban context, where slaves were not primarily used for production, or in the pastoral economy of the Cape where they formed a minority of the total labour force, profit levels of slave output cannot be calculated with any precision. Yet there are two major reasons why such a process should be attempted for the arable regions in which slave labour predominated. First, the variety of farming enterprises in the colony, the variables of prices fetched for produce and the high capital costs required in some sections and regions of the Cape economy meant that differential levels of profitability led to considerable diversity in the use of slavery as a labour system even within the arable sector. This was to cause a notable disparity of wealth in the rural districts which closely correlated with slave ownership and use.

The second reason why an indication of slave rates of return is of interest is in a comparative context. In terms of the preconditions which have been determined for slave profitability elsewhere, the Cape seems an unlikely candidate for a flourishing slave economy.[4] Agriculture was not carried out on a large plantation scale with high demands of labour per unit, and only a few of the largest farmsteads at the Cape approached the size of the New World plantation or the Roman latifundium. There were limits to the fertility levels and the slave population did not reproduce itself at a high enough level to keep up with labour demand. Moreover, the slave supply system was erratic, and although divisions of property led to an active internal market, there was no systematic breeding of slaves in one region for sale to an expanding rural economy in another. Alternative labour was available from the nominally free Khoikhoi, although less so in the earlier decades in the western districts than inland. Finally, the cost of slave purchase rose in the course of the century, and the capital required for investment in slaves could be considerable.

It would appear therefore that profits made from slave production in such a society would be minimal. Indeed, some writers during the nineteenth century indicated that this was so, and farmers often complained that they were hardly able to make any profit at all.[5] Yet analysis of rates of return, despite considerable variations caused by conflicting sources and the differences between certain products and scales of output, shows that at the Cape, arable slave production produced profits comparable to, and possibly even exceeding, those calculated for the British Caribbean or the southern United States. It is the purpose of this chapter to demonstrate this, and to explain the continued dependence upon slavery at the Cape in economic terms, as well as to assess the effects of slavery on the economic development of the colony. Although a slave, as a marketable item, possessed a value in himself whether or not he laboured, his full value could only be realised in terms of the output of the agrarian system in which he worked.[6] It was a major concern of the Heren XVII from the early days of slave importation at the Cape that they 'may be supported by their own labour',[7] and it was some time in the seventeenth century before the slave system of production did begin to yield a profitable return on the capital invested.[8]

Following the example of American and West Indian slave profitability studies, an attempt will be made to assess the productivity levels per slave unit of each crop or livestock system, and the value of these levels in terms of the prices obtainable for farming produce in the colony (S). Against this gross income from slave labour will be set the necessary annual costs of the farmer to maintain his farm and his slave labour; food, clothing, the need for supervision by overseers and medical expenses (E). To assess the rate of return per unit, this net income must be divided by the total capital investment per slave made by the farmer to produce his crops; land, equipment, and the cost of purchasing slaves (K). The calculation by which this data will be used to produce an annual rate of return per unit of slave labour (r), is:[9]

$$ r = \left(\frac{S - E}{K} \right) \times 100 $$

1 THE PRODUCTIVITY OF SLAVE LABOUR (S)

Despite the relatively well-documented census returns for the colony, the lack of farm records such as the plantation accounts that survive from the West Indies or the United States has meant that little study has been made of the economy of the western Cape farmsteads as individual units.[10] Precise estimates of slave productivity per *morgen* of land are therefore hard to assess, although the census does enable some calculation of the rate of crop output according to the size of the labour force. There are two major problems in assessing such a productivity return for the Cape. First, the census returns give no indication of the hired labour force or the Khoikhoi labourers permanently attached to the farms, and secondly, the lack of a monoculture and the wide variety of prices for each crop or livestock type over time and the differential between them in any one year, give a range of variables for the value of each unit of slave productivity. By using some of the examples given by contemporaries and matching them to the census returns, with valuations for certain periods of the century, some typical models can, however, be constructed.

The most straightforward farms to analyse are the relatively large-scale monoculture grain or wine farms. Several estimates by contemporaries are available for grain productivity per slave. In the early 1740s, burghers complaining that they could not afford to accept a lowering of the price offered for their produce by the Company, estimated that a middle-sized grain farmer, producing 300 *mudden* of wheat for sale, required fifteen slaves.[11] There was an incentive to exaggerate the costs of their production, although a scribbled calculation made by Blankenberg, a Cape burgher, in 1746 who was considering buying a farm, reckoned on purchasing sixteen slaves to produce 300 *mudden*.[12] At the end of the century, Van Ryneveld estimated that thirty slaves were required by a grain farmer producing 800 *mudden* of corn and 400 *mudden* of barley.[13] If production on a large scale gave a higher return per slave, this estimate accords approximately with the 1740s figures. Barrow, however, writing in the same year, allowed only six slaves in his reckonings for a farm producing 300 *mudden* of wheat and 100 of barley, which is considerably lower than the estimates of the 1740s.[14] Barrow was concerned to stress the inefficiency of Cape Dutch farming, and would have been unlikely to minimise the size of the labour force deliberately. It seems more likely that the smaller-scale grain producer in Barrow's calculations was relying more heavily on hired and Khoikhoi labour than Van Ryneveld's large farm; the maximum period of slave use in the 1740s gave way by the end of the century to a higher level of non-slave labour employment.[15]

All of these estimates refer to grain monoculture by middle- to large-scale producers. Comparison with the census records reveals a high degree of correlation, although precise figures are distorted by under-representation of grain yields. For the Cape district in 1741, where slave labour most closely correlated with output, farmers producing grain only, and with a livestock size at only a level to support grain farming, held, on average, one adult male slave for every 24 *mudden* of grain harvested.[16] This compares with one slave per 20 *mudden* in the burgher complaint and 18.75 *mudden* in the Blankenberg papers calculation. Some of the difference may be explained by the amount of grain retained for seed and for feeding the farmstead; the calculated estimates only included grain marketed. Overall, an average of 20 *mudden* of grain per slave seems reasonable for this scale of production. On Van Ryneveld's larger grain farm, the return per slave increased to 40 *mudden*. This implies a higher rate of return per slave as the scale of the total farming enterprise increased. It seems likely that small grain farms had a lower yield per slave than 20 *mudden*. The census records are too inaccurate to be precise at this level, and slaveholding size only approximately corresponded to output, but the Cape census for 1741 shows that exclusive grain farmers producing less than 150 *mudden* of grain had a mean adult male slave output of 16 *mudden*; considerably less than the average of the whole sample. In the other districts the output was higher, but Khoikhoi and hired labour use distort the census figures.

In the case of wine production, there appear to have been considerable variations of productivity per slave which depended on the quality of the wine produced. Johannes Colijn's estimate of 1789 for his large estate producing high quality Constantia wines, included fifty-two slaves used to produce 80 leaguers of wine per annum; a unit productivity of 1.5 leaguers per slave.[17] Barrow's calculation of 5.3 leaguers per slave is high by comparison; the mean figure for Stellenbosch exclusive wine producers in the 1773 census was 1.9 leaguers per slave, and in the Cape district in that year was only 0.8 leaguers.[18] As in the case of grain, the figures for Drakenstein are higher, but the use of Khoikhoi and hired labour in this region distorts the labour size as represented in the census returns and this may also have been a factor which Barrow neglected. For wine farms using only slaves as a labour source, between 1 and 2 leaguers per adult male slave seems to have been the average productivity per annum.

These estimates are based on the models of monocultural farms. Many Cape farms produced both wine and grain, and the slaves on them worked at different seasons of the year to produce both crops. In these cases, productivity levels as represented in the census have to be modified accordingly for each crop. Estimates from the Cape district in 1741 show that the productivity level of mixed farmers' male adult slaves when divided between both the grain and wine yields, was approximately equal to that of monoculturalists; in total, 860 adult male slaves were owned by farmers producing 356.5 leaguers of wine and 8,105 *mudden* of harvested grain.[19] Taking the average for monocultural grain producers of that year, 24 *mudden* per slave, and applying it to these figures for mixed farmers gives a distribution of 337 slaves for grain and 522 slaves for wine; 1.46 leaguers per slave, which is slightly higher than the monoculture wine figure calculated above for the Cape district. As expected, farmers producing both grain and wine obtained a slightly higher rate of return in terms of output per slave, resulting from the use that they could make of their slaves in the cultivation of each crop.

It has been pointed out that the use of slaves by exclusive pastoralists bore little relation to the size of the herds.[20] Mentzel estimated that 'a shepherd is required for every 500 sheep' and that five or six slaves were needed by a farmer with a flock of 3,000 sheep with 'additional assistance needed for the cattle and horses, as well as for agricultural work'.[21] In most cases, however, Khoikhoi were used by pastoralists as shepherds, and slaves were considered to be less suitable. In the calculations that follow, only arable farming will be included, although most arable farmers also owned some livestock which was tended by slaves and this increased the value of output per slave.

In order to obtain an estimate on the value of these productivity levels, the market prices of wine, grain, cattle and sheep must be considered. The VOC fixed prices which it was prepared to pay for the amount of grain and wine required for its own purposes and for export. The remainder was sold on the local market, normally by auction. There was a considerable difference between the Company price, which took little account of variables of supply and demand and was determined in Amsterdam, and the market price fetched at auctions. Table 6.1 indicates the official prices set by the Company and the average prices obtained in public auctions for specified products and periods during the eighteenth century. There were variations of price between each decade and around the average values shown, but some of the limits of returns are indicated.

Table 6.2 links these prices with the output figures per slave for each product already shown to produce some indication of the ranges of slave unit productivity.

Clearly the whole range represented in this figure includes exceptional circumstances. Grain prices only fell as low as 1.0 Rxd per *mud* in 1770, and although the Company price was higher than that obtained in auctions, most

Table 6.1 *Average prices of agrarian produce obtained at public auctions, 1716–1800 (in rixdollars)*

	Price	
Year	Wheat (per *mud)*	White Wine (per leaguer)
1716	2.0	21
1720	2.2	22
1730	2.4	26
1740	2.4	28
1750	1.6	30
1760	1.5	38
1770	1.0	22
1780	2.4	38
1790	2.6	35
1800	2.8	30
Official Company price	2.6 (to 1741) 2.5 (after 1741)	27

Sources: CA MOOC 10/1–10/18, Vendurollen, 1716–1800. Wheat prices are converted from guilders to rixdollars at the rate of three guilders to the rixdollar, following the exchange value of the Cape guilder, which was valued at sixteen stuivers rather than the Dutch guilder of twenty stuivers; one rixdollar equalled forty-eight stuivers

Table 6.2 *Range of values of slave productivity per unit (in rixdollars)*

Product	Output per slave	Range of prices per unit of output	Range of values of slave productivity per unit
Grain	16 *mudden*	1.0–2.5	16–40
	20 *mudden*	1.0–2.5	20–50
	40 *mudden*	1.0–2.5	40–100
Wine	0.8 leaguers	22–38	17.6–30.4
	1.5 leaguers	22–38	33–57
	2.0 leaguers	22–38	44–76

farmers were unable to sell all their grain in such a way. The estimate of 40 *mudden* output of grain per slave made by Van Ryneveld was untypical for the VOC period. The normal range of value of slave productivity per unit for grain producers was thus between 35 and 50 Rxds, depending on the fluctuations in market prices. Wine prices varied more than those obtained for grain, and quality was a critical determinant. High quality wine required more intensive labour use, however, so that the higher price obtained was offset by a lower level of output per slave. The range of values of slave productivity per unit averaged between 25 and 45 Rxds.

Many arable producers marketed both wine and grain. Such mixed farms were able to derive labour from their slaves at a higher level of productivity since the peak labour demands of each product did not overlap.[22] The value of slave unit productivity for mixed farmers was thus higher than that obtained by monoculturalists, although it is difficult to estimate precisely by how much. If the figure for monoculturalists are used in the calculation of the annual rate of return on slaves, it may be assumed that this was minimal and that many mixed farms were in fact deriving a greater profit, although the capital outlay required for a mixed farm was greater.

2 COSTS OF MAINTAINING THE SLAVE LABOUR UNIT (E)

From the annual gross value of return per slave labour unit must be deducted the 'pocket expenses' involved in maintaining both the slave population on the farm each year, and the capital assets of land, buildings and equipment necessary for the production system. Such information is extremely scanty for the Dutch Cape because of the lack of records kept by the farmers themselves; official records or estate papers rarely indicate the running costs of the farm. Moreover, on farms with only a handful of slaves, costs of clothing, food and maintenance were minimal and a section of the household expenses of the whole farm rather than separate identifiable items. There was also considerable variety from farm to farm in the quality and quantity of food, clothing, housing and medical attention given, a fact made clear when legislation to regulate slave treatment was passed in the nineteenth century.[23]

Some broad approximations can, however, be made. The Blankenberg papers estimate allowed an annual expenditure of 240 guilders for clothing for the sixteen slaves in 1744 or 5 Rxds per slave; in 1787, H. Cloete stated that he spent 7 Rxds on overgarments, trousers and shirts per slave and by the end of the century, Barrow estimated 15 Rxds per slave for clothing, triple the Blankenberg figure.[24] Inflation of prices by the 1790s may account for this difference. By 1827, when prices for cloth had increased still further, an estimate of 21 Rxds per slave was made for a large grain farm.[25] Johannes Colijn estimated an annual expenditure of 488 Rxds for cloth for this fifty-two slaves, or 9.4 Rxds per slave, on his Constantia wine farm.[26] A steadily increasing figure from about 5 Rxds per slave in 1740 to 10 Rxds in 1789 and 15 Rxds by the end of the century, gives an average expenditure of about 10 Rxds per slave for clothing.

The variety of food given to slaves was considerable. Many farmers fed their labour force from their own produce. A survey of grain farmers taken in 1797/8, showed that all farmers kept an average of just over 2 *mudden* of wheat a year per head for bread for their slaves; a market value of about 5 Rxds Presumably non-grain producers bought an equivalent amount at auctions. Near the coast slaves were often given fish caught locally, and the meat from game shot near the farm was sometimes distributed amongst them.[28] Apart from such windfalls, normal rations could be meagre; in 1750, slaves on a Stellenbosch wine farm received only rice and wine twice a day.[29] Rice was imported from the East Indies, but was mainly used for Company slaves.[30] Some slaves were more fortunate; Johannes Colijn calculated that he spent 865 Rxds per annum on butter, fat, beef and lamb for his slaves; 16 Rxds per head, and these rations would have been well supplemented by the farm's wine. H. Cloete slaughtered an ox worth 6 Rxds each week for his sixty labourers as well as providing bread and herring.[31] Such fare was unusual, and most slaves probably received no more than 10 Rxds value of food and drink per annum, although at some periods their diet could be supplemented, such as during the grape harvest.[32]

Johannes Colijn also lists 60 Rxds spent each year for the services of a 'surgeon to tend to the slaves'; just over 1 Rxds per annum per slave. Such medical attention was rare; treatment given to the slaves on most farms consisted of herbal remedies, normally administered by the Khoikhoi, or a tot of brandy.[33] Even the estimates for the Constantia estate are insignificant to the total annual expenditure per slave.

A major cost which affected most of the larger farms, and certainly those farming units which consisted of lands in more than one area, was the employment of one or more *knechts* hired on a contract basis from the Company. *Knechts* were hired at various rates; normally those listed as *bouwknecht* or with practical skills were paid about 10 Rxds to 15 Rxds per annum, plus the cost of maintenance, food and tobacco; the wage levels rose slightly to about 20 to 25 Rxds by the end of the century. Some of the more trusted and long-term *knechts* were paid up to 40 Rxds per annum.[34] In the Cape district, *knechts* were rarely employed on farms with less than ten adult male slaves; in 1741, the mean number of adult male slaves per *knecht* on farms with *knechts* was twenty-four. In Stellenbosch and Drakenstein far fewer *knechts* were employed, but the mean slaveholding size was less: only seven adult males in 1741. Allowing an average wage of about 25 Rxds plus 30 Rxds maintenance costs, the cost of a *knecht* per male adult slave lay between 2.3 Rxds and 7.8 Rxds. An average of about 5 Rxds may be deduced.

Despite considerable variation, the average cost of slave clothing, food and *knecht* supervision may thus be estimated at roughly 25 Rxds per slave per annum; farms without *knechts* spent about 20 Rxds per slave per annum, although earlier in the century the figure could have been as low as 12 Rxds. In addition to these constant annual slave maintenance costs, must be added incidental costs; a Cape district farmer in 1736, for example, had to pay 4 Rxds to the authorities for the capture and punishment of his slave, and masters were sometimes liable to pay costs incurred by the criminal activities

Table 6.3 *Models of annual costs of maintaining slave labour farming unit (in rixdollars)*

	(*a*)	(*b*)	(*c*)
Clothing	5	5	15
Food	5	5	16
Knecht wages	–	10	25
Other slave costs (medical, incidental)	1	1	5
Farm maintenance, transport, etc.	7	10	35
Total	18	31	96

of their slaves.[35] Such incidental expenses were an added liability to farmers of the slave production system.

Annual costs of farm maintenance and marketing of produce at the Cape could be considerable, although again, there was great variety and general estimates are difficult to make. The Blankenberg writer allowed 100 Rxds for bills to the carter and blacksmith, 6 Rxds for the hire of a 'cellar in which to store the corn' and 15 Rxds for levies to transport the grain to the market; a total of 121 Rxds, or 7.5 Rxds per slave.[36] Barrow estimated 170 Rxds duty for grain brought to market and a further 150 Rxds for 'contingencies, wear and tear'; 320 Rxds in total, or 52 Rxds per slave, counting only the six slaves he indicates, although in fact many more slaves would have been required if the farm was working with a labour force of only slaves.[37] Taking the labour demand of the Blankenberg farm, this gives 20 Rxds per slave. Johannes Colijn estimated that he spent annually 350 Rxds on the maintenance of his farm equipment, 150 Rxds for manuring the vineyard, and 1,400 Rxds for barley and rye for animal feed; a total of 36 Rxds per slave, although he may have been over-estimating his costs.[38] Certainly, however, the annual costs of maintaining the farm in all sectors of the Cape economy increased dramatically with the price inflation of the 1780s. Only the wealthiest farmers had their own forges and were able to escape the fees charged by smiths and wagon-repairers; despite attempts to fix the scale of charges in 1744, both of repairs and new farm equipment, by the end of the century prices had doubled.[39] Moreover, transportation costs increased the further away the farm was situated from the market.[40] In general, it seems that the annual costs of maintaining farm equipment and marketing produce in the western districts rose from a minimum level of about 7 Rxds per slave to between 20 and 30 Rxds per slave by the end of the century.

The higher and lower limits of the annual costs of maintaining the slave labour farming unit may be summarised as in Table 6.3. The three models represent the costs of a small to medium-sized without a *knecht* in the period to c. 1780 (*a*), a medium-sized farm with a *knecht* such as the Blankenberg grain farm (*b*), and a large-scale high-quality wine farm at the end of the century as represented in the estimates of Johannes Colijn (*c*).

3 CAPITAL COSTS (*K*)

Against these annual returns and costs must be set the total capital investment required by the Cape farmer to purchase his farm land, stock, equipment, housing and slaves. Once again, there was considerable variety in the capital outlay of farmers, depending on the point in time and the nature of the farming enterprise.

The slaves themselves formed a major item in the capital investment of the farmer, according to Guelke between 13% and 17% of the value of total estates of arable farmers in the period 1731–80, and this percentage increased in the final two decades of the century to about 20%.[41] The percentage value of slaves in the estates of stock farmers was lower; Guelke estimates a figure of 12.5% in the 1730s, falling to 7.7% in the 1770s which reflects the lesser use of slaves by pastoralists.

The cost of purchasing slaves was therefore of major concern to the profit margins of the Cape farmer. Whilst there is a large amount of surviving data on slave prices fetched at public auction, a problem of the source material is that such records give no indication of the age or health of the slave: the major factors determining price levels in any slave society.[42] No precise correlations can therefore be made between slave prices and age. Nevertheless, since the auction records of estates include the total slaveholdings of each farm, the range of prices obtained in any one period may be linked to the age distribution of the total slave population. As auction prices, they reflect the market value of each slave related to the demands of the locality and time, rather than being artificial figures of the kind listed in estate valuations.[43] Auctions were designed to procure the maximum price for each item, and although there were occasional reports of malpractice, they were carried out by special agents under supervision.[44]

Table 6.4 indicates the distribution of adult male slave prices fetched at auctions for selected periods of the eighteenth century and the median price for each period. The median reflects the price of a slave of age and health, or labour utility value, in the middle of the distribution, and is thus less distorted than the arithmetic mean by the very low prices of useless slaves or the high levels of skilled slaves of prime age. Since all slaves had to be sold at estate auctions, those who were old, 'worn-out', blind or dangerous were sold at minimal sums; often less than 10 Rxds.[45] Sometimes slaves of poor health fetched lower prices than expected, although a young male who had a hernia was sold for 640 Rxds in 1783, considerably higher than the median; age was of prime importance.[46] Slaves with special skills and who were young and healthy also skewed the distribution; skilled vine-dressers, smiths or wagon-

Table 6.4 *Percentage distribution and median price of adult male slaves in rural auctions, 1692–1795 (in rixdollars)*

Year	Total number of slaves	Price (Rixdollars)											Median price
		1–99	100–99	200–99	300–99	400–99	500–99	600–99	700–99	800–99	900–99	1,000 and over	
1692–1715	103	29.1	62.1	8.8	–	–	–	–	–	–	–	–	103
1715–21	67	16.4	50.7	28.3	4.6	–	–	–	–	–	–	–	130
1722–9	131	38.2	48.8	12.2	0.8	–	–	–	–	–	–	–	105
1730–7	197	21.3	58.8	13.2	5.0	1.0	–	–	–	–	–	–	134
1738–48	151	32.4	44.4	16.5	5.9	0.8	–	0.7	–	–	–	–	120
1743–8	55	9.0	45.5	32.7	10.9	1.8	–	–	–	–	–	–	185
1748–56	123	17.8	40.6	30.9	6.5	4.1	–	–	–	–	–	–	192
1757–64	123	17.0	52.0	17.9	4.1	6.5	1.6	0.9	–	–	–	–	156
1765–72	219	18.7	47.5	20.1	9.1	4.1	0.5	–	–	–	–	–	163
1773–9	175	13.7	35.4	28.0	14.9	4.6	3.4	–	–	–	–	–	195
1780–4	189	3.3	16.6	23.2	19.8	14.4	7.2	6.1	1.7	2.2	–	5.5	310
1785–90	199	6.5	14.6	19.1	23.1	14.6	4.5	7.6	4.5	1.5	1.5	2.5	305
1791–5	201	5.4	15.9	21.9	26.4	16.9	6.0	2.5	2.0	1.5	0.5	1.0	345

Sources: CA MOOC 10/1–10/18, Vendurollen, 1692–1795

drivers could fetch two or three times the price of an unskilled slave of the same age.[47] H. Cloete wrote in 1787 that an untrained but 'well-built' slave could be purchased for 150 to 180 Rxds, one skilled in agriculture for 330 to 450 Rxds and a young and good driver for up to 600 Rxds.[48] Some slaves could thus be sold well above the median price; in 1773, for example, a skilled vine-dresser was sold for 1,000 Rxds.[49] Cloete added that the best-trained slave who 'knows his job well' would probably be Cape-born, since imported slaves 'seldom learn more than pick and shovel work unless they come to the colony very young'.[50] Such variables are not reflected in a median figure which can only represent a male adult of labour utility neither at absolute prime no beyond a useful age for farm work.

In general terms, it is clear that the distribution of slave prices was becoming wider as the century advanced. The median price rose gradually to c. 1740, more sharply between then and 1748, and then fell again. It slowly rose to 1780, and then increased dramatically–almost doubling–in the final two decades of the century. These trends may be closely related to the factors of supply and demand indicated in the previous chapters. There was a higher median price in the period 1715–21 than in the subsequent decade, which may have been as a result of the high slave mortality of the 1713 smallpox epidemic.[51] The slave shortage of the 1740s caused by a fall in the slave population by mortality and an increase in labour demand of agrarian production led to an increase in slave prices which is evident in the figures for 1743–8, and which continued into the 1750s.[52] The sudden increase of prices in the 1780s was the beginning of a lengthy period of inflation, which in the case of slave prices continued well into the nineteenth century and was caused primarily by the cut-back and ultimate stoppage of slave imports into the colony.[53] By the time of the first British Occupation, farmers were complaining that slaves could only be obtained at between three and four times their previous prices, and that the possibility of setting up a new farm was severely limited since 'there is required almost a Treasure to purchase the necessary number of slaves'.[54] The fall in supply and rise of population increasing demand led to an immense inflation of slave prices at this period.

The main effect of this steady increase was to widen the distribution of slave prices in auctions. Thus, for example, whilst it remains true that in the later 1780s a slave purchased at the mean price fetched in the 1730s was at the very bottom of the scale and unlikely to be much use as a field labourer, farmers in the later period were able to choose from a much wider price range, and, as the median figure suggests, obtain a useful slave at considerably less than prime cost. Some of the increase in slave prices must have been compensated for by a decrease in the prime value of slaveholdings, and purchasers later in the eighteenth century would have had to balance the amount they could afford to buy a slave with the scale of returns from the labour of one who was not of prime age or value. Moreover, the wide spread of slave prices indicates that buyers were acutely aware of the widely different values and labour utility of each human they purchased. It is likely that new farmers, or heirs purchasing

Table 6.5 *Models of capital costs for arable farmers (in rixdollars)*

	Land	Equipment	Number of slaves	Slave price	Capital costs per slave
Medium–large arable farm	2,300	1,200	10	1,200	470
(1740s)	2,300	1,200	15	1,800	353
Small–medium arable farm	1,500	800	5	600	580
(1740s)	1,500	1,000	10	1,200	370
Medium wine farm	15,000	3,500	10	3,500	2,200
(1790s)	15,000	3,500	15	5,250	1,580
Medium grain farm	7,000	4,700	10	3,500	1,520
(1790s)	7,000	4,700	15	5,250	1,130

some of the family slaves with their inheritance portion, would have obtained slaves of widely differing prices and age. The median price for each period may therefore be taken as typical.

There was also considerable variation in the other major capital cost to farmers: land. Geographical location, the quality of the soil and access to water or pasturage were all critical in determining land values. Guelke has estimated that land prices remained at a fairly steady level throughout much of the century, but started to increase notably in the general price inflation of the 1780s. There were enormous variations between prices obtained for land in the wealthier regions of the Tijgerberg or Hottentots-Holland and Drakenstein or Waveren. He has estimated, however, that the average value of land on arable farming estates was approximately 2,000 to 2,300 Rxds in the decades 1731–42 and 1751–62, rising to almost 4,000 Rxds in the 1770s.[55] These figures include the *opstal,* or farm buildings. The Blankenberg papers estimate allows 3,000 Rxds for 'a good corn farm' in 1744, but by the end of the century, Barrow estimated 15,000 Rxds for a wine estate land and *opstal,* and 7,000 Rxds for a grain farm.[56] As in the similar geographical conditions of classical Italy, there appears to have been a need to make a higher capital investment in a wine farm than in a grain farm; moreover, it took longer before the capital invested in wines yielded a marketable crop.[57]

Land and slaves accounted for about 60 to 70% of the capital investment of most farmers in the western Cape. The remainder was made up of farm equipment and livestock: ploughs, wagons, trek-oxen and horses necessary to carry out agricultural production. The Blankenberg grain farm estimated 1,130 Rxds for wagons, oxen, sheep, horses and ploughs, or 20% of the total capital assets of the farm; Barrow estimated such costs at 4,730 Rxds for a grain farmer (40% total assets), and 3,660 Rxds (16% total assets) for a wine farmer in 1797/8, needing wine leaguers, implements for distilling and pressing, oxen, horses and wagons.[58] The inflation of prices on farm equipment and livestock between the middle and the end of the century had a notable effect on the capital outlay required by the farmer; new ox-wagons increased from 45 Rxds in 1744 to 100 Rxds in 1793, and a ploughshare from 3 Rxds to 7 Rxds in the same period.[59]

Some of these figures may be drawn together to give an indication of the types of capital costs required in setting up arable farms at differing decades of the eighteenth century (Table 6.5). It is clear that the capital costs per slave were reduced by an increase in the number of slaves, since land and equipment costs did not rise proportionately: a factor favouring the use of larger-scale slave units, where there was sufficient means to keep all slaves fully employed. The capital costs rose dramatically at the end of the century for all arable farmers.

4 ANNUAL RATES OF RETURN PER SLAVE (*r*)

These estimates made of the costs of farmers per slave unit permit some broad conclusions to be drawn on the annual rate of return to farmers of their slaves. Table 6.6 indicates such a rate based on the estimates of the contemporary sources. These figures give a rate of return on slave units which are comparable to those of the plantation systems of the Deep South and the Caribbean, for which figures of between 5 and 10% have been calculated.[60] Certainly it appears that many Cape burghers were obtaining a higher return from a slave production system than the 6% normally paid on invested capital in the colony.[61] Nevertheless, contemporary figures are not always a very accurate indication of the costs of farmers; Barrow, for example, does not include the expenses of hired labourers which would have been necessary on the larger farms, nor the personal expenses of the maintenance of the household. A proportion of the profit indicated would thus have been absorbed in the costs of the farm unit. Moreover, these estimates seem to represent the kinds of farms which would have been most profitable; those producing a marketable crop on a large scale. The output value per slave (*S*) figures are considerably higher than those estimated as an average for arable producers.

Table 6.7 indicates some of the rates of return per slave when the models already discussed for each component in the calculation are combined. Although there is considerable variation in the values of the components, it is evident that the most likely combinations of values usually produce a percentage rate of return per slave of between 5 and 10%. Yet these figures only indicate averages during the eighteenth century. Very large-scale farms, such as Johannes Colijn's wine estate, or Martin Melck's wine and grain farm in Stellenbosch, were able to obtain a higher return on their slave labour by distributing the capital costs and marketing expenses amongst a large number of slaves. Rates of return on farms with fewer slaves were lower. For the

Table 6.6 *Annual percentage rates of return per slave from contemporary Cape sources*

Source	Slave productivity Value (S)	Annual maintenance costs (E)	Capital costs (K)	Percentage rate of return per slave unit (r) ($[S - E]/K \times 100$)
Blankenberg papers (grain farm 1740s)	37.5	19.5	358	5.02
Barrow (grain farm 1797/8)	200	68	1,955	6.75
Barrow (wine farm 1797/8)	266	54	1,544	13.73
J. Colijn (Constantia wine estate 1789)	250	75	1,615	10.83

Sources: CA MOOC 14/36/iii, Blankenberg papers, J.A. Sichterman folder; Barrow 1801, vol. II, pp. 396–7 and 399–400; CA C 184, pp. 229–31, Memorial of Johannes Colijn, presented to the Council of Policy, 27 November 1789

seventeenth century, adequate records of farm production costs are lacking, but profit levels may not have been as high when markets for produce and the commercialisation of arable agriculture were less developed. Moreover, farmers were threatened by variations in prices of goods: reduction in the prices obtained for produce in auctions or from the Company or increases in slave or farm equipment and other capital expenses. It is not therefore surprising that farmers complained bitterly when slave prices rose in the 1740s, or costs rocketed after 1780.[62]

One indication of the problems of finance which some farmers faced is the number of slaves which were obtained on credit, especially in the earliest years of burgher farming and in the period after the 1770s when rising prices meant that many were unable to afford the large capital outlay of a new slave. Many farm estates also had debts showing in their inventories, and there was not infrequently nothing left for the inheritors of smaller estates once the creditors had been paid. There were difficulties in accumulating sufficient capital to obtain a new arable farm, especially towards the end of the century, a factor which, together with the prospect of profits on the pastoral frontier, gave considerable impetus to the move of the colony inland.[63] Those who inherited sufficient capital, or farming goods and slaves to enable them to establish a farm of their own were more fortunate. It appears that Cape rural slaves produced a rate of return on the capital invested in them by their owners which

Table 6.7 *Models of annual percentage rate of return per slave for Cape arable producers (in rixdollars)*

Output value per slave (S)	Maintenance costs per slave (E)	Capital costs per slave (K)	percentage rate of return per slave (r)
200 (Mixed/large farm, after c. 1780)	96	2,200 (10 slaves)	4.7
		1,580 (10 slaves)	6.0
		1,130 (15 slaves)	8.4
100 (Mixed/medium farm, after c. 1780)	96	2,200 (10 slaves)	1.8
		1,580 (10 slaves)	2.5
		1,130 (15 slaves)	3.5
75 (Medium/large farm in good auction price year, pre-c. 1780)	31	580 (5 slaves)	7.5
		470 (10 slaves)	9.4
		353 (15 slaves)	12.5
50 (Medium farm, Company/average auction prices, pre-c. 1780)	31 (with *knecht*)	580 (5 slaves)	3.8
		470 (10 slaves)	4.0
		353 (15 slaves)	5.4
	18 (without *knecht*)	580 (5 slaves)	5.5
		470 (10 slaves)	6.8
		353 (15 slaves)	9.0
25 (Small/medium farm, low auction prices)	18	580 (5 slaves)	1.2
		370 (10 slaves)	1.9

was not in general any lower than that of New World plantation slave societies.

It is less easy to determine the rates of return on domestic slaves, whether in Cape Town, the inland villages or on farms. Artisans and craftsmen could obtain considerable profits for their owners, but the range of variables was immense. An estimate was made in 1826 that slave artisans in Cape Town could bring in a return of 18% per annum, considerably higher than that of rural slaves, although this is difficult to verify for the VOC period. Thunberg commented after his visit in the 1770s that every slave selling wood in Cape Town was 'obliged to earn for his master, two skellings daily, which makes about 80 rixdollars in a year; so that in a few years that master gets his purchase-money back again'.[64] Certainly skilled slaves could be highly profitable to their owners.

Other sources of profit by slaveholding resulted from speculation in slave purchase and sale, hiring out of slaves to others and slave breeding.[65] Speculation provided greater opportunities for urban residents than for farmers, and there is evidence that sales up-country from Cape Town were made at profit throughout the VOC period, especially at times of rural labour shortage.[66] The Company itself was the major beneficiary of profits made from the slave trade and from sales in Table Bay by foreign traders.[67] Nevertheless, the rather haphazard nature of the slave trade and the demands for slaves to be used for labour rather than speculation meant that there was no large-scale accumulation of profit by such activities.

The same was true of slave breeding. As has already been indicated, the Cape slave population was not self-reproducing. Many colonists had no, or very few, female slaves, although where they were present the levels of fertility could be high and were encouraged by the master. Van Ryneveld maintained that 'women are a charge if they do not serve for procreation'.[68] A *knecht* told Sparrman in the early 1770s that 'a female slave who is prolific is always sold for three times as much as one that is barren'.[69] Analysis of auction records indicates that female slaves of potentially fertile age could fetch higher prices than males, but that other females were normally valued at lower levels.[70] A few burghers were able to benefit from the offspring of their female slaves, and, with the introduction of the *inboek* systems, that of their male slaves with Khoikhoi females. There appear to be few cases, apart from the largest farms, however, where colonists could rely solely on this means of slave supply. Moreover, the high mortality rates for the slave population meant that many owners lost a valuable part of their capital invested in their slaves at one fell stroke.[71] The costs of replacing slaves therefore need to be added to the running costs of farms and households. As slaves became more expensive, this was an increasingly difficult task. Moreover, the costs of raising slave children could outweigh their return value. American slave studies have shown that planters only 'broke even' in their expenditures on slaves against the returns obtained from their labour after their twenty-sixth year.[72] The annual return from Jamaican slaves in the eighteenth century increased in proportion to the number of years for which they had worked on the farm.[73] This was clearly also true of the Cape, and a mortality crisis, such as that of the 1740s, could cause severe financial crisis. Many owners could not afford to replace their slaves, and either were forced to reduce their output or turn to alternative labour sources. This was especially true of the 1780s and 1790s when slave prices increased, and is a major factor in the lesser correlation of slaveholdings with output towards the end of the century.

One of the alternatives to purchasing a new slave for farmers was to hire slaves from others during the peak labour periods. This in turn provided a means of profit to the farmers who had invested capital in slaves which they could allow out of the farm: especially wine farmers, who had less use for their slaves during the harvesting period when they could be hired to grain producers. Mentzel comments that this could be a profitable business; the rates of monthly hire being 4 Rxds plus food and tobacco.[74] In Cape Town, some slaves worked permanently on a hired basis and were a considerable source of profit to their masters, although there is little evidence of this in the rural areas.[75] In 1783, the official monthly rate increased to about 6 Rxds, which gave a higher return on slaves at a time when purchase prices were increasing.[76] Slaveowners could also hire their slaves to the Company for public works, or for work at the local Landdrostdies. The records of the Stellenbosch Landdrostdy reveal that some farmers hired slaves to the Landdrostdy on almost a permanent basis for a number of years, whilst others did so only occasionally. Many of these were wine farmers; Jan Nel, for example, obtained a total of 255 Rxds for hiring two of his slaves over the period between March 1730 and November 1737: an amount which would have almost covered the cost of replacing them at current auction prices.[77]

Slave hiring could therefore provide a means of increasing the rate of return on slave investment for some owners, especially in Cape Town. Against this and the possibilities of slave breeding, however, must be set the cost of maintaining slaves in old age, or after their period of maximum labour utility.[78] Older slaves could be used as shepherds on mixed farms, for domestic work or in less arduous farm labour, but clearly the rate of return on their labour declined notably in the case of those who lived beyond an age of maximum strength. Since the calculations above are based on the total number of slaves, the age distributions must have been kept even for farmers to obtain a profitable rate of return.

The need to maintain slaves beyond their maximum labour utility age, and the problems of capital risk by death, was a major drawback of any slave production system. At the Cape, there was little compensation of high breeding rates. The problem was, however, to change to any other major form of labour which would be both feasible and more profitable. There were two alternatives: free white labour, produced by increasing dramatically the level of immigration to the Cape, and the indigenous Khoikhoi.

The response of the Council of Policy to the suggestion in 1716 by the Heren XVII that slavery should be replaced by free labour, was that hired immigrant labour would be considerably more expensive than slaves. Estimates of wages were made on the basis of the amount paid to the Company-hired *knechts*. One member of the Council concluded that wages and board and lodging of a free labourer would cost 58 Rxds per annum, in comparison with the 13 Rxds spent on the maintenance of a slave. This ignores the capital outlay necessary to buy the slave, of about 100 Rxds, but even allowing for this, the cost of a slave would be exceeded by free labour within three years. Another estimate made was that 'the wages paid to a farm-labourer for a year and a half would often pay for a slave'.[79] Van Ryneveld came to the conclusion at the end of the century that the average arable farmer would certainly be unable to afford hired free labour.[80]

Apart from the inability of farmers to afford hired labour, there were major problems in obtaining it. Discussion of the issue remained theoretical; no large-scale immigration scheme had been carried out, and, as Van Ryneveld indicated, there was no sign that sufficient free white labourers could be obtained, nor that they would be able, or willing to perform the kind of hard field labour carried out by slaves in the unmechanised agrarian system of the Cape.[81]

Moreover, at the Cape, as in other slaveholding societies, there were considerable advantages of slaves over free labour. Although their capital cost involved a greater initial outlay, they required no wages, were less able to demand good food or clothing, and were owned for life, with any offspring becoming the property of the master. They could not move away to other employers who offered more attractive wages, or drift to the town to seek work outside the rural sector. In a rural production system which was relatively inelastic in its demand for labour, and in which wages of free labour could not be afforded on a large scale, slavery had considerable advantages. The costs of the slave trade and of maintaining the structures of control of a slave system were outweighed by lower maintenance costs and a more constant supply of labour.[82] The only form of free labour which was of greater economy than slaves was the unpaid work of the family and kin on farms. On smaller-scale poorer farms, and especially in the pastoral regions, this was certainly used, especially at peak periods. In general, however, it was inadequate to maintain commercial agriculture.

A possible alternative and one which compromised between the costs of capital investment of a slave labour force and the lack of control over free hired labour, was the use of Khoikhoi and San labourers in a social system which reduced their mobility and access to the free labour market. The story of the gradual imposition of labour controls over the Khoikhoi has been told elsewhere. The existence of a system of labour repression conditioned by slavery provided a framework for the control of Khoikhoi labourers, who, with limited access to courts and Company, and with loss of their own system of production, could be relatively easily persuaded to enter burgher service at very low wages, and with none of the disadvantages of maintenance or potential loss of capital that slaves possessed.[83]

It would thus seem that Khoikhoi labourers were potentially an economically more viable labour force than that of slaves. There were, however, several problems. First, the Company initially discouraged the use of Khoikhoi labour by colonists because it wanted to preserve indigenous cattle supplies and links with the interior. Secondly, with the breakdown of Khoikhoi society, there was a demographic collapse, attributed by many contemporaries to the 1713 smallpox epidemic, but by recent historians to the loss of land and cattle as a result of colonial settlement.[84] Khoikhoi labourers were in short supply in the western areas, although they were used very much more in the pastoral frontier together with the San, and increasingly on arable farms in Stellenbosch and Drakenstein as their numbers recovered, or more were forced to seek employment by the loss of their own means of subsistence. In the western districts they were mainly used to supplement, rather than to replace slaves; only 6% of Stellenbosch and Drakenstein farmers in 1806 employed Khoikhoi and no slaves.[85]

The third reason, and that most often cited by contemporaries, against the use of Khoikhoi labour, was that they were 'lazy' or unsuited to heavy field work.[86] This reflects partially the preference of the Khoikhoi for, and their greater skill at, the pastoral herding work which was part of their indigenous subsistence mechanism, although Khoikhoi were also used in arable production, and especially as hired labour in seasonal periods of labour demand. It is mainly, however, a comment on the lesser ability of the farmers to extort labour from the Khoikhoi than from their slaves; despite cases of individual cruelty to Khoikhoi, and attempts to keep them at work against their will, the ultimate authority that a farmer possessed over his slave did not apply to his Khoikhoi labourer. The corollary to low wages was a lesser output or incentive on the part of the Khoikhoi to contribute to the profit margin of his employer.

The question of slave and Khoikhoi labour efficiency raises the wider issues of the effects of slavery on the economy of the Cape. One of the classic, although now controversial, views of slavery in the American South is that its use inhibited the development of agrarian innovations, and that intensive labour use exhausted the soil.[87] There are signs that soil fertility in the western districts of the Cape was decreasing notably as the eighteenth century advanced and that grain yields per morgen of land were falling.[88] This may be attributed to the lack of manuring, although the rates of profit from slave production farmsteads was not so high that farmers ignored the prospect of increasing their output deliberately. In contrast to northern Europe at the time, there was very little evidence of change in farming techniques or labour mechanisation at the Cape. Possibly the existence of slave labour reduced the incentive to develop labour-saving devices; threshing, winnowing and wine-pressing were carried out by hand and ploughs were crude and heavy. Yet the lack of intensive farming and the availability of land to absorb demographic increase, together with the limited resources of many arable producers in the colony, were as significant in explaining the apparent backwardness of Cape agriculture.[89] Moreover, as in ancient Rome or the American plantations, it was not the case at the Cape that slavery inhibited entirely the development of skilled labour. In fact, as in the ancient world, the permanent slave labour force often carried out the skilled tasks, such as vine-dressing, whilst the hired Khoikhoi acted as unskilled labour. Certainly in Cape Town the most skilled artisans were slaves.[90]

The limited size of slaveholding units at the Cape was, however, an inhibiting factor in the efficiency of slave labour. In the plantation systems of ancient Rome, the Caribbean or the Deep South, the most efficient use of slave labour was by organisation into work teams and gangs, each slave having a specialised role to play according to his age and skills.[91] Slave production seems to have been most profitable when the scale of the production unit was large. The rates of return in Table 6.7 indicate that this was also true of the rural Cape. The most profitable slave estates were the large-scale units where slaves developed specialised skills, and the burden of capital investments in the farm was relieved by the returns from the labour of a large number of slaves.

The main problem facing the small-scale producer was that the ownership of slaves tied up a great deal of the available capital, which was at high risk and could be lost entirely if a slave fell sick, escaped or died. There was certainly an acute capital shortage at the Cape by the end of the eighteenth century. De Chavonnes, the only advocate of the replacement of slavery by free labour in 1717, had prophesied that slavery would have the effect of inhibiting economic development in the colony, since 'the money spent on a slave is dead money'.[92] During the period of inflationary prices in the 1780s, the Company itself became worried at the very large amounts of capital which were being tied up in slave purchases by the farmers.[93] Capital shortage considerably inhibited the development of farming, and the unusual inheritance system was one of the few ways in which it could be released, or rather, re-distributed.[94] By the 1780s, the lack of ready capital led to a situation where arrears on land rents, and even the cost of slaves themselves, were paid for in kind.[95] The amount of capital invested in slaves was in itself a contributory factor to the inflation which increased their price. The fact that slave prices increased three- to four-fold in the period between 1770 and 1800, whilst prices of agrarian produce remained relatively stable, or increased only gradually, suggests that the slave-worked rural economy of the Cape was becoming over-capitalised.

The other major drawback of a slave production system was that, in comparison to a free labour economy, it inhibited the development of a market for goods and was unable to adapt itself readily to change. The market for foodstuffs created by the presence of the slaves could be considerable; the Stellenbosch miller, for example, complained at the loss of his trade during the slave mortality crisis of the 1740s and when the numbers increased again in the 1770s, a stimulus to the internal grain market was given.[96] Yet the existence of a substantial body of wage-earning labourers may have provided more impetus to trade and craft or industrial development within the colony. Perhaps more serious, however, was the check that the slave economy made on innovation or change within the agrarian sector.[97] This was most notable in the nineteenth century, when the market for grain and wine slumped and there was little to replace it. The developing part of the rural economy at the Cape during the eighteenth century was mainly the pastoral sector in which slavery was little used.

The slave production system of the western Cape tended to favour large-scale farmers rather than the smaller producers, but many arable farmers obtained considerable profits from it, and it provided the basis for a system of cultivation which expanded throughout the VOC period. By the end of the eighteenth century it was still a viable system. As the abolitionists of the nineteenth century were told and as the Cape government discovered after emancipation in the 1830s, there was little alternative labour system originating in the Dutch period with which burghers could profitably farm, unless a cheap and readily available supply was provided with legislative controls over the Khoikhoi, San and later, the Bantu-speaking peoples. Profits obtained by some slave owners could be limited, but they were only possible at all because of the existence of slavery around which the rural economy of the western districts had been moulded. Moreover, the rates of return on slave labour were not significantly different to those obtained in other colonial plantation slave societies or to interest rates in the Cape on capital loans. In Cape Town and as domestic labour in the pastoral districts, slaves were less directly linked to the profit levels obtained by their owners, although the hiring of slaves for employment in Cape Town could be a major source of income for urban inhabitants. The dependence upon slavery was not without economic disadvantages, especially in the amount of capital which it tied up in labour, and the inhibiting effect which it had on the development of interstitial labour positions. Ultimately, however, the social costs of such dependency were to be more far-reaching in the development of early colonial South Africa.

7

Slave life and labour

The purpose of the second part of this study is to examine some social aspects of the Cape slave system. Study of many other colonial slave societies has shown that slaves developed a 'world' of their own, shaped by common cultural traditions, religious beliefs and relatively stable family units.[1] In the rural Cape under the VOC, however, this was not possible. The lack of a self-reproducing slave population meant that slaves from a wide variety of areas of origin were constantly being brought into the colony, where they worked alongside Cape-born slaves and, increasingly, the indigenous Khoikhoi with very different cultural traditions. Slaves were frequently sold at the death of their owner to conform with the inheritance laws, and religious conversion was actively discouraged. The small size of most farms limited the potential for a thriving 'slave quarter' life, and many slaves lived in virtual isolation from each other. Rural slaves thus lacked the support of a strong cultural or social environment of their own. Only in Cape Town did closer contacts between slaves of differing masters and the greater fluidity of an urban environment provide some opportunity for the development of a specific slave community, marked especially by the growth of Islam. This contrast between rural and urban slave life emphasises the dependence of social structures on the organisation of slave life and labour in differing economic circumstances.

As in most slave societies, the living and working conditions of the rural slaves were considerably more restricted and arduous than those of the town.[2] The dominating feature of the life of the rural slave was work. 'I work the whole day long; I need to rest sometimes', grumbled one slave who was ordered to stop loitering and get on with his allotted task; another claimed in court that he had attacked the farm *knecht* because although he worked 'like blazes', he was still hit by him.[3] In common with most rural slave labour systems, the hours of labour were long and arduous. Work could begin well before dawn and continue after dusk, although most owners and their slaves were asleep by 10.00 p.m.[4] During peak labour periods, such as harvesting or wine-pressing, the working day could be much longer than usual. A proclamation of 1823 specified that slaves employed in field labour were not to work for more than ten hours per day in winter and twelve hours in summer, 'except during ploughing or harvest seasons or on extraordinary occasions when a remuneration shall be made to them in money or by an additional proportion of food'.[5] This suggests that many masters were previously demanding more than this number of hours from their slaves, and comparison with other societies indicates that rural slaves could be made to work for at least fifteen hours a day at peak periods.[6] Hours could also be long for domestic slaves, both on the farmsteads and in the town, although they were less subject to the intensive demands of seasonal work than field hands.

On most Cape farmsteads, slaves performed the variety of tasks described earlier related to the keeping of livestock, the cultivation of grain and the making of wine. Most farmers also kept a few slaves to undertake the domestic chores of the household, which could include tending to vegetables, making butter and cheese and feeding poultry. These were normally women who undertook the chores of both domestic servant and farm-girl, although occasionally male slaves milked the cows and worked in the house of the farmstead.[7] Field slaves were also used for other chores. The collection of wood was a task which almost all of the male slave labour force of the farms had to undertake at some time, and increasingly so as the forested areas around Table Mountain and Stellenbosch became denuded in the course of the eighteenth century. This was always a major burden for slaves living in Cape Town, and by 1797–8, Barrow described it as 'an arduous and daily task' for rural slaves as well, even citing it as a cause of slave mortality.[8] At least one case is recorded of a slave who died of exposure on the side of the Hottentots-Holland mountains when he had gone there to gather wood.[9] Slaves were also used as wagon-drivers, although in some cases Khoikhoi, whose skill at oxen-driving was renowned, were preferred for this task. In addition, slaves could always be called upon to act as messengers, or porters and guides to travellers, especially in Cape Town, but also in rural areas.[10]

Only on the largest Cape farmsteads was there any training of skilled slave craftsmen in the countryside. Groot Constantia was sufficiently large to have its own slave workshops and a forge, and there are occasional indications of slave smiths or carpenters on other large estates.[11] On most of the farms, however, such work was either carried out by specialists in the villages or in Cape Town, or by hired smiths. Some slave carpenters or smiths were hired out to farmers from Cape Town or large farms with their own craftsmen.[12] Craftsmen thus formed only a minimal proportion of the rural slave population, and the majority were field labourers who performed a variety of tasks throughout the year.[13] Skilled slaves were concentrated in the town and villages.

It was quite common for slaves to be sent to work on other farms. This could be as hired labour, particularly slaves owned by wine farmers who hired them to grain producers during the harvest, or, as frequently happened in the small-scale and closely knit settler community, loans of slaves to other members of the master's family to help out at peak labour demand periods.[14] Some farmers who could not fully use their slaves were able to hire them out to the local landdrostdy, and occasionally privately owned slaves were ordered by the Company to assist in public works projects, such as the banking up of rivers, the building of drifts or maintaining roads, paths and mountain passes. Cape Town residents were also called upon to provide slaves for public works, such as clearing the parade ground in front of the Castle.[15] There were thus a number of ways in which slaves could be fully utilised by their master, even if specialisation in rural areas was limited to the largest farms.

Few farms worked on a large enough scale to permit the organisation of specialised slave 'gangs', although slaves who were used to such tasks as vine-pruning or threshing, which required some knowledge and acquired skill, were obviously likely to be used for the same work from year to year. Age and sex were of prime importance, although farms were not large enough to permit the kind of absolute divisions of labour by age that existed, for example, on many New World plantations.[16] At times of peak labour demand, women and children as well as all available male slaves could be co-opted into the main labour activity of the farm. At other times, it was rare to find women slaves working in the fields; the few examples that have been traced significantly stress that it was normally a man's work, and in one case the woman was dressed in a man's clothes.[17] Certainly slave women at the Cape were not used regularly in field work, as for example in Jamaica, but were all involved in domestic labour. Some could become specialised seamstresses, and those of the right age were used as wet-nurses for white children.[18] Slave children could be employed in seasonal work such as sheaf-binding, or in domestic occupations.[19] Some were 'companions' to their master's children or required to guard younger white children or babies when they became of a responsible age.[20] Older farm slaves often worked with the livestock either as shepherds or leading the oxen in ploughing.[21] Yet in comparison with the Deep South or the Caribbean, there were few women or children in the slave population, and many slaves did not survive into old age. It seems likely, therefore, that the majority of the rural slave labour force at the Cape was fully employed, and that a lower percentage of slaves owned by farmers but not in full use existed than the 18 to 25% that has been estimated for Barbados.[22]

The lack of specialisation on most Cape farmsteads meant that fewer distinctions emerged of rank or position within the rural slave labour force than on the plantations of the New World.[23] Only on a few of the largest farms which approached the size of slaveholdings of the plantations of other colonial societies were slave drivers or *mandoors* used who had a privileged position within the slave group given to them by the master. Robert Ross has described the privilege given to the slave *mandoor* on Martin Melck's farm of sleeping with slave women.[24] Slave drivers were normally only used when there was a sufficient division of labour amongst the work force to make supervision of all of them by whites on the farm impossible. Melck's *mandoor* was controlling the other slaves working in the wine cellars at pressing time, when the majority of slaves were cutting grapes in the vineyard. Some farmers used slave *mandoors* if they had separate pasturage from the main farm, as supervisors over hired Khoikhoi labourers.[25] Such slaves could evidently be trusted to maintain their master's interests and to control temporary workers who were not themselves slaves. They did not work alongside other slaves in a position of authority, however, and direct control of slave or free black drivers over other slaves, as in many plantations of the Deep South, appears to have been very unusual at the Cape.[26] Significantly, Melck's *mandoor* was murdered by another slave who resented being given orders by him.[27] Moreover, the few references to slave *mandoors* in the available sources all date from the later decades of the eighteenth century, with the emergence of a few very large farmsteads and the presence of second or third generation slaves who may have been more trusted by their masters than imported slaves.

On the vast majority of the farms, the work of the slaves was supervised by whites. This was often the master himself, especially on the smaller farms, or his sons and step-sons. Occasionally, male relatives helped to organise the slaves on the farms of widows. On farms where there were not enough members of the family to cope with the number of slaves employed in different tasks or split over several units of the farmstead, or whose owners were resident in Cape Town, *knechts* were employed. These were not of burgher status, and were hired from the Company on annual and renewable contracts, at an agreed annual wage plus provision of food, housing and often specified amounts of brandy and tobacco.[28] They were generally unmarried and as Company servants only temporarily based in the colony, although some later settled there permanently. Some farmers employed a new *knecht* each year, whilst others could stay for ten or more years. Of the twenty-six *knechts* employed on farms in Stellenbosch and Drakenstein districts in 1752 whose contracts survive, only four worked for that year alone, ten were employed on the same farm for between two and ten years, and the remaining twelve for over ten years; the longest period of service was twenty-four years on one farm.[29] Comparatively few farms had *knecht* overseers; in 1752, there were only eighty-eight altogether in the colony, of which fifty-nine (67%) were in the Cape district, and the remainder in Stellenbosch and Drakenstein. Thirty-two per cent of the Cape district farmers, but less than 1% of these in Stellenbosch and Drakenstein, had *knechts*. Of the sixty-two farms with *knechts* in 1752, forty-two (68%) had only one, whilst fifteen (25%) had two, four (6%) had three and only one had four.[30] Hired overseers of slaves were thus used only on a minority of farms at the Cape and were not nearly as widely distributed as on the plantations of the southern States in America or the West Indies.[31] They were placed on the largest and most important farmsteads, however, where they replaced the master in the role of supervisor. In some cases, *knechts* worked alongside the slaves; they were responsible for giving the daily orders and for making sure that work was carried out satisfactorily.[32] They were called out first when trouble arose on the farm amongst the slaves, and when the master was away were left in control of the farm.[33] As such they were often hated and feared by the slaves, and were not infrequently the victims of assault by them.[34]

The *knechts* and *mandoors* were also given control over the non-slave labour which the farm employed; the Khoikhoi hired and permanent workers and the indentured *bastaard hottentots*. In the course of the eighteenth century, these became more and more closely integrated into the slave labour system, and performed the same tasks alongside them. Although nominally free and wage-earners, the slave control and labour structures absorbed them as well. They were also conscripted to help in public works, their wages were sometimes not paid, and their mobility was restricted.[35] The close contact in work and life on the farm of slaves with the Khoikhoi provided an element within the society of the farmstead which gave slaves a link with their surroundings; most Khoikhoi maintained some contact with their own kraals.[36] It could also be a point of tension; at least one case is recorded of a Khoikhoi who jeered at a slave on the same farm because he was not free.[37] Use of Khoikhoi against slaves by the masters was a significant aspect of slave control, and they accompanied commandos against runaways or betrayed them, but the relationship was not always antagonistic; Khoikhoi contacts with the interior could also be used by the slaves to advantage, and in one case at least, a Khoikhoi repeatedly incited slaves to escape inland.[38]

One distinction amongst the slaves that was clear on the Cape farmsteads was between the field workers and the domestic slaves. As in other slave societies, household slaves generally had a more privileged position in relation to their masters, and on the larger farms were distinct from the others not only by the kind of work which they performed but also by their greater involvement in the daily life of the burgher family.[39] They normally slept in the farmhouse, rather than in the special quarters provided in a separate building for the field slaves. The differences between the majority of the slaves and those few who worked in the house could be a cause of tension on the farmstead or division amongst the slaves. 'You are just an old house slave', one field slave said contemptuously when he left his sleeping place in the slave building in the yard and broke into the farmhouse at night, where he was apprehended by the domestic slave sleeping in the kitchen.[40] Sparrman records a violent argument that took place between the house slave and a cattleherd on a farm he visited, which only ended when the house slave 'was forced to buy him off with a large slice of meat'; an indication of the kind of advantage such as access to the master's pantry which a domestic slave could have.[41]

Circumstances in Cape Town were very different. All of the privately owned urban slaves worked in domestic labour, although there were variations between skilled and unskilled, those who were hired out and those who worked within the master's home. The organisation of labour was much less rigidly controlled. Only the Company slaves who worked together in large numbers required close supervision and Valentyn records both a *mandoor* and *ondermandoor* who allotted work to the 600 slaves in the Company Slave Lodge.[42] Privately owned slaves in Cape Town were not concentrated on the same tasks in such numbers and there are no records of urban *knechts* or *mandoors* supervising them.

The kinds of living conditions of slaves was individually determined by the wealth and level of consideration given to food, clothing and shelter by each owner. In general, slaves living on the farms were likely to be better fed from the produce of their surroundings than those with urban masters. De la Caille commented that on many farms, 'masters and slaves eat the same bread', which was of poor quality, 'although there are a few of the farmers who make good bread for their own table'.[43] At times of grain shortages slaves could be deprived of their bread rations, which were replaced by vegetables. Despite a recommendation as early as 1681 by the Company that farmers should give their slaves corn, pumpkins and sugar-cane as well as their 'usual' allowances, there was no legislative control over the feeding of slaves until 1823.[44] Sparrman ate tea and bread with a domestic slave, whilst Damberger shared the slave rations of meat and fish on two separate occasions.[45] Some wealthier owners with large numbers of slaves slaughtered sheep, or even oxen, for their labourers, and Company slaves in Cape Town were given regular meat and fish rations, although Mentzel commented that 'their food is scanty and coarse'.[46] On the wine farms, slaves were normally given tots of wine at regular intervals; at one farm, a basin-full each at 8.0 a.m. and another at midday with some rice.[47] The tot liquor system was thus becoming well established.

Slaves sometimes complained that they were not being given enough to eat, and some made a bid to escape because they were always hungry or, more often, stole food from their masters or from others.[48] Slave shepherds were in an especially advantageous position in this respect. Sparrman came across a shepherd slave roasting a lamb in the fields, and commented that many shepherds kept back one of twin lambs produced by a ewe for their own food without telling the master.[49] One slave shepherd defended his action of killing and roasting one of his master's sheep by saying that some of the slaves of the farm had come to him begging for food because they were hungry.[50] Percival commented that many slaves were given bad food which would otherwise have been thrown away: 'black bread, half sand, and the offal of sheep and oxen are their general fare', and according to Barrow, bad or insufficient food was a major cause of slave mortality.[51] However, in the rural areas, slaves could normally obtain enough food either from the produce of their master's farm, or by their own endeavours; tortoises caught locally were one delicacy which slaves ate.[52] There is evidence that on some of the larger farms slaves were given a piece of ground to cultivate their own vegetables, although this practice was not as extensive as on many New World plantations. As early as 1676, vegetables produced by slaves were sold to the fleet in Table Bay, and occasional indications are given of slaves planting their own onions and cabbages for their own consumption or for sale; on one farm in the Wagenmaker's Valley, each slave was given his own plot of land which he jealously guarded.[53] Normally at least one meal at midday was given to all the work force on the farms, sometimes eaten in the fields or vineyards.[54]

It appears that Cape slaves were poorly provided with clothing, although there were variations, particularly in Cape Town. By the nineteenth century, some urban slaves were dressed in livery or rich 'Malay' costume and at least one urban slaveowner hired tailors to make leather trousers for his slaves, but a more general picture is given by a Russian observer in the city in 1808 who commented that, 'the slaves in this colony are kept very poorly – they are dressed in rags, even those who serve at the tables of their masters'.[55] Engravings such as Illustration 1 (page 22) or the cover illustration show slaves wearing a minimum amount of clothing, although both portray hard manual labour in the summer. Descriptions of slave clothing in available records indicate that slaves normally wore only a shirt and trousers made of coarse cloth or leather and occasionally head-cloths as in Illustration 2 (page 38). Shoes and hats were rare; Thunberg stated that their absence was a 'token of their servile condition', whilst a manumitted slave wore shoes, stockings and a hat 'as a mark of his freedom'.[56] Company slaves were provided annually with a doublet and trousers made up by the garrison tailors and females with 'smocks imported from Batavia', according to Mentzel.[57] Rural slaves were less fortunate; many farmers acquired second-hand clothes for their slaves when visiting Cape Town, although the wealthy Johannes Colijn purchased one piece of coarse cloth annually for each of the slaves on his Constantia wine farm and some clothes were made by Khoikhoi or slave women.[58] Slaves sometimes protested that they were not given sufficient clothing, and as a result most slaves jealously guarded their clothes and at least one dispute over a missing shirt led to murder.[59]

The quality of the living quarters occupied by slaves also varied considerably. Few Cape farms were large enough to warrant slave 'villages' of the kind that existed on some of the New World plantations. Stavorinus described the extensive slave quarters on Martin Melck's farm, in which each of his 200 slaves 'had a separate brick building to sleep in', but this was very exceptional.[60] Only the larger farms had separate slave sleeping quarters, which were sparsely furnished; inventories which include slave 'houses' normally list only wooden plank 'bunks' and surplus or old farm equipment which was stored there.[61] On most smaller-scale farms, slaves slept in odd corners of the farmstead; in the kitchen, the attic, or even in the warmer weather out of doors in the garden, or the cow pastures. On some farms, slaves slept in the barn or the farm outhouses.[62] Slave shepherds and herders sometimes slept in the open or in sheep-pens with their flocks.[63] At night during the Cape winter temperatures in the slave quarters could be very cold; arguments about sleeping near a fire made in one of the slave-houses led in one case to a slave murder and blankets were treasured possessions.[64] Usually the slave women and children slept apart from the men; often, as domestic slaves, in the house whilst the field slaves were outside, but this was not always the case. In Cape Town it appears that most privately owned slaves slept in the attic, kitchen or outhouses of the master's home, and there is no evidence for the large yard slave enclosures of cities in the Deep South.[65] The exception was the Slave Lodge in which Company slaves were housed, where conditions were described as being far from sanitary and there was overcrowding.[66]

Slaves who were sick, and therefore of little use to their masters until their health was restored, could be given special treatment. In Cape Town, some slaves were treated by physicians, but in the rural districts brandy or extra wine was often the only remedy given, and there were no specialist slave doctors as in some other colonial slave societies.[67] Thunberg commented that his medical abilities made him especially welcome in the countryside where slaves were 'less accustomed to the use of remedies' than in Cape Town.[68] Tobacco was also given to slaves by some masters as an incentive or a reward for good work. In general, however, the working and living conditions of Cape slaves was far from pleasant.

Comparative studies of other slave societies have shown that even in the oppressive circumstances of the slave plantation or farmstead, slaves have developed their own norms and patterns of living, and have produced a strong and enduring cultural tradition which could give an element of solidarity and protection from the full onslaught of the slave system. At the Cape, however, circumstances prevented the emergence of a distinctive slave cultural tradition in the rural areas where the majority lived, and only in Cape Town was there some development of such a tradition in the VOC period. This was partly because the extreme diversification of place of origin of the slaves weakened the degree to which elements from their own cultures could be preserved in a new environment. Unlike the slaves on the New World plantations who came, broadly speaking, from societies with similar languages, belief systems and musical traditions, slaves at the Cape could come from such diverse regions as Madagascar and Mozambique, the Indian coastline and the Malay communities of the East Indies. The system by which rural slaves were acquired individually through sales from Cape Town or by the splitting up of rural estates, meant that a unit of slaves on a farm from a common origin was extremely unlikely. Although some visitors, mainly on the basis of their observations in Cape Town, stressed that the 'Negroes' of Mozambique and Madagascar more often undertook the heavy labour tasks, whilst Indian and Indonesian slaves worked in domestic labour, the evidence from the farmsteads shows that there was no such clear-cut division.[69] Variations in the ethnic composition of the slave labour force resulted from the main sources of slave supply at any one period, but often on the farms 'Negro' slaves were outnumbered by Indonesians or Indians. In addition to this ethnic diversity, a large proportion of the slaves throughout the century were imported, and there was little development of a cohesive Cape-born slave group with its own traditions and ways of life similar to that which existed in the ante-bellum southern States. There is some evidence that locally born slaves were valued more highly by their owners than those who were imported, since they had no need to adapt to a new life in servitude, but most owners had a mixture of Cape and foreign-born slaves. This could be a source of tension; at least one case is recorded of a Cape-born slave who called a Malagasy slave *Moer* after the latter had told him to help with the work, and was attacked by him as a result.[70] Assertions of area of origin were often a source of pride, and a cause of division within the slave population.[71]

Something of the effect of this diversity of slave origins and weakness of a common slave culture is evident in the languages that slaves used at the Cape. Slaves in any society quickly need to adopt the language of their masters to survive, and much of the intense debate about the origin of Afrikaans centres on the degree to which slave and Khoikhoi use of Dutch produced a simplified morphology and syntax.[72] Certainly most of the slaves whose speech is recorded in the records used a simplified form of Dutch which they had learnt from their masters. As Franken has pointed out, the Dutch spoken by the colonists was in itself far from pure, and many slaveowners were German, Scandinavian or French.[73] Other languages were also used by the slaves, however. Many Indonesian slaves spoke Malay; a Malay interpreter was required at the Council of Justice, and there is a surviving letter in the criminal records written by a slave in Bugis.[74] Portuguese, the lingua franca of the Indian Ocean, was also often heard. This was reflected in the criminal records, although Franken believed that it was untypical.[75] Nevertheless, there are clear signs that both Portuguese and Malay were increasingly used by slaves and masters also used a kind of 'Low-Portuguese' to communicate with them. As Mrs Kindersley commented in 1769, 'what seems extraordinary is that [the slaves] do not learn to talk Dutch, but that the Dutch learn their dialect, which is called Portuguese and is a corruption of that language'.[76] In this the Cape was following the pattern of the VOC possessions in the East Indies, where Portuguese survived and actively competed with Dutch as a language of communication with local peoples long after the Portuguese had left, in spite of Batavian legislation which encouraged the learning and use of Dutch, and refused manumission to any slave who could not speak it.[77] Similar attempts were made to enforce the speaking of Dutch amongst slaves at the Cape during the earliest period of the settlement, but this was largely unsuccessful, with the constant introduction of new slaves from diverse areas.[78] Sparrman visited a farm on which the slaves spoke only Portuguese to each other, and Thunberg had a slave guide who spoke no Dutch but communicated in sign language.[79] As late as 1822, Burchell records making a trip up Table Mountain with a 'polyglot party' of slaves who spoke their own languages as well as those of the colonists, although he also stated that some slaves could only speak Dutch.[80] Slaves often showed greater linguistic ability than their masters; there are several examples of slaves using Malay or Portuguese to each other in order to conceal what they were saying from the colonists.[81]

Whilst some slaves were doubtless proficient at several European, Oriental and Khoikhoi languages, others were handicapped by their lack of knowledge. This was especially true of newly imported slaves, of whom there were many at the Cape. Problems could arise when slaves did not understand each other; in one case the failure of a slave who spoke 'no Dutch and little Portuguese' to understand an instruction given to him led to a serious accident.[82] One runaway slave who was recaptured and died in prison, could not be identified because the *Caffers* who acted as guards in the Landdrostdy could not understand him.[83] In a society where a large number of slaves were new arrivals speaking a variety of tongues, there were evident limitations to the speed and extent to which a common culture could develop. A slave patois did emerge, much influenced by Dutch, Portuguese and Khoikhoi languages, but there were always those who did not understand their fellow slaves well. As Mullin has pointed out for colonial Virginia, language was an important aspect of slave acculturation; at the Cape it was a major obstacle.[84]

Linguistic disunity, reflecting the diversity of slave origins, was not the only factor inhibiting a thriving slave culture at the Cape. The two major stabilising foci of slave life on the American plantations were the slave family and the belief system and patterns of behaviour structured around religion, especially Christianity. In the eighteenth-century Cape, both of these elements were restricted. The relative stability of slave families which has been identified in North America was unusual.[85] At the Cape, the sexual imbalance of the slave population, especially in the farming districts, meant that very few male slaves were able to find slave partners. Until the nineteenth century no slave marriage was recognised in law, marriage being 'incompatible with slavery'.[86] The possibility of sale or the splitting of partners and their children at auctions of estates limited any permanence of slave family units.[87] Nevertheless, some slaves did form unions, although they had no official recognition, and referred to themselves as *man* and *vrouw*, with deep emotional attachments. One slave woman drowned herself and her children after the death of her slave husband.[88] Lacking slave partners, some rural slaves formed alliances with Khoikhoi women and lists of their offspring, the *bastaard hottentots*, show that some co-habited for a period of between ten and twenty years.[89] There were, however, limits to the number of Khoikhoi women permanently living on the farmsteads.

One of the main problems in the development of a stable slave family life at the Cape was the small scale of many of the farms and domestic slave holdings. Lacking special housing and in close proximity to their master and his family, most slaves were unable to find even the minimum amount of privacy necessary to maintain a family unit; farms such as that of Martin Melck in which 'married' slaves were given their own lodgings were very rare.[90] The subordinate position of the slave to the master and his family always overrode his function as a spouse or a parent. For example, slaves were powerless against the sexual desires of their masters, both towards themselves and for their children. An example of the ways in which interference by a master could disrupt slave family life was the case of Reijnier van Madagascar, who lived on a Drakenstein farm with a female slave, Manika van Bengal, in the 1730s. They had a daughter, whose beauty at the age of fourteen so attracted their master that the farmer's wife became jealous of her and tried to persuade her husband to sell her. She beat the girl constantly, and after doing so one afternoon when Reijnier was working, and then rubbing salt into the wounds, Reijnier attacked his master in rage when he returned and discovered what had happened. Fearing punishment, he ran away and hid for eight years in the hills by the Berg River, until he was captured and identified by Manika.[91]

Slave control over their own children could also be severely limited. One slave who clipped his son around the ear for being insolent to his mother, was challenged for doing so by the *knecht*. He replied that 'I can hit him if he is naughty. He is my son, and if the Baas were here he would say "Go ahead."' The *knecht* disagreed, and hit the slave so severely that he fell unconscious to the ground.[92] The effect of such actions on the parental authority of slaves must have been considerable. The slave, as a subordinate of his master, could not effectively act as head of his own family. Where slave families did exist, the weakening of the role of the father tended to lead to matriarchal families.

Some masters made conscious attempts to preserve the unity of their slave families by bequeathing them to one person in their wills or selling them as a unit. It was not until 1782, however, that a ban was made on the sale of young slave children separately from their mothers. As late as 1830, the British official responsible for the administration of slaves (the Protector of Slaves), stated that slave children who remained with their mothers 'to a later period than 10 years, are in no respect benefited by it but far otherwise'.[93] Certainly there were at the Cape no conscious efforts by slaveowners to encourage stable slave families. The sexual imbalance together with the disintegrative effects of close physical contact with the master made such developments unlikely. As a result, some owners faced problems from slaves or Khoikhoi who had been forcibly separated from their partners by sale and who attempted to follow those they loved.[94] A more frequent difficulty to slaveowners, and one which caused considerable tension especially on farms, was the lack of any sexual outlet to the majority of the male slave work force. Slave murders or assaults because of 'jealousy' were relatively common in a society where there were few females.[95] In one case, an owner accused a female slave of causing so many fights and discontent because of jealousy amongst his male slaves that he 'wished I had not bought you', and Sparrman records the case of a farmer who refused to keep any female slave because it would 'cause jealousy'.[96] Rape, homosexuality and bestiality can be seen as extreme responses to the sexual frustrations of rural slaves, which the prevalence of women in Cape Town helped to alleviate for those in the town.[97]

The majority of Cape slaves and especially those on farms therefore lacked family organisation or a common cultural heritage which would have aided them to create a 'world of their own'. There was, for example, no sign of a continuity of slave names which accompanied the kinship network that Gutman has identified on the American plantations; Cape slaves received arbitrary names from their masters, normally of the months, figures from classical mythology or the Bible, to which, in official records, were appended their place of origin.[98]

Not only were slaves at the Cape unable to develop a strong unified cultural tradition or family life of their own, but they were also largely excluded from the cultural system of their masters. In contrast to the southern States, where slave churches and missions were established, or Cuba, where there were resident clergy on some of the plantations, there was at the Cape little attempt to evangelise the slaves until the very end of the eighteenth century.[99] Decrees passed in Batavia and at the Cape in the earlier years of the settlement had encouraged masters to bring up their slaves in the Christian faith and there is evidence of some slave baptisms in both urban and rural districts in the seventeenth and early eighteenth centuries.[100] Lists of slave baptisms in records of the Dutch Reformed Church in Cape Town show that during the VOC period there were never more than forty per annum, and the vast majority of these were of Company-owned child slaves or of privately owned adults who were then manumitted. This practice lessened later in the eighteenth century.[101] Even in the city, the number of adult slaves who were baptised was minimal, and in rural areas was even more restricted. The religious enthusiasm of the farmers was limited; as early as 1727, the Landdrost of Stellenbosch complained that burghers in his district led 'a very godless and scandalous life' and in 1714 Valentyn commented that despite the efforts of preachers they had made little headway amongst the colonists, 'due in no wise to the faltering of their zeal, but to the stupidity and indolence of the burghers'.[102] This was not true of all, of course; Sparrman visited one farm where the slaves sang psalms with the rest of the family. Nevertheless, he commented that this showed 'a zeal for religion quite unusual in this country' and that the master had not permitted his slaves to be baptised.[103] There was considerable hostility of masters toward slave baptism; after 1770 baptised slaves could legally obtain manumission if they could afford it, and as Christians could not be sold.[104] Not only did masters thus lose economic control over Christian slaves, but baptism also gave them access to churches and preachers which would reduce their dependence upon their owners. De la Caille commented in the early 1750s that the farmers 'never talk to their slaves about religion'.[105] Only in the 1790s was much attention paid to the conversion of rural slaves to Christianity by the Dutch Reformed minister of Tulbagh, Reverend Vos, who realised the harmful effect of the law forbidding the sale of Christian slaves and worked for its repeal.[106] Although several Dutch Reformed and foreign missionaries began work amongst the slaves from that time, by 1831 one missionary commented that neglect of religious education meant that 'vast numbers of the slaves profess no religion whatever: the vast majority of those who do are followers of the doctrine of Mohammed; few, very few, make any profession of Christianity... the number of baptised is extremely small, and to be found chiefly among the rising generation'.[107]

Islam certainly provided a more attractive form of religious expression for some slaves, although its influence in the VOC period was almost entirely restricted to Cape Town and there were few converts elsewhere until it was taken to the eastern Cape in the early nineteenth century by a group of escaped slaves.[108] Islam was introduced to the Cape by the Indian and, to a lesser extent, Indonesian slaves imported from regions of Moslem control, and was also given impetus by the presence of Batavian political exiles, some of them notable Islamic teachers.[109] Although there was no official recognition of Islam by the authorities and permission to build a mosque was not granted until the period of the British Occupation, its spread amongst the urban slaves was evident throughout the eighteenth century.[110] In part this was the result of the restrictions on the sale of Christian slaves which encouraged masters to permit their slaves to turn to Islam, and several writers noted a preference for the sobriety of Moslem slaves.[111] It appears that the increase in Islam was most notable towards the end of the eighteenth century, when it began to play a role in the assertion of a slave identity. Robert Ross cites the case of slaves escaping from Cape Town in 1786 who obtained Islamic talismans from a 'Mohamedan priest' to protect them from capture, and by the first decade of the nineteenth century the extent of the spread of Islam amongst slaves had been noted by the authorities and attempts were made to control it.[112] The precise extent and effects of the growth of Islam amongst the urban slave population still remain to be investigated but it is clear that it was beginning to play a role in the formation of an urban society in which slaves played an important part.

Access to education was extremely limited. On many of the farms, education for burgher children was limited to the occasional teaching of *knecht* schoolmasters, but their qualifications and efficiency were often suspect. Some slaves may have benefited from the private education given to their master's children, but the overall effect was minimal. Certainly there was no rural equivalent to the schools for white and slave children established in Cape Town.[113] A slave school was not established in Stellenbosch until 1823.[114] In the town, Company and some privately owned slave children were given a rudimentary education but the overall impact was restricted. There is only one surviving example of slave writing, and that is in Bougies, evidently learnt before the slave arrived at the Cape.[115] In all of the criminal records, slave testimonies are signed with a cross.

Deprived of family stability, access to the culture of their master's society and a common heritage from their own homes, slaves at the Cape during the Dutch period were thus left very few resources with which to construct their own world and values to face the onslaught of the coercive labour structure into which they were forced. Only in Cape Town was there some emergence of a specific slave life and culture in social circumstances and an environment which differed strikingly from that of the majority of slaves who worked in rural areas. Masters seemed to concern themselves little with what occupied their slaves' free time or thoughts, provided it did not interfere with their labour or obedience. Lacking any accounts of slave life by slaves themselves, only a few hints of some of their occupations may be obtained from the legal records and accounts of travellers. The musical gifts of slaves were particularly noted. According to Lichtenstein, 'there are many freedmen in the town who gain their living by instructing the slaves in music but neither master nor scholars know a single note: they all play entirely by the ear', and slave musicians were in demand in Cape Town for private and public functions.[116]

Little is known, however, of the kinds of entertainment which slaves provided for themselves. Although there was no legislation on hours of work until the nineteenth century, it appears to have been common usage during the Dutch period to give both rural and urban slaves a holiday on Sundays, and in one case slaves on a farm refused to work on a Sunday when ordered to do so by the *knecht*.[117] Burchell also states that the slaves were given a holiday at New Year, and after the harvest was completed.[118] Attempts, however, were made to prevent slaves from leaving their farmsteads on Sundays and holidays by legislation in 1766, since they were 'meeting up together in remote places and there perpetrating many rowdy actions'.[119] Success at controlling them was limited, however, and in 1786 and 1788, Stellenbosch farmers complained at the difficulty of restraining their slaves from visiting the drink shebeens in Stellenbosch village.[120] This was a major problem for owners of slaves in Cape Town, where the many taverns provided refuge for slaves. Legislation was passed forbidding slaves from gambling or buying liquor, but this was often broken in Cape Town, and drink houses in False Bay and the Hottentots-Holland area were frequented by slaves from the surrounding farms.[121] In addition to drink as an escape from the realities of their lives, some slaves also smoked dagga, to which they were introduced by the Khoikhoi.[122]

Taverns were also seen as a threat as they were often places in which stolen goods could be sold or exchanged. As in other slave societies, Cape slaves distinguished between theft from their masters, which they saw as partly theirs by right, and that from each other. Often thefts of food or clothing were a necessary prelude to a bid for escape with provisions, but sometimes slaves were able to obtain goods whilst still on the farm or in their master's household. A problem in rural areas was where to hide the goods until they could be disposed of. One slave hid brandy and wine which he had stolen from his master's wine cellar in a hole which he had made in the thatch of the farmhouse itself; others made false keys to the wine cellar which they used on several occasions, in one case taking the keg of wine into the slave quarters where it remained hidden from the master for several weeks.[123] Theft of money, silver or valuable goods was more dangerous, since it could often be traced, although underground channels were available in Cape Town.[124] This was especially true when paper money was introduced in the last decades of the century.[125]

Most thefts by rural slaves from their masters were of food or drink and were condoned by the other slaves on the farm. The rudimentary internal discipline that slaves maintained over each other in case of thefts from their fellows was an entirely different matter. One slave who was accused by his fellows of stealing a shirt, fled from the farm and told his master when caught that he 'had been made afraid by the other slaves and had run away for fear of a beating by them'.[126] Slaves could also inflict a rudimentary justice on each other for other activities they saw as harming their own interests, such as sleeping with each other's women or, as in one case, a father who killed his own son after he had been found sleeping with his sister.[127] There is no evidence surviving of the kinds of slave trials found on some Jamaican plantations but Cape slaves clearly maintained certain rules of survival and taboos in their restricted and deprived environment.[128]

Cape Dutch slave society was thus still a society in the making. It lacked the stability of cultural or family traditions established later on some of the plantations of the New World or Zanzibar, being constantly supplied with new arrivals who needed to adapt to their position and with a severe sexual imbalance. On the small-scale farms of the Cape, the presence of the master was often more direct than on the New World plantations, and the living conditions of many slaves poor and rudimentary. Moreover, on many remoter farms slaves lived in almost complete isolation from a wider community; on those where there were only a handful of field slaves, excluded from the life of the farmhouse, life must have been lonely as well as harsh. In Cape Town, the potential for contacts with slaves and others was much greater, living conditions in general better than on the farmsteads and the growth of Islam provided some basis for slave cultural identity. Nevertheless, even in the urban context, there was little development of the vibrant slave culture of the kind that emerged in the Afro-American societies of the New World. To this extent, the Cape example supports Patterson's suggestion that a flourishing slave culture can only emerge in a society with a significant free population whilst 'a society with only masters and slaves cannot sustain a slave culture'.[129] Only in Cape Town where a group of Free Blacks and other freemen who did not own slaves existed, was there some evidence of such a development. In general, however, without the backing of a strong 'world of their own', Cape slaves resorted to other methods to cope with the control mechanisms of their masters and the authorities. It is to these aspects of authority and response within the Cape slave system that we now turn.

8

Slave discipline and Company law

The nature of the control system is a key element of any society in which a sector of the population is held against its will. All slave societies were by definition coercive in structure. To the modern mind, all slavery is morally repulsive, and reference to a 'mild' slave system an abuse of terminology. Some contemporaries also realised the implications of a slave system. As one writer, commenting on the treatment of slaves at the Cape at the beginning of the nineteenth century, stated: 'it is self-evident that the comfort and happiness of the slave must necessarily depend upon the temper, habits and character of his master. We need not cite examples to demonstrate that cruelty is the necessary and inseparable concomitant of slavery, even in its mildest form'.[1] Examination of the ways in which authority was exercised reveals much about the dynamics of slavery, and the attitudes of those who controlled the system. It operated at two levels; the individual relationship of master and slave involving personal subordination, and the wider context of the administrative system in which both master and slave lived, expressed most clearly through the rule and operation of law.

Slavery at the Cape is often presented both by contemporary observers and more recent writers as having been of a particularly mild nature. De Mist, for example, stressed that 'There is a great difference between the treatment of these [the Cape] slaves and that meted out to those who are yearly shipped to America from the Congo and Angola. At the Cape they are, in the majority of cases at least, looked upon as permanent family servants... their lot in life quite tolerable.'[2] Such views have been reflected in the comments and writings of officials and historians ever since.[3] Some of them were based on the assumption that Cape slaves were mainly the personal servants of their masters who performed domestic work only, 'domestic rather than predial'.[4] In the rural areas this was clearly not the case. The majority of slaves were field labourers who had little personal contact with the life of the master's family in the household, especially on the larger farms of the western areas. Many contemporaries distinguished between the treatment of slaves in Cape Town and on the farms. Barrow, for example, commented that 'The field slaves belonging to the farmers are not, however, nearly so well treated as those of the town... they are ill fed, ill clothed, work extremely hard, and are frequently punished with the greatest severity; sometimes with death, when rage gets the better of prudence and compassion' and Percival, by no means the critic of the slave system that Barrow was, wrote of the good treatment of urban slaves but added that 'the treatment of the different classes of slaves at the Cape is by no means the same... the people of Cape Town universally treat them well in comparison to the farmers and planters of the country parts'.[5] The distinction between Company and privately owned slaves in Cape Town was stressed by Mentzel: 'The slaves belonging to the Company are, undoubtedly, the most rascally of all. They also receive the worst treatment... those who are owned privately are, with few exceptions, much better treated and much more amenable to good treatment.'[6] Certainly the favourable impression that many visitors had of Cape slavery seems to have been based on their observations of domestic slaves in Cape Town, rather than the realities of life for the majority on the farmsteads or in Company ownership.[7] Just as there were distinctions between the living conditions of slaves, so variations in the means of slave control were also of significance.

A further aspect of the argument that Cape slavery was mild is that slaves were protected from abuse by their masters by the VOC government and its legal structure, to which they could complain and receive redress.[8] In general, however, the impact of the legal system at the Cape was to reinforce the authority of the master over his own slaves, except in cases where life was taken. Even then the protection offered in practice to the slave population was considerably less than that in theory. Finally, the argument that the high value of slaves prevented them from being badly treated can be reversed; the need to extract the maximum profit from the slave as quickly as possible to redeem the purchase price could lead to heavy labour demands in an expanding economy.[9] Moreover, the need to maintain authority by masters especially on relatively isolated farmsteads meant that fear of slaves could be expressed by forceful and violent punishment which often overrode such economic considerations. Examination of the workings of the slave control system by individual actions of owners and in law provides a picture which seriously qualifies the orthodoxy of a lenient slave system at the Cape.

In most of the colonial slave societies, as well as those of the ancient world, the property aspect of slavery has been to the fore, despite whatever feelings of paternalism may also have existed between master and slave.[10] This seems to have been especially true of the Cape under the VOC partly because the whole ethos of the colony, as far as its government and many of its inhabitants were concerned, was dominated by the desire to make profit and record losses. In this, attitudes of colonists towards their slaves were largely shaped by the policy of a mercantile company which regarded them in inventories, estate valuations, wills and auction records, alongside furniture and cattle, as objects solely for sale and valuation. Like material objects, slaves could be bought 'on trial' for a year and returned if unsatisfactory, or loaned for a year and returned on demand of the vendor if required.[11] They were described in inventories as *kleijn* or *groot* on the same sheet as oxen and sheep bearing similar labels.[12] The rights of ownership of a master over a slave were established by Company law and were absolute; Van Ryneveld commented that they were assumed unless the slave or someone acting on his behalf could prove otherwise, even if there was no deed of sale available.[13] In a society in which census records which included slaves as stock were taken annually, and estates and slaves were valued on the death of either the owner or his spouse and redistributed amongst numerous heirs, the slave retained a property valuation which was constantly expressed in financial terms. Absolute possession and treatment of the slave as property could lead to extreme brutality. One of the most sadistic slaveowners of the VOC period, Johannes Kuuhn, said to his nephew, who wanted to hit one of Kuuhn's slaves with a spade, 'Go right ahead, since I bought him with my money, if he dies from the blow all I need to do is to buy another one.'[14]

This was an exceptional circumstance, but it is indicative of an attitude that was likely to develop in a society where slaves were comparatively easily available by inheritance or local auctions, where the slave trade was still open, albeit with a sporadic supply, and where the property concept was to the fore. Some slaves clearly demonstrated to their master that they were more than mere property and on a small-scale farm or in an urban household there must have been much interaction of master and slave. This did not always take a coercive form; there are examples of slaves who protected their masters from attack by others or who took a lively concern in the affairs of the family to which they were attached.[15] Sparrman even came across one slave in the Langekloof region who 'had absolute management of the farm' and had developed a system of irrigation for wheat cultivation.[16]

Clearly, as in any slave society, there could be a wide variation in the relationship between master and slave at the Cape. Nevertheless, the ownership of the slave by his master and the control this implied was normally expressed in terms of discipline by force or threat of its use. One master demonstrated the loyalty and devotion of his slave by stating that he had not needed to punish him for thirteen years; another stressed that he did not want to corporally punish one of his slaves who had been returned to him after escape.[17] The absence of punishment in these cases was clearly a noteworthy feature. As in many slave societies, corporal punishment was the most evident means or asserting authority. At the Cape this was made necessary not only by the structure of coercion but also by the circumstances of the slaveowners themselves, especially in the rural districts.

Sparrman, visiting a farm in the Paarl region which was left in the control of a *knecht*, and seeing the slaves in the house that had served him 'in such good humour and so kindly and familiarly treated', observed to his host that 'his mildness and kindness was the best pledge for their good behaviour, and the surest preservative against their attacks'. He received the answer, however, that the isolation of the farm and the fear of attacks from gangs of runaways in the district, together with 'instances of the blacks becoming furious at night, and committing murder, more particularly on the person of their master but sometimes, if they cannot get at them, on some of their comrades or else upon themselves', required the exertion of a strict discipline; 'I am here in the place of a master to them, and am obliged to punish them whenever they behave ill to me or to each other.'[18] The *knecht*'s attitude may have differed from that of his master, but the incident indicates that behind an apparent facade of benevolence could lie a darker picture. The *knecht*'s reasoning was significant. Despite the fact that the farm was located well within the boundaries of the south-western settled arable region of the colony, he lived in fear of attack by runaways and roving gangs. The relative isolation of many Cape farmsteads led to a situation in which farmers had considerable fear of their own slaves and of danger of attack from others. Sparrman was prepared to spend the night in the open rather than stay on a farm near Cape Town where the master was absent, 'for everybody in this country is obliged to bolt the door of his chamber at night, and keep loaded firearms by him, for fear of the revengeful disposition of his slaves', and on another farmstead he set a chair against the door of his room and 'laid down to sleep with a drawn knife'.[19] In one court case in which a slave was accused of attempting to murder his master, the prosecutor commented that 'in this country everyone places himself daily in great danger by the frequent contact with slaves'.[20] Such fear was endemic in the colony and rose to great heights when slave plots were unearthed or suspected.[21] In Cape Town there were also periodic fears of revolt and feelings of insecurity by masters despite the presence of the Company garrison.[22] Much of the hostility to the legislation of the early nineteenth century attempting to 'improve' the treatment of slaves came from owners who felt it would reduce effective control over them: 'a flame will be kindled only to be quenched in blood'.[23]

The fear of masters of their slaves is reflected in the kinds of ways in which they were controlled. Percival stated that slaves on farms were locked up in their quarters at night and the Company Slave Lodge was locked at 8.0 p.m. and a roll call held, although the visiting sailors were let out at 9.0 p.m.[24] This was not universal, but the fear of slaves moving around at night led most farmers to keep packs of dogs to guard the farmstead against them.[25] Measures were taken against slave movements in Stellenbosch village, and towards the end of the century between the farms by the use of passes. Slaves could be apprehended and shot on sight if they were not provided with a letter or pass from their master when seen on pathways between farms.[26] In the less ordered structure of an urban environment, the need to control the movement of slaves was even more acute.[27] Legislation passed in 1754 imposed curfews on slaves, forbade them from riding horses or wagons in the streets, singing, whistling or making 'any other noise' in the evening, meeting in bars or buying alcohol, or gathering at the entrance of church during services. A sixteen-year-old slave boy was publicly whipped for the latter offence, and for his 'great impertinence' in telling the Fiscaal that he had come there to bring his master's coat.[28]

The major concern of masters was with control of slaves within their homes or farms. This depended primarily on maintaining clearly the division of power between master and slave, and the constant expression of the authority of the master and the inferiority of his slave. In a situation where contacts between master and slaves were close as on a small farm or town house and slaves not always distinguished by separate living quarters, family life and daily living patterns, the maintenance of such a division was all the more crucial to the master's authority. The master needed to emphasise the complete dependence of his slaves and their duties to him.[29] Visible marks of deference were thus vital. The son of one burgher resented that he was not acknowledged by his father's slave when he met him one evening in the farmyard, and asked him why he did not say 'Good evening' to him. The slave's reply indicated a lack of due respect in the eyes of the owner: 'If I do my work during the day and come home in the evening, that is enough.' It was not enough; deference was also required, and the slave was beaten for his 'insolence'.[30] Another slave did not say 'Good day' to a burgher who was not his owner, saying that he was obliged to greet his master and mistress but no other.[31] Domination was thus structured into the daily life of the slave.

The slave was bound to obey the order of his master or those appointed by his master. The slave who complained that he wished to stay up later than the time he was told to go to bed or who asked to be given other work when the daily orders were given out, was punished for his 'insolence'.[32] To rest even briefly after being ordered to work was to threaten the authority of the master and the structure of control.[33] Female slaves were obliged to submit to their owner's sexual appetites if so ordered, and risked beatings if they refused.[34] Under a master's orders, slaves were obliged to carry out actions to which they themselves strongly objected, such as holding down fellow slaves while they were whipped or beating up slaves of other masters who occupied disputed grazing lands.[35]

Some studies of other colonial slave societies have suggested that loyalty of a slave for his master could be developed by a system of rewards on the plantation.[36] Most of the means of offering incentives were, however, lacking at the Cape. The privileges of position within a specialised labour force based on rank and seniority did not apply to the small-scale farms, slave family life was minimal, and the breakup of the slave unit at the death of the master or his spouse limited the close association of master and slave. One slave was offered a money reward for helping to recapture a fellow slave who had escaped, but this was a unique example.[37] Closer bonds could develop between masters and their domestic slaves, who were distinct from the field workers, and as wet-nurses to the family children could play a very personal role in the life of the master.[38] Whilst this might have applied more in Cape Town, domestic slaves formed only a small percentage of the total slave population in the rural areas.[39]

In general, the use or the threat of force dominated the relationship between master and slave and assured the authority of the former. Such a position might be expected in a society where a minority group was exerting absolute authority and control over the lives and labour of slaves who were living in poor conditions, deprived of family life or a firmly rooted culture. Many slaves were imported and had memories of freedom. In addition, most farms were relatively isolated and even in Cape Town, dominated by a mountain which provided refuge for runaways, masters lived in a potentially hostile environment surrounded by fear. The male burghers were greatly outnumbered by adult male slaves. Their one advantage was a monopoly over the instruments of power. Master control had to be seen to be maintained by the use of force, either threatened or actual.

The corporal punishment of slaves was the most common means of control. By inducing fear of pain, masters obtained co-operation, albeit often grudgingly. The first instinct of virtually all the slaveowners encountered in the records when faced with a threat of breakdown of authority by slave disobedience to orders, 'insolence' or disruption of the daily routine of labour was to reach for the *sjambok* whip which seemed usually to be close at hand. As in the New World, the punishment of slaves for offences which threatened the authority of the master was a private action carried out within the confines of the farm or home, and was sanctioned by the law. On the small-scale farmstead, removed from eyes of all but the slaves themselves, the master had powers of more or less arbitrary action.[40] Provided the punishment did not lead to the death of the slave or he was not tortured without good reason, there was no attempt by the authorities to exert regular control over domestic discipline methods until the nineteenth century.[41] On remote farmsteads such control by any external body would have been very difficult.

Whipping was the most common form of slave punishment. It inflicted considerable pain, which could be increased by rubbing salt into the wounds, providing a striking impact to the victim and the other slaves on the farm of the visible authority and supremacy of the master, and yet it did not greatly reduce the labour efficiency or time at work of the punished slave. After a severe whipping for trying to escape, Jacob van Malabar was ordered by his master to immediately get on with the ploughing. When he collapsed in the field, saying he could not go on because of the pain, his master's wife replied, 'I can't help that; you have only got what you deserved, and you must get on with your work.' His inability to do so only led to more flogging.[42] The *sjambok* was a whip with particularly painful effects, and was a speciality of South Africa. Burchell described it as 'a strip, three feet or more in length, of the hide either of a hippopotamus or of a rhinoceros, rounded to the thickness of a man's finger, and tapering to the top. This is universally used in the colony for a horsewhip, and is much more durable than the whips of European manufacture.'[43] That *sjamboks* were not solely used for horses, however, is clear from the many examples in the legal records of the domestic punishment of slaves. One house in Cape Town recorded three *sjamboks*, 'kept in a box', in its inventory of 1755. There were no horses recorded, but many slaves.[44]

Whipping could be given for a wide variety of reasons. Crimes, such as stealing or assaulting a fellow slave or member of the household, could be immediately punished, in which case the master exerted a rudimentary, but effective system of justice for actions committed by slaves against each other or himself. A very common cause for whipping was an attempt to escape, often administered as soon as the slave was caught and returned to the farm. The inevitability of such an action is clear from the several examples of slaves who begged their captors to 'put in a good word' for them to their master in an attempt to reduce the severity of the punishment.[45] Whipping could also be a punishment for bad work and neglect of duties. An attempt to enforce greater working efficiency was to whip slaves who took too long in the master's opinion to carry out specified tasks, especially when carrying out errands away from the farm and staying away for longer than necessary.[46] Punishment for 'insolence' was more dependent on the master's whim and his own feelings of insecurity, and indicates the points at which he may have felt himself most threatened and liable to lose control, such as when a slave refused to work or answered back.[47] Violent punishment in such cases could be a desperate attempt of a master on an isolated farmstead to assert control over his slaves when he felt it was being challenged. Whipping could also express personal feelings of jealousy; a relatively common feature of farms where the attractions of female slaves imposed a threat to a master's wife and provided motivation for her to 'continually beat and maltreat' her rival.[48] Domestic slaves working with the master's wife during the day were most subject to this kind of chastisement.

Part of the purpose of whippings was not merely to mete out punishments for crimes or offences already committed, but to demonstrate to the victim and to other slaves the supremacy of the master's power. Other slaves would frequently be ordered to stand around and watch the flogging, or to hold down the victim while it was administered. The message was clear to all. The fear of punishment was thus well established amongst the slaves. When a slave shepherd was encouraged by *drosters* (runaways) whom he encountered to join them, he replied that he had done that once before and been punished for it, and he did not want to repeat the experience.[49] Another slave who had been caught stealing hung himself from a beam in the barn 'for fear that he would be punished'.[50]

The master was normally responsible for the punishment of his slaves. The organisation of the labour force on the larger farms of the Cape, however, involved the use of *knecht* overseers and, in a very few cases, slave *mandoors*, who also needed to be invested with some of the master's authority if they were to be able to carry out their supervisory role effectively. The only reference found to the control measures taken by a slave *mandoor* indicates that he 'gave several blows' to a slave who had drunk too much wine while working in the cellars of Martin Melck's wine farm and had fallen asleep on the job. There is no mention of use of a whip, or indications of a flogging such as those meted out by slave drivers in the Deep South, although such an argument from silence is inconclusive.[51] Slave *mandoors* were anyway very rarely used at the Cape.

More common, particularly on the larger slave farmsteads, were *knechts* as overseers. Their position was much clearer, and they were fully invested with the authority of the master. The *knecht* that Sparrman met described himself as 'acting in my master's place', and the Fiscaal in a court case of 1743 declared that the murder of a *knecht* by a slave warranted the same punishment as that of a master since 'he was placed as overseer on his master's farm and was representing him'.[52] There could, however, be problems if the slaves did not recognise the *knecht*'s authority as representative of the master. As an employee, the *knecht* lacked the supreme control on the farmstead, and was therefore more often in a position of insecurity, especially since his work involved the most direct and unpopular means of contact with slaves on a large farm. A *knecht* who was left alone on a Stellenbosch farm in 1791 in charge of the slaves while the master was away, tried to punish one of them and met with the response 'Take me to Cape Town, to Baas Lijbrand; he is my Baas and his full power allows him to do what he wants with me.'[53] On another farm the attempts of a *knecht* to force the slaves to work on a Sunday whilst he sat drinking the master's coffee led to a general revolt; they refused to work or to co-operate in holding down another slave while he was being whipped, and threatened to report the overseer to their master.[54] Such incidents indicate that stability on the farmstead could easily be disturbed if the authority of the master or his overseer was weakened. Considerable alarm could be caused in the whole community if a farm was left without a master or someone to represent him.[55]

The need to preserve control primarily by the use or threat of punishment, and the rather tenuous nature of that control under certain circumstances, meant that not infrequently masters, or those representing them, treated their slaves with considerable brutality that went beyond the norms. In most slave societies, the unequal distribution of power and the dependence of the slave on the master led to examples of extreme brutality and sadism. The Cape was no exception. Summing up the case against one particularly sadistic slaveowner in 1770, whose speciality was in drawing sharpened cattle horns across the bare flesh of his slaves from neck to buttocks, and for whipping them into unconsciousness without any given reason, the prosecutor of the Council of Justice stated:

> It is indisputable, and pitiful findings indicate all too well, that in the lands where slavery exists there will be plenty of people, even those who call themselves Christians, who are in fact no Christians but rather inhumane creatures. It is a great misfortune for those who come under their authority, since these men hardly think that the slaves and heathens, being paid for with money, are also human beings.[56]

Examples of such sadistic treatment abound in the court records. There seem to have been two particular circumstances in which extreme brutality was most likely. One was where *knechts* were left in control. Psychologically, the position of the *knecht* was very different to that of most slaveowners. As has been seen, his authority was subject to greater challenge. Moreover, as in many slave societies, *knechts* were faced on the larger farms with the daily problems of control, but lacked any of the incentives of the master to limit maltreatment of their own property or to restrain punishment to a level where it would not severely hinder labour productivity. Most *knechts*, being hired out for short periods from the contracts with the East India Company, had little vested interest in the welfare of the farm. Van Imhoff commented on the 'unlicensed conduct' of many of them on short-term contracts.[57] It was also stressed by one of the members of the Council of Policy in the 1717 debate that slaves were preferable to free labourers because they could be more easily controlled, the wild behaviour of many *knechts* being cited as an indication.[58]

There are many cases in the records of maltreatment of slaves by *knechts*.[59] Some became notorious. One case is recorded of a slave who committed suicide rather than be punished by the *knecht* on his master's farm.[60] A Swellendam farmer in 1770 praised the *knecht* who had been working for him because he 'kept a good control over the slaves', although he admitted that he was inclined to be 'rather strict' with them, a concession made after it was found that the *knecht* had clubbed a slave to death for allowing a cow to go loose.[61] Clearly there were some exceptions to these pictures of overseer severity. There were a few cases of *knechts* who tried to restrain the master from abusing or maltreating his slaves, or who testified to such behaviour to the courts.[62]

Another general factor which can be discerned in the records was geographical location. Evidence from the American slave colonies suggests that severe maltreatment of slaves tended to be worst in newly settled areas.[63] This may be explained by the greater isolation of farmsteads both from the authorities of government and from each other. There are similar indications at the Cape. Some of the worst cases of maltreatment came from the Bokkeveld and Roggeveld areas, and the threat of selling a slave 'up-country' or 'over the mountains' was used by masters in the more settled areas of Stellenbosch and its region.[64] Isolation of such farms accentuated a tendency that existed throughout the rural regions of the colony where fear of losing control by masters and removal from restraint of others led to, in the words of the Protector of Slaves in 1827, many farmers 'taking the law into their own hands'.[65]

In Cape Town, by contrast, owners were less able to maltreat their slaves without such actions coming to the attention of the authorities. This is not to say that domestic punishment was any less harsh than in rural districts, and there are cases in the records of urban slaves receiving severe corporal punishment. In general, however, the absence of overseers in the town and the less isolated circumstances of owners tended to inhibit the worst abuses. On the other hand, urban slaves, especially those with female owners, were often handed over to the Fiscaal for punishment by the *Caffers*. Such punishment

109

was much feared and the threat of it alone sufficient to retain control by many urban masters.[66] It was, however, carried out under the aegis of the law.

This factor implies a necessary qualification to be made to the picture of absolute authority of the master over his slaves. The role of the colony's legal structure and its interaction with the slave control system was of critical importance. This was evident in three main ways. First, masters could turn to the authorities for help when the internal discipline and authority over slaves broke down. Secondly, the local authorities, backed up by the legal code and institutions in the local districts and Cape Town could intervene on the slave's behalf in exceptional cases, although often with limited effect. Most significantly, slaves who had committed criminal offences were taken over by the government, which imposed a severe system of punishments. By such means the authority of the master could be superseded by that of the government. This was not in itself an unusual feature of slave societies. At the Cape, however, the personnel and systems of government were part of the wider organisation of the VOC, over which slaveholders had no control. The division of interests between the Company and groups of colonists was a consistent source of tension and one of the complaints of the Patriots in 1779 was that the VOC restricted the absolute rights of masters to punish their own slaves without any outside interference.[67] This position seems to contrast with many New World slave societies in which plantation discipline was not subject to external oversight or in which masters were also the rulers of the whole community.[68] As Robert Ross has pointed out, as far as the authority over slaves was concerned, Cape society in the VOC period was three-tiered; government, master and slave.[69]

Whilst this was certainly true, in theory at least, the division between the interests of those operating the law of the VOC at the Cape and the slaveowners of the colony must not be exaggerated. In many crucial respects relating to the slave population, the Company and its officials actively supported the masters. Batavian law as applied to the Cape strongly bolstered the authority of slaveowners. Despite differences of opinion between farmers and the government over prices and marketing of produce, it was clearly in the interests of both that control over slaves was effectively maintained and that sufficient produce was extracted from their labour to keep the colony self-sufficient and to provide the necessary surplus for Company and burgher requirements. The concept of rights in slave property and the attitudes towards slavery that this inculcated in the colonists derived from the Company's introduction of the system and its maintenance by law. Moreover, local administrators in the rural areas were appointed from the most important landholders, who were inevitably major slaveowners.[70] The divisions between government and colonists were thus by no means as absolute as some orthodox histories of the early Cape would suggest.

The three-tiered structure acted primarily in the interests of the slave owners. Company authority could be called upon when discipline and control was in danger of breaking down. Some masters went as far as ceding their ownership of slaves to the authorities when they became too troublesome; on suspicion that they were plotting some 'evil', were 'too dangerous to control', or that they continually ran away and could not be restrained.[71] Thunberg claimed that an owner was obliged to sell his slave to the Landdrost 'if he takes a liking to him', although no evidence of such an enforced transaction by a Company official has been found.[72] More common was the sending of a slave to be punished by the *Caffers* both by urban and rural masters.

Batavian law had placed restrictions on the kinds of domestic slave punishment that could be given. A decree of 1642 forbade the keeping of slaves in leg-irons, or their torture, and gave them the right to report abuses to the authorities. It added, however, that slaves who could not provide 'major and wholly convincing' proof were to be severely punished and returned to their owners.[73] Qualifications to this legislation were made in 1681 by a decree (re-issued in 1765) which permitted masters to chain their slaves if the authorities had been previously notified.[74] Batavian law was applied to the Cape and reinforced by decrees issued there; from the first year of private slave use in the colony attempts were made by the Company to prevent their maltreatment, and occasional repetitions of the Batavian ban on chaining without permission were made.[75] The fact that such laws had to be repeated, each time with a preamble stressing the barbaric behaviour of some slaveowners, indicates that their efficacy was limited.

A major problem was how to enforce such regulations that attempted to intervene in the internal control system of masters, especially in rural districts. The responsibility rested on the local Landdrost and Heemraden.[76] Instructions given in 1793 to the Landdrost and Heemraden of Stellenbosch and Drakenstein by the visiting commissioners from the Netherlands included 'the oversight of all domestic punishment of slaves' and the institution of an enquiry if severe maltreatment was suspected.[77] They were, however, dependent upon reports given to them by the slaves themselves or by others who had witnessed the maltreatment. It took great courage for a slave to escape from a master who had already demonstrated his power and to go to the authorities. Moreover, if convincing proof could not be obtained the slave risked punishment. One slave who 'falsely' accused his master of killing another slave in 1718 was flogged, branded and returned to his master 'as an example to others'.[78] Ironically, the slave code of 1754 included the stipulation that slaves guilty of false accusations against their masters were to be whipped and kept in chains, despite the Batavian legislation against chaining.[79]

Such legislation and actions could hardly have inspired great confidence in slaves of the protection given to them by the authorities against their masters. Owners could threaten their slaves if they attempted to complain; sometimes they could only be induced to report what had happened by other burghers.[80] The period of time that elapsed between a report of maltreatment and the bringing of a case to the courts was also dangerous for the slave. He could be kept in the Landdrostdy jail, hardly an enviable proposition for a witness while the wheels of Cape justice slowly turned. One slave was kept in the Stellenbosch jail for two years until the truth or falsity of his complaint had been determined.[81] His fate was nevertheless preferable to that of another slave in 1792 who was taken back from the Landdrostdy by his master and severely beaten.[82]

In cases where maltreatment was so severe that it led to death, another theoretical control of the authorities was a regulation requiring a permit from the Fiscaal or Landdrost before a slave could be buried. Batavian legislation of 1681 had specified that two witnesses were needed to testify that no maltreatment had led to the death, and this was also applied at the Cape.[83] In 1731, the need for such permission was emphasised since,

> some of the inhabitants, forgetting their Christian responsibilities, do not hesitate to so maltreat their slaves by cruel floggings and other barbaric treatment that these miserable creatures lose their lives. These wicked masters then try to conceal this blood by burying their murdered slaves anywhere under the earth to avoid their justly deserved punishment and so as not to come into the hands of the law.[84]

Means of enforcing such legislation were limited, however. The Council of Policy noted in 1793 that masters were not reporting the death of their slaves and the decree was re-issued.[85]

In an attempt to ensure that such legislation was not being abused, it became usual practice for Heemraden and a surgeon to visit the farm in person and inspect the body; not only in cases of suspected maltreatment, but also in those of accident or suicide.[86] This seems to have been done in many cases, but there could be lapses. One embarrassed Landdrost of Stellenbosch had to report to the Fiscaal in 1737 that he had given permission for a slave body to be buried without inspecting it because he had believed the sixteen-year-old son of the master who said the slave had died naturally and 'did not suspect maltreatment'. It was only when a slave from the same farm escaped and reported to the Fiscaal that his fellow slave had been murdered that the body was exhumed and found to be 'covered in severe wounds and blows from head to foot'.[87] Other excuses could be found by the Landdrost for not making personal visits to farms, such as the danger of travelling during the smallpox epidemic of 1767.[88] Delays were caused in cases involving more than one district when Landdrosts claimed that they should be dealt with by the authorities of another district than their own.[89] Often the evidence presented to the visitors could be inconclusive; in the case of a *bastaard hottentot* who was killed when hit over the head with a piece of wood by his master, the Landdrost commented that blood found near the body 'could just as well be that of an antelope as of the Bastaard Andries', although in the end the murderer was convicted.[90]

Even if cases of maltreatment were brought to the attention of the authorities and a case formed, it could be a major problem to bring the accused to the central Council of Justice in Cape Town. The remoteness of some farms and the weakness of local authorities meant that a summons could be repeatedly ignored. The wife of one Swellendam burgher accused of maltreatment and murder of his slave laughed in the face of a representative of the courts and told him that 'I will no more listen to the Landdrost than to my slave.'[91] Certainly effective control of the central authorities over regions further inland was limited. As Barrow stated at the end of the century, not only did the Landdrost have little effective authority in 'distant parts of the colony' but 'if a man, after being summoned [by the Council of Justice] did not choose to appear, there was no force in the country to compel him; and they knew it would have been fruitless to dispatch such a force from the Cape. Hence murders and the most atrocious crimes were committed with impunity.'[92] Cases of extreme delay were also not unknown in the rural districts nearer to Cape Town.

In short, there were numerous means of evading the laws which were supposed to protect slave interests. As Le Vaillant commented after his visit in the early 1780s, 'these wise laws do honor to the Dutch government, but how many ways are there to elude them!'[93] In spite of this, there were a few masters who were convicted for maltreatment of their slaves when the evidence against them was overwhelming. Usually these were cases in which slaves had been beaten to death and the owner admitted guilt. In 1729, the Landdrost of Stellenbosch brought successful prosecutions in two separate cases in which farmers had ordered their slaves to be severely flogged, leading to their death. Despite the attempted defence by both of them that death had been caused by the slaves drinking a large amount of stagnant water after their punishment each was fined; 100 Rxds in one case and 50 Rxds in the other.[94] When convictions were secured, the normal punishment was a fine which, although described by Thunberg as 'considerable', was never as much as the market value of the slave.[95] In 1770, Johannes Kuuhn, who had been convicted of severe maltreatment and torture of several slaves and Khoikhoi labourers, was fined 100 Rxds and slaves who had given evidence against him were ordered to be sold, never to come into his hands or those of his family again.[96] This stipulation as a means of protecting a slave from retaliation by his master after the trial was frequently used, and recorded with the deeds of sale of slaves at estate auctions.[97] In 1767 one burgher was banned from owning any slaves at all, although he was permitted to keep one female domestic slave, and the following year made an appeal to buy two field-hands, which was granted.[98]

Sometimes other punishments for slave maltreatment could be given. In 1796, one master convicted of beating his slave to death with the recommendation of the prosecutor that 'the full force of the law' should be used against him, was sentenced to a period of three weeks in prison on a diet of bread and water, which was shortened to four days after his wife claimed that he was sick. The slaves who had brought the accusation were kept in the jail at the Stellenbosch Landdrostdy, after which they were put to work for the Company.[99] Punishments could be more severe; although there is no case in the VOC period of the murder of a slave equivalent to that of a master who in 1767 was sentenced to death for killing a *bastaard hottentot* labourer by beating him, in 1801 a farmer who beat his slave to death was himself flogged and exiled from the colony.[100] It was not until 1822 that a burgher was executed for murdering a slave, a case which caused a major uproar in the colony. Throughout the eighteenth century, however, punishments for those few farmers who were convicted of maltreating their slaves were not severe.

More ignominious for the slaveowner than fines or restrictions on slave ownership was the actual process of being brought to trial. One master, guilty of keeping a slave in chains, begged the Stellenbosch Landdrost 'with tearful eyes, that he not be brought before the Council of Justice and thereby bring shame upon himself and all his family and bearers of his name'. His request was granted, and he was fined 100 Rxds on the spot.[101] In most cases, however, the accused was brought to Cape Town by the local authorities on the instructions of the Council of Justice.[102] He was there detained for the duration of the trial, although intervention of relatives in one case ensured that he was allowed freedom during the day.[103]

Limitations on the effectiveness of Company law in protecting slaves against their masters therefore provide a major qualification to the view that Cape slaves were less subject to maltreatment than those in other slave societies. Indeed, the very existence of such laws and their frequent repetition indicates that slaves could suffer considerable abuse. The contact which most slaves had with the Company's legal system was not, however, as victims of maltreatment but as the accused in criminal cases. The efficiency and harshness of the law courts were considerably greater in prosecuting slaves than their masters. In this most important aspect of the inter-relation of central Company authority and the slaveowners, the legal system acted as an alternative to the disciplinary control of the master over his slave. A corollary of the legal restrictions on masters over domestic punishment of their slaves was the principle that 'power over their lives belongs to the magistrate'.[104] There were no plantation courts of the kind sometimes found in New World colonies. The master therefore had to decide whether to send a slave who had committed a crime on his farm to the authorities and risk losing the value of his property if the punishment decided by the courts was death or maiming. Unlike some of the American slave states, masters were not compensated for such loss and also had to pay for the costs of the trial; following Roman legal principles, they were also liable for the damages and actions of their slaves.[105] Several cases are recorded of masters who gave over control of their slaves to the Company to cover legal costs incurred by them.[106] Giving over slaves to the authorities for trial under the law could therefore be highly disadvantageous to the master. Most of the cases that came before the authorities involving slaves are of crimes that seriously threatened the master's control such as attacks on his person, his family or his property, murder of one slave by another or rape. The other possibility was that runaways who caused damage to burghers who were not their masters were caught and turned over to the local Landdrost, at no risk to their own investment in slaves.

Some minor crimes could be dealt with in the local districts by the courts set up by the local Landdrost and Heemraden; in such cases slaves were punished locally by imprisonment or beatings and sent back to their masters.[107] In most cases, however, the testimonies were taken by the local Landdrost and then forwarded to the Council of Justice in Cape Town, where the Landdrost normally acted as prosecutor. It was there that the full force of the legal system was felt in relation to the control of the slaves.

Law administered by the Company at the Cape derived from a variety of sources; the decrees of the United Provinces were adapted to a colonial situation by the statutes of Batavia under whose authority the Cape fell, to which were added occasional decrees from the Governor and Council of Policy in Cape Town. The law of the Netherlands was greatly influenced by that of Rome, and in the new situation of a slave society, Batavian and Cape authorities turned to Roman precedent in their legal definitions of slaves and slave status.[108] Slaves were unable to marry, had no rights of *potestas* over their children, and were unable to make legal contracts, acquire property or leave wills. As the exclusive property of his master, a slave was obliged to obey any order that did not involve a criminal offence, and could be sold or bequeathed at will. Following Roman example, unlike the slave laws of the Americas, masters were also liable for the actions of their slaves, unless a crime had been committed, but unlike Rome in such a case, the master gave his slave up to the courts for punishment thus absolving himself of responsibility but risking the loss of his property.[109]

The slave was thus liable in law for the actions he committed. In addition to the criminal law which applied to freemen, he was also subject to a series of regulations passed in the Company period to maintain strict control over the slave population. The most notable summary of these is the 'slave code' passed under Governor Tulbagh in 1754, which controlled the meeting of slaves in groups, especially in the potentially dangerous circumstances of Cape Town streets, taverns or in rural districts on holidays. The clearest indication of the role of the law in relation to the position of slave and master was that article of the code which stated that any slave who should 'culminate, affront or treat his master with despise, or accuse him falsely with any disgraceful act should be scourged, put in irons or punished according to the circumstances of the case', and that a slave who 'laid hands upon his master or mistress, with or without a weapon, should be punished with death'.[110] A similar punishment was decreed for any slave who made sexual advances to his master's wife or daughter.[111]

Roman precedent led to a legal definition of slavery at the Cape which denied any theoretical concept of legal equality, in contrast to the American states.[112] There was little indication of the kind of protection offered, for example, by the Spanish slave laws of the period, although, despite the restrictions of Tulbagh's code, neither was the Cape slave legislation as severe as the Danish Virgin Islands or the British West Indies, where masters were compensated for the loss of their slaves, and killing a slave was not an offence brought before the courts.[113]

The division of interests between the slaveowners and the Company officials who ran the courts and administered the colony meant that at the Cape masters could be made to account for the maltreatment of their slaves in public, even if in practice the protection of slaves was limited. The most significant divergence of Cape law from that of the Americas followed from this: slaves were able to give evidence, even in cases against their own masters, although only 'when convenient' and not on oath.[114] This is not to say that such evidence was accepted without question.[115] Normally slave evidence needed some form of corroboration from a freeman; in a case in which the wife of a farmer wished to prove adultery of her husband with a female slave, she arranged for the old slave woman who had observed the couple in bed to fetch a 'white witness' who could confirm the evidence in court.[116] The Cape Fiscaal, summing up one case in 1740 in which slave evidence against his master was crucial, stated that it should be viewed with some suspicion since 'slaves inevitably hold a measure of hatred and bitterness towards their masters', although he concluded that where no freeman evidence was available, slave testimony was necessary if law and order were to be maintained, since many people lived in areas in which 'there is not a single Christian freeman to be found for miles around'. In this case, a conviction was secured, since the *knecht* of the farm gave some corroborating evidence, but an appeal was made by the accused that slave evidence was unacceptable and the whole case was transferred to Batavia.[117] There was considerable prejudice against the evidence of slaves; in 1798 the Procurator claimed that a slave witness, 'being a heathen can scarcely be considered capable of giving trustworthy evidence'.[118] As in the case of slaves complaining against their masters to the local authorities, there were severe limitations on the amount of freedom which a slave had to speak out in court, when they knew that they might have to return to their masters on the farmstead and face the consequences of their statements. The control which masters exercised over their slaves also placed some of their evidence in doubt; in several cases slaves claimed that their masters had forced them to give false testimony in court.[119]

Despite this feature of the Cape legal system which could lead to some checks on the control of the master, the main weight of the law as it was practised was to support the master group in the control of slaves. This was most clearly indicated in the legal punishments meted out. Required by the new British governor in 1796 to justify the wide disparity between punishments given to slaves and freemen, the Council of Justice stated that, Experience has taught that gentle means are inadequate, even amongst free persons to maintain good order ... consequently, altho' strongly actuated by motives of humanity, and viewing the Slaves in the most favourable light, it becomes necessary to adopt severe measures to deter them from revolting against their Masters and taking advantage of their superior strength.'[120] The fear of slaves which played such a significant part in the domestic structure of control was thus also expressed in the legal code. The nature of slave punishments was directly linked to the degree to which their crimes had threatened the social order of the colony; attacks on masters or other freemen and on property by arson being the most severely punished.[121] Contemporary visitors to the Cape were horrified by the barbarity of some punishments of slaves in an age not noted for its leniency. Mentzel described the habit of breaking slaves alive on the wheel, often without the *coup de grâce*. Other means of carrying out the death sentence included pulling out pieces of flesh with red-hot tongs and mutilation, impaling, and slow strangulation.[122] Such 'Republican severity', as one observer described it, served to fully demonstrate to the slaves the power of the authorities representing the interests of the slaveowners, and the folly of resistance. Bodies of executed slaves were left hanging on gibbets or exposed after mutilation in Cape Town or on farms.[123] Although legal punishments in Europe were also severe at the time, there was no sign at the Cape of the debate taking place in northern Europe during the eighteenth century on the use of torture and effectiveness of capital punishment.[124] Attempts to abolish breaking on the wheel after the ending of VOC rule met with considerable opposition amongst slaveowners who believed that it would weaken discipline and slave control in the colony.[125]

In addition to such agonising punishments which served as clear warnings to others, slaves were also tortured to obtain evidence and confessions of guilt. Confession was necessary under Dutch law before sentence could be passed, but at the Cape torture seems to have been mainly applied to slaves and occasionally to the rank and file members of the Company.[126] Evidence and confessions obtained under torture in one case were found afterwards to be false when the real culprit was located by chance, but such circumstances were rare.[127] There were few slaves who were acquitted by the courts.

The role of the law in the colony in relation to both masters and slaves was exemplified in the case of an urban slaveholder, Daniel Braun, who in 1766 maltreated his slaves so severely with beatings that two of them in revenge set fire to the thatch of his house. Both were sentenced by the court to be burnt alive at the stake; a punishment frequently reserved for slave arsonists. The court admitted, that there was clear evidence of maltreatment, and Braun was therefore forbidden to own any other slaves. A year later, he submitted a request to do so, saying he had learnt the folly of his ways, which was granted.[128] Any slave action which threatened the control system of the colony met with severe punishment, whilst a master's abuse of his authority over slaves was liable to punishment of a mild and temporary nature. The legal system thus supported the control mechanism of farmers as a response to fear of slaves. In one case, a slave was sent to Robben Island for life, merely on the unproved suspicion of causing arson.[129] Towards the end of the century, some slaves were freed from the island, only on condition that they be removed from the colony altogether, and under the British Occupation, slaves could be transported to the West Indies for crimes such as theft.[130] The problem of control was thus removed from the Cape owners and authorities.

The circumstances of relative isolation and highly developed fear of masters, together with a lack of alternative control mechanisms could thus lead to a very high level of coercion in the master–slave relationship. The Cape did not produce an overtly paternalistic society which studies of other small-scale non-plantation slave systems might lead one to expect. A theoretical qualification to the power of the slaveowner especially in the town was the potential intervention of the authorities, although the efficacy of such action in rural areas was limited by the difficulty of penetrating the master's control system on the farms. In all parts of the colony, the government played a more significant part in exercising control over slaves when masters needed support, and especially in the ruthless methods and punishments which it inflicted by its criminal law system. Anomalies such as slave complaints against masters, or the use of slave evidence in courts, arose out of divisions of power and interest between colonist and government. Nevertheless, for the vast majority of the slaves this was little comfort in a highly coercive society. Rather than resorting to the authorities, many slaves responded to their circumstances by methods of their own.

9

The slave response

One of the most notable developments in the historiography of slavery over the past two decades has been the examination of the variety of slave responses in relation to the social environment in which they lived and worked. The debate following Elkins' suggestion that the closed system of the North American plantation produced a docile 'Sambo', has directed attention to individual responses of those who did not overtly resist their enslaved position rather than those who made bids to escape by running away or organising collective rebellion.[1] Such slaves sought to maintain their dignity and humanity in the face of extreme coercion whilst remaining with their masters; actions which were in many ways as heroic as the more dramatic bids at resistance and escape.[2]

Elkins and others have thus usefully qualified Aptheker's assertion that it was a fundamental tendency of all slaves to resist their enslavement by revolt.[3] Nevertheless, as Craton has pointed out, 'slavery distorts the personality and all human relationships, so that only in resistance can the self be realised and dignity restored'.[4] Moreover, the problem with the study of many slave societies outside the Deep South – and the Cape is no exception – is that evidence of internalising grievances, 'playing Sambo' or preserving dignity is very hard to find, whilst that for overt resistance and escape forms a major part of surviving criminal records. Analysis of the response of Cape slaves to their condition must therefore be primarily concerned with resistance as a feature of slave response. The structures of Cape slave society would indicate, however, that this is not a great distortion. In the rural districts, farm discipline could be harsh and paternalism was limited, and yet the possibility of escape from the dispersed farmsteads was relatively high, and they were certainly less 'closed systems' than the plantations of the Deep South, whilst the opportunities for escape in Cape Town, as in all urban slave communities, was also high. Furthermore, the absence of a developed slave family life and limits to the development of separate religious and cultural support systems meant that the maintenance of dignity or the adoption of a 'dual personality' must have been very much more difficult for the Cape slave than his North American counterpart.[5] Some indications of the wider range of slave response can be deduced from the available material, and the specific forms of resistance expressed reveal much about the nature of Cape slave society.

Studies of other slave societies have indicated general features which conditioned the levels and means of slave response.[6] Broad aspects such as the nature of the whole political economy, the unity of the slaveowning class and the mechanisms of state control, provide one level of analysis; more specifically, the organisation of the labour force and the composition of the slave population indicate likely responses on a more localised level. The proportion of fully acculturated slaves with a common identity and that of newly imported slaves was particularly significant. Societies with a culturally homogeneous slave population, large slaveholding units, a differentiation of labour skills producing a slave 'elite' and a master class divided within itself or lacking the coercive apparatus of a strong state, were more likely to produce slave rebellions and collective acts of resistance than those in which slaves were fragmented by diversity of origin, and where masters had a strong degree of cohesion and measures of control. The pattern of work routine and the physical environment also determined the responses of those who demonstrated more 'passive' resistance, by refusing to actively co-operate with the interests of the master beyond direct orders.

At the Cape, one of the most significant factors was that the continued dependence on slaves imported from differing areas, the lack of a strongly developed slave cultural identity and the isolation of many slaves on farmsteads with small labour forces, severely limited the potential for collective slave resistance. In Cape Town, where there was a concentration of slaves and a greater degree of cultural homogeneity, the presence of a garrison and patrols by watchmen kept a continuous control over the town. No attempts were made at widespread rebellion in the colony; only in the nineteenth century were there two threats of slave revolt, both of which were swiftly overcome and had little potential for success.[7] Unlike North America, where all imported slaves were African, 'the variety of nations occasions a variety of inclinations and opinions also, and of course a lesser apprehension of rebellion'.[8] On the other hand, individuals or small groups of slaves frequently attempted to escape, aided by the physical environment which provided mountain hideaways and hopes of refuge further inland, although lack of contact with others, together with the unity of owners and the local authorities in organising commandos and capturing *drosters* made escape a hazardous business.

On the farms and in urban households slave resistance more often took individual forms: in particular the spontaneous attack by a slave on his master or the *knecht* in the face of punishment, but also planned acts of sabotage, murder or theft. Other means of 'passive' resistance were conditioned by the working routine and social contacts of each slave. There is some evidence of contact between slaves on differing farms and 'underground' networks of communication in Cape Town, but in general the small scale of each slave labour force, the frequency of sales and lack of a strong sense of community amongst slaves limited the potential for collective actions, especially in rural districts.

In spite of this, Cape colonists lived in a constant fear of slave violence and rebellion. The importance of this fear in determining the control mechanisms within the colony has already been stressed, but it is also significant in that the perceptions of the slaveowners reveal much about the nature of slave resistance and response. The Cape was unquestionably a violent society, and as such, it was those at the lower end of the social hierarchy, the slaves and the Khoikhoi, who suffered the most.[9] Contemporaries blamed the slaves for much of the violence. Mentzel, for example, concluded that slaves were in general a dangerous group: 'It is not an easy matter to keep the slaves under order and control. The condition of slavery has soured their tempers. Most slaves are a sulky, savage and disagreeable crowd.'[10] The attribute of 'sulkiness' or gloom and depression is one that many North American slaveowners noted in their slaves, and was one response to excessive work and punishment.[11] Sparrman made the connection between the bitterness of slaves as a result of their captive status and the prevalance of violence in the Cape more explicitly, and more sympathetically:

> You will be apt to think with me that even the most supportable kind of tyranny always brings with it its own punishment, in troubled sleep and an uneasy conscience. Slaves, even under the mildest tyrant, are bereaved of the rights of nature. The melancholy remembrance of so painful a loss, is most apt to arise during the silence of the night, when it ceases to be dissipated by the bustle of the day. What wonder then if those who commit outrages on their liberties, should sometimes be forced to sign and seal with their blood the violated rights of mankind?[12]

Violent reprisals by slaves on their masters, and the fear of them, were common features of most slave societies and the isolated nature of some Cape farmsteads made the problem especially acute.[13] Farmers were particularly anxious that slaves should not have access to firearms; there were several decrees forbidding the use of guns by them, and even ineffective attempts to prevent slaves from owning knives.[14] Much consternation was caused in the Picquetbergen in November 1742, when slaves left alone on a farm were seen shooting game with their master's guns.[15]

Alarm was heightened at several periods in differing areas of the colony. After one particularly gruesome murder of a Cape Town family by *drosters* in 1760 urban slaves were forbidden to go into the hills in search of firewood where they might encounter runaways, a widespread search was made for fugitives and a strict curfew imposed.[16] In the remoter pastoral regions the threat of combined attacks by the Khoikhoi and runaway slaves led to the organisation in 1758 of commandos in Swellendam to 'calm the fears of the good inhabitants.'[17] In 1793 the Veldwachtmeester of Stellenbosch reported to the Council of Policy that there was a 'general fear' in that district and in Drakenstein of an uprising of Khoikhoi and slaves who planned to 'attack the farms of Christians and murder the inhabitants', although the Landdrost denied that the danger was real but was merely rumour spread by certain 'malevolent persons'.[18] Such rumours of slave rebellion were common in North America, as Aptheker has demonstrated, although often little related to the facts.[19] Nevertheless, it was significant that colonists feared both individual slave reprisals and organised attack in conjunction with the Khoikhoi. The attitude of most was reflected in the comment of the prosecutor in a case of severe maltreatment by one master, that despite such occasional sadistic behaviour, 'there are many creatures amongst the slaves who seem to be devoid of all humanity and whose rage, ingratitude and lack of trust is beyond all comprehension'.[20]

More specifically, many believed that certain kinds of slaves were more likely to resist than others. Most contemporary writers drew distinctions by the place of origin; slaves from the East Indies, and especially Bougies being generally accepted as the most 'capricious and vindictive', 'violent and barbarous' or 'revengeful'.[21] Somerville believed that this was the reason why the Cape government banned the import of eastern slaves in 1767, and certainly the prevalence in the legal records of Indonesian slaves is partly attributable to the cases of escape, attacks and running *amok* by such slaves which considerably alarmed the authorities.[22] African slaves, on the other hand, were often presented as being 'faithful, patient and good', lacking violent passions, or alternatively, as Percival believed, 'sulky, untractable and treacherous'.[23] It might appear that a distinction is being made here between the stereotype 'rebel' and 'Sambo'. The records do not reveal, however, such a neat contrast of slave response by area of origin. Moreover, such impressionistic comments reveal little about the conditions which determined the nature of individual slave response, and are best explained by the belief often expressed by contemporaries that African slaves worked on the farms whilst eastern slaves were employed in Cape Town. Differentials of slave response based on the nature of work and the status of the slave in the labour hierarchy offer a more promising approach, particularly in the rural areas.

A more useful distinction which may be made in broad terms relating to the origins of slaves is that related to the degree of acculturation or adaptation to the slave society determined by the proportion of newly imported slaves and those born within the colony, or 'creolised'. Comparative slave studies have often revealed that slaves recently landed were more likely to attempt to escape, whilst those born in the host society or long adjusted to it developed alternative means of resisting the full impact of slavery whilst remaining within its broad confines.[24] Genovese has listed the preponderance of African over locally born slaves as a factor increasing the possibility of rebellion, but this assumes a degree of cohesiveness amongst imported slaves of common origin which was lacking at the Cape.[25] Escape was normally by individuals or small groups, with limited success; the existence of nearby maroon communities could encourage more creole involvement and slave rebellions were normally led and supported by locally born and creole slaves. Since the high proportion of imported slaves at the Cape was only gradually reduced during the eighteenth century and even by the end of the period locally born slaves were in the minority, this framework of analysis would indicate that the risk of slave escape in the colony was high, but that of rebellion less so.

This was indeed the case. The records of both local Landdrostdies and the central Council of Justice in Cape Town are filled with accounts of slave escapes and the actions of *drosters*. Estate inventories and valuations often indicated that slaves were missing. Even some surviving place names in the western Cape stem from the existence of *droster* communities.[26] Yet there was no slave rebellion in the VOC period and only very limited attempts were made later, significantly perhaps, after the ending of slave importation. The prevalence of foreign-born, unacculturated slaves at the Cape was only one broad factor explaining the high incidence of slave escapes and the absence of rebellion at the Cape. Others include the geographical nature of the colony which made running away and concealment in the mountains surrounding Cape Town and the rural hinterland possible for limited periods of time, until permanent escape from the colony could be made inland or as stowaways in ships.[27] Some places, notably Table Mountain as a refuge from Cape Town and the Table Valley, and Hangklip promontory became regular hideaways for *drosters*, and the latter survived as a maroon community by raiding farms in the Hottentots-Holland region and by fishing in False Bay throughout the eighteenth century and beyond.[28] A further major factor aiding escape attempts was the difficulty of immediately organising search parties or commandos by owners or the local authorities, and much attention was given to this problem in the course of the century.

The most useful distinctions to make concerning the motivation, means and impact of *droster* action is by level of acculturation of slaves, work status and the degree to which rebelliousness was a conscious protest against the whole slave condition or temporary truancy to avoid a crisis point on the farm: a distinction which Mullin makes in his study of eighteenth-century Virginia between 'inward' and 'outward' resistance.[29] Such analysis reveals much about the extent to which slaves saw themselves as an identifiable group with actions of a political nature, and the response of the wider society to them, with which the following chapter will be concerned.

The nature of the Cape economy and labour structure already examined contained several notable features which may be related to the patterns of slave escape. Complete quantification of the incidence of escape is impossible for the whole century, since many of the local records are incomplete and the central Council of Justice only dealt with a small percentage of the *droster* cases.[30] Some trends are clear, however. There was a distinction between escapes which appear to have been planned and aimed at rapidly leaving the settled areas, and those which were spontaneous, often the reaction to punishment or fear of punishment, when *drosters* remained in the neighbouring area. The former can be seen as acts of deliberate rejection of slavery, and appear to have been most often carried out by foreign-born slaves, the earliest example being the slaves brought by Van Riebeeck from Angola, who attempted to escape to return home.[31] Often such planned escapes were accompanied by deliberate acts of destruction before flight.[32]

The problem for such slaves was that the terrain was wholly unfamiliar to them and they were dependent upon being shown the way by others.[33] This was particularly true for Cape Town slaves who had no knowledge of the hinterland. Often the Khoikhoi were crucial in determining the success of such an escape bid, either by acting as guides or by giving protection in surviving Khoikhoi communities. The Company's original scheme of giving rewards to the Khoikhoi for the return of *drosters* had only limited success by the eighteenth century.[34] In 1778, a Khoikhoi was sent by the Stellenbosch Landdrost to the Council of Justice to be placed on Robben Island for repeatedly inciting slaves to run away to Cafferland'.[35]

Such planned escapes sometimes involved slaves from more than one farm, although communication between widespread farmsteads was often difficult. Contact could sometimes be made when slaves from one owner were hired out to work on another farm, or when slave shepherds met others away from the farmstead itself.[36] In Cape Town contacts between slaves of different owners was much easier, and escapes from the town tended to be of larger groups than those from farmsteads. As the centre of administration, captured slaves met other *drosters* in the town. In 1751, a group of sixteen Eastern slaves who had been sentenced to imprisonment on Robben Island, in Table Bay, plotted to murder the whites on the way there and then to sail the ship to Batavia.[37] Often, however, groups of *drosters* who had made individual escapes from different farms or from Cape Town, met up afterwards by chance rather than by plan. Some of these groups caused concern amongst farmers as they raided farmsteads for food and clothing, sometimes injuring the slaves or Khoikhoi whom they found there or persuading them to join the group.[38] The existence of groups of *drosters* on Table Mountain and at Hangklip was well known and chance encounters with a member of a *droster* group could lead to an escape bid by slaves based on the farms or in the town.[39]

There are some cases recorded of slaves who clearly planned their escape as a reaction against their slave condition, even if they were less certain of where they would seek refuge or how they would survive. Augustus van Batavia, a slave in his mid-twenties, was sentenced by the Council of Justice in December 1728, because he had repeatedly tried to escape and, 'being of a godless and malicious nature ran away three or four times on the abominable pretext that he was getting no food but a great amount of work from his master'.[40] The majority of escape attempts that came to the attention of the authorities, however, were not pre-meditated but were immediate responses to some point of crisis: after the committing of a crime such as theft or arson or the imposition of a flogging. Such actions were more 'inward' looking, being a spontaneous response rather than a conscious rejection of slavery *per se.* Cape-born slaves were as likely to be involved as those who had been imported, and, most significantly, such *drosters* often remained in the vicinity of the farm or town rather than trying to escape from the colony altogether. Fear of retribution or death if found by a commando unit drove some to the maroon groups or to attempts to flee inland, but this was less prevalent than in the case of the planned escape bids.

Some examples of this sort of slave response indicate the kinds of circumstances involved. In 1738, four slaves escaped from a Constantia farm after one had been beaten, and hid for almost a month near the farm (presumably in the hills that form part of the Table Mountain range), feeding on vegtables which they stole from the garden of their master, hens and ducks which they took with them, and food brought to them by other slaves from the farm. Only after a dispute broke out between them did one attempt to escape by boat across False Bay to Hangklip.[41] A Madagascan slave, Reijnier, who escaped from a farm in the Simonsvallij, after his master's wife had severely beaten his daughter, lived in the hills near the Berg River for eight years before being captured, surviving on fish and dassies he caught there.[42] In 1738, five slaves, all of them born in the Indies, escaped from a Drakenstein farm after they had stolen wine, food and a gun when one of them had by chance found the keys to the farmhouse while their widowed mistress and her family were away. Their decision to run away was on the spur of the moment, and several were unwilling at first but were persuaded by the others. Three of them lost their way, and were so afraid of being seen and shot on sight that they returned to their owner, one was caught begging for bread on a Tijgerberg farm as he was making his way to the town in the hope of getting on board a ship, and the fifth was captured on another farm.[43] Such a range of responses after escape indicates the distinction between slave 'truancy' and planned escape.

The chances of successful escape were limited. There was at the Cape no sizeable group of skilled farm slaves who could escape to town and pass as Free Blacks, as in, for example, colonial Virginia.[44] Moreover, apart from the Hangklip community whose existence was always precarious, there was no permanent point of refuge in the western Cape after the expansion of the settler farming region. The settlements of the Khoikhoi further inland or of the Xhosa on the eastern regions of the colony provided security for some slaves, but there was less certainty of refuge there than, for example, in neighbouring regions of Dutch slave colonies in the Americas.[45] The Council of Policy commented in 1680 that conditions for escaped slaves were exceptionally difficult, although 'neither hunger nor thirst, the fury of ravenous animals, nor the murderous hordes of the more distant Hottentots, nor finally the certainty of death, will suffice to shake their wicked resolution'.[46] The Council certainly exaggerated the position, but the isolation of the colony was a limiting factor on the ultimate success of slave escapes, although it made initial flight relatively easy.

In spite of this, slave escape continued unabated. Variations over time are hard to assess since there is no complete record, but there are indications that the problem was especially acute in the later 1670s, when the rural sector of the colony was rapidly expanding and the Council of Policy stated in a despatch of

1680 that 'desertion has become more prevalent than formerly'.[47] A decree of 1714 referred to the increase in the incidence of slave escape; this was a period of high slave mortality and increasing labour demands.[48] There are a higher number of deserted slave cases in the records of the central Council of Justice during the 1740s than for other periods during the century, which may be related to the intensity of demands on slaves at a time of expanding production and falling slave numbers in the rural sector. Such an impression cannot be quantified, although it is notable that the farmer petitioners in the Cape district of 1744 mention the increase in slave escape as a factor in their losses.[49]

More apparent than broad chronological distinctions are the variations of escape numbers during the course of each year. The harsh climate of the Cape winter limited escapes during that season, and bodies of *drosters* who had died of cold and exposure were sometimes shown to others as a warning.[50] Pasques de Chavonnes commented in 1717 that slaves generally ran away at harvest time 'and leave their masters in the lurch' during the period of heaviest labour intensity.[51] A similar observation was made by the Protector of Slaves over a century later, whose attitude to slaves was less sympathetic:

> In the harvest and sowing times when the Services of the slaves are most required, frequent desertions take place, and it is no uncommon occurrence for a slave to misconduct himself for the purpose of inducing his Master to punish him that he may absent himself from his work under the plea of going to make his complaint.[52]

Despite the dubious logic of the final sentence, it is clear that farmers faced a greater risk of desertion at such times, both of slaves and of *knechts* and white labourers.[53]

The success of an escape bid by a slave was dependent upon the degree of aid he could obtain either from Khoikhoi or freemen directly, from other slaves or by raiding and stealing food from farms.[54] The existence of groups of *drosters* searching for food and weapons was a major cause of the fear of many colonists. A series of thefts in Stellenbosch village in August and September of 1793 was attributed to a *droster* gang.[55] Sometimes *drosters* who visited other farms at night searching for food attacked slaves or Khoikhoi there when they were discovered.[56] Occasionally farmers obtained warnings of impending attacks by *drosters*; in one case in 1744, two Khoikhoi labourers of a Drakenstein farmer told him that they had been approached whilst in the fields by a group of escaped slaves who had asked how many guns were kept in the farmhouse, and when the owner would be away from it.[57] The presence of *drosters* thus considerably threatened the stability of the rural districts. A traveller visiting the Cape in the 1760s wrote that travelling to the Caledon Springs was a hazardous business since escaped slaves 'infest the area and are rendered desperate by their unhappy condition'.[58] In 1781, the Council of Policy received reports that travel on the road from Swellendam to the Cape

126

was dangerous because of attacks from *drosters*, particularly on the mountain pass near Hangklip.[59]

The existence of a high level of escape, if not necessarily successful, thus contributed to the violence of Cape slave society, but it was also at least in part a product of that violence. Many desertions followed punishment and it appears that the need to maintain the order mechanism of the master on the farmstead by such means overrode the risk of subsequent bids for escape by slaves.[60] Unless other crimes had been committed, captured *drosters* were not usually brought before the courts, but the punishments meted out to them by their owners often perpetuated acts of violence by master and slave. There were cases of slaves being flogged to death after recapture, and one who preferred to be shot rather than be recaptured.[61]

The high incidence of slave escapes made the problem of control both by individual owners and by the Company administration a difficult one. It should be noted that the Company was not only concerned with the escape of slaves. There was also a number of cases of Company employees and *knechts* breaking their contracts and escaping into the interior. Isolated regions of the colony and the difficulty of control over the rural areas provided shelter for a wide range of fugitives, including army deserters and escaped prisoners.[62] For slave refugees, however, the problem was one of detection by their skin colour, especially in the earlier decades of the century when foreign-born slaves were clearly identifiable from the indigenous Khoikhoi and San. As time passed, however, and more slaves were of mixed Khoikhoi and slave blood, or Cape-born of slave parentage from different origins, it became less easy to identify slaves by pigmentation. A particular problem in the remoter districts where more Khoikhoi labour was used was that escaped slaves could pretend to be *bastaard hottentots*. The Landdrost of Swellendam complained to the Governor in 1774 that many deserted slaves were doing this, 'and thus procure a free passage and obtain employment among the farmers, to the great injury of their owners, who are thus not only deprived of their property and the work of the slaves, but are put to great expense and trouble in vainly endeavouring to find out the said evil-disposed slaves'.[63] Similar problems occurred in Stellenbosch, and the Landdrost of that district recommended in 1780 that a pass system be adopted for all *bastaard hottentots* as a means of preventing such actions.[64] These difficulties occurred in other slave societies where slaves of lighter skin colour could pass as freemen, but the existence of the *bastaard hottentot* labour indenture and hiring system at the Cape made the problem especially acute by the later eighteenth century.[65]

The mobility of slaves between pasturage and the farmhouse, or between the rural districts and Cape Town, also made identification of *drosters* difficult. The lure of the females of the Slave Lodge in Cape Town for male slaves from the rural hinterland could also lead to absenteeism and in at least one case to severe retributions by the owner.[66] It was a constant fear of masters that slaves who had been sent on errands would escape, and those who took longer than expected were often punished severely.[67] Attempts were made to control this by issuing slaves with passes when they were away from their owners on legitimate business.[68] The pass system for slaves only seems to have been fully implemented towards the end of the eighteenth century, however, and moreover could be evaded; a group of slaves who escaped from Cape Town in 1786, for example, obtained forged passes.[69]

Despite attempts by the Company to organise a regular system of patrolling for *drosters*, the efficiency of the system for slave recapture in the rural districts was limited and sporadic. An alarm system was organised in Stellenbosch in the earlier decades by flying a blue flag which could be seen at the Castle, but this had fallen into disuse by the eighteenth century.[70] Slaveowners were constantly enjoined in the later seventeenth century to report the desertion of their slaves immediately so that action could be taken to recover them, and occasionally fears of increases in the number of *drosters*, as in 1690, led to intensified action by the Company.[71] A Veld-corporaal was appointed to deal specifically with the problem of slave *drosters* in the Cape district in 1740, two were chosen for Swellendam in 1753 and in 1782 an appeal made by the Veldwachtmeester of the Rodesanta area for an extra Veld-corporaal to deal with the large number of reports of *drosters* was granted.[72] The suggestion that the 1740s were years of particularly high slave escape numbers is supported by the organisation of special commandos to deal with the Hangklip *droster* community in 1741.[73] Concern about Hangklip had been shown earlier; local farmers and their slaves were consulted for sightings or traces of the *drosters* in the 1730s.[74] In 1748 another commando was sent out to deal with the 'vagabonds and drossers on the Paarl mountain'.[75]

Some of these organised commandos against *drosters* had a measure of success, but overall their impact was limited. A slave captured in 1736 by a commando managed to escape again when being taken to Stellenbosch jail.[76] Complaints were made in 1741 that a commando leader had kept a *droster* for his own use without reporting it to the authorities.[77] Much of the problem was the lack of contact or co-operation between the Company and the farming burghers. The commandos were drawn up with the support of the farmers themselves, and were part of the military obligations of burgher companies which all male freemen had to undertake.[78] The delay between the sighting of *drosters* or reports of their escape and the sending out of a commando could thus be considerable. In September 1731, a Veld-corporaal reported to the Stellenbosch Landdrost that his commando had come across a group of *drosters* about a week earlier, of whom two had been shot when they tried to give flight and four were captured, and one burgher was shot by the slaves. It was suspected that 'European *drosters*' were also part of the group and had provided them with firearms, but it took another three days before agreement was reached to send out a further commando against them.[79] A further problem was that slaves captured by commandos could often not be identified; in one case an unknown slave was taken to the Stellenbosch prison where he died before his master could be established.[80] The usual practice in the 1740s was for a *droster* to be taken from farm to farm until he was identified by his owner; in one case a farmer kept a *droster* who did not belong to him and the slave managed to escape again.[81]

In Cape Town, control of the slaves by the Fiscaal and *Caffers*, the exiled convicts from the East Indies under the Fiscaal's orders, as well as the night patrols of the burgher watch provided a more immediate and effective measure of control than the rural commandos. Nevertheless, their powers were limited to the town alone and were by no means entirely successful even there. The underworld of Cape Town provided ready channels for escape and disguise, and the existence of a free black community made ready identification of *drosters* difficult.[82]

Clearly, therefore, VOC administration could not rely on its own resources alone for recapturing escaped slaves. Rewards were offered for *drosters*, which were increased in 1743: again, a possible response to the increase in escapes during that crisis decade.[83] Different rewards were offered depending on the place of capture which reflected the increasing difficulty of control and capture of slaves further away from the western farming districts.[84] Individuals were thus encouraged to capture *drosters* themselves. At the same time masters of escaped slaves had to pay for their recovery: according to a Batavian statute of 1768 one-fifth of the amount went to the commander of the outpost where the slave was captured; at the Cape payment went to local officials.[85] Decrees were issued which absolved burghers from responsibility if they fired on a *droster*, and several cases were recorded of slaves being shot on sight.[86] There were also severe penalties for anyone assisting or hiding escaped slaves. A Cape Town free black woman was sentenced in 1737 to be whipped and to work in chains for the Company for three years after harbouring a slave deserter for two nights.[87]

Every attempt was thus made to improve the means of recapturing slaves by exhorting the colonists to aid the authorities. In 1714, a year of major concern at the high number of *drosters,* and again in 1717, the Stellenbosch Landdrost appealed to farmers to keep a look-out for them and to recapture them if possible.[88] This was not always easy. One farmer who found four *drosters* by chance bathing in the Breede River, took their clothes and returned home; when they came naked to his farm at night and demanded them back, he refused, telling them to 'go home and I'll send the clothes to your master'. They responded by attempting to set fire to his farmhouse.[89] A burgher was given permission in 1773 to make an expedition into the interior to recover slaves, provided he did not barter any cattle with the Khoikhoi, which suggests that he may have had mixed motives for the journey.[90]

A point of major significance was that very often the best informants on *drosters* were the Khoikhoi and other slaves. As in many societies, Cape slaves were encouraged to inform on deserters and were sometimes offered the possibility of emancipation if their information led to capture.[91] Khoikhoi were often used in commandos where their knowledge of the terrain was of great use.[92] Masters sometimes offered their slaves money if they would help find *drosters*, and sometimes slave tip-offs led to their recapture or slaves took part in the hunt for *drosters*.[93] In Cape Town, Company-owned slaves occasionally reported *drosters* from rural areas to the authorities.[94] Not all slaves were so co-operative, however; in one case when a Hout Bay farmer ordered his slaves to run after a *droster*, they refused and hid from him.[95]

The participation of slaves in the hunt for *drosters* and their co-operation with masters against fellow slaves indicates that by no means all of the slave population attempted to escape or to resist their owners. Some slave *drosters* were killed by other slaves, especially after they had attacked their master's property or attempted to steal food or ammunition.[96] Clearly any system of coercive labour produces those who realise that their interests can best be served by co-operating with their employers, and there were some notable cases of slaves who showed marked 'devotion' to their masters.[97] Occasionally, mentions were made in estate inventories or wills of slaves who were not to be sold because of their loyalty.[98] Some court cases reveal examples of slaves who held down other slaves whilst they were beaten, or even themselves carried out the punishment on orders of their master. Normally these were on the orders of the master and the slave had little option.[99] Attacks made by slaves on each other were either the result of quarrels between them alone, such as disputes over rights to women or property owned by the slave, or after attack on the master's possessions or farm for which the slave might later be blamed. The fear of retaliation was critical in slave response; in one case a master warned his slaves that if they attempted to give water to a slave whom he had just flogged they would receive similar treatment.[100] Such slaves were effectively powerless and their apparent acquiescence must be seen in this light.

There was one group of slaves who appear to have more readily co-operated with their owners, and that was the domestic house slaves, many of whom were female. This indicates a closer relationship between master and slave which grew up in the farmhouse, where slaves acted often as personal servants to the burgher family. One such slave told her master's wife that the mistress's husband and daughter were committing incest, and warned the daughter that she was doing wrong; another reported to the wife her master's adultery with female slaves on the farm.[101] Of course, such cases were themselves informing on their owners, and using evidence against a master, but they indicate the closer bonds that could grow up between female slaves and the master's wife and daughter. Such slaves normally slept in the house; when a burgher family and *knecht* were murdered by a gang of slave *drosters* in 1786, the female slave sleeping with them was also killed.[102] Domestic slaves often had closer ties with their master and his family than with the field slaves on farms, and were particularly numerous in Cape Town.

By no means all house slaves were undividedly loyal, however. The closer proximity to their masters also gave the opportunity for some to take action against their owners. Mullin has suggested that the direct contact of house slaves with the master's family imposed a more severe psychological strain, and that the attempt to conceal feelings that field hands could express out of sight of the master produced sharper resentments rather than greater loyalty.[103] Farm hands could express their dissatisfaction with their condition, not only by attempting to escape but also by a number of actions designed to limit their effectiveness as labourers or to damage the property, and in some cases, the persons of their owners whilst remaining on the farm. Such 'internal' means of resistance can be seen as one of the more important aspects of the slave response. It could take the form of overt reaction or of less evident means of limiting the full impact of the master's control and of preserving the individuality and dignity of the slave. The former methods were most often represented in the criminal records, either because of the nature of the slave action itself, or the violence of the master's response to it. Nevertheless, there are signs in the sources of more passive means of resistance, particularly in the rural areas.

The most obvious way in which a slave could limit his master's intentions was to deliberately work inefficiently or slowly, and in some extreme examples, to refuse to work at all. This was at the risk of severe punishment if detected, and could be resented by other slaves who were working alongside.[104] Slowness at work was hard to identify, although masters and their *knechts* or slave *mandoors* were alert to attempts to slacken; Melck's slave *mandoor* whipped a slave who was drunk, and had failed to work as ordered.[105] There are several cases of slaves who were punished by their masters for ploughing badly although whether this was deliberate or not is difficult to determine.[106] Certainly masters were aware of the potential for slaves to perform tasks slackly and were quick to punish them as a result, occasionally leading to their death. Sometimes slaves took more direct forms of resistance and refused to work at all. One Bougies slave, who had been ordered to plant vegetables in 1759, was later found by his master 'lying on the ground smoking a pipe of tobacco', and when asked what he was doing replied, 'I work the whole time; I must also rest a little; if the Baas wants to sell me after this, then go ahead and sell me.'[107] In 1751, another Bougies slave told his owner that he was tired of chasing birds away from the crops all day and refused to do so any more.[108] Refusal to obey orders to work could be a means of expressing the resentment built up over a period of time by a slave and marked the breaking point at which internalised reaction turned to overt resistance to the master or *knecht*.[109]

Such *brutaliteijd* (insolence), as it was described in the court records, warranted severe punishment by the master. The realisation that such treatment would follow a stand against carrying out orders could lead slaves to more desperate means of resistance. Direct attacks on the master or his property were often the result of punishment or in anticipation of it, and most such actions appear not to have been pre-meditated. Usually they were fruitless expressions of frustration, unless the slave managed to escape afterwards. The breaking point for Caesar van Madagascar came in 1793 when he demanded to know why he had to go to sleep so early and 'I must have my right to speak my mind.' When his master attempted to hit him with the *sjambok* he drew out a knife and cut it in two.[110] Such actions reflect the spontaneous outbreak against the orders of a master which reduced the status of the slave to that of a child resisting the time at which he is told to go to bed. One slave from Sambouwa attacked the son of his owner, a Drakenstein widow, in 1787 after being given *sjambok* blows on the shoulders for refusing to immediately obey orders when he was still eating his lunch; the freeman was only slightly wounded on the hand by the slave's knife, but although the latter claimed that he had acted purely on impulse and had no intention of seriously harming the man, he was sentenced to be beaten with rods and sent to work in the Company quarries on Robben Island for life.[111] His fate was preferable to that of Thomas de Croes van Trancquebaar who in 1719 retaliated to blows given by his master by picking up a pole lying nearby and hitting him on the head. Overcome with remorse, he begged for forgiveness, but was found out when his master died and he reported the death to another burgher, claiming that two Khoikhoi had been responsible. After 'freely' confessing in court, he was sentenced to have his hand chopped off, to be hung and then dragged through the streets of Cape Town and his body to be left exposed 'to the ravages of the air and the birds'.[112]

In such cases violence clearly engendered violence. Other cases of slave attacks on masters indicate the circumstances of extreme frustration to which slaves had been reduced; such as one male slave whose daughter had been severely beaten by his owner's wife in jealousy of her good looks, or another who discovered that his master, the sexton of the Waveren church, had been sleeping with his Khoikhoi lover.[113] Jonas van Monado murdered his owner's daughter after being told that he would never be manumitted.[114] These were the only actions which slaves could carry out to establish their interests, given the failure of the Company's system of justice to recognise such behaviour of the masters as criminal offences.

Some slaves attempted to set fire to their master's property or to kill his livestock; arson was a major hazard in a dry climate and with farmsteads of thatch roofs, and slaves could start fires by throwing bundles of burning cloth, often lit by burning tobacco, onto the thatch. There were several cases of deliberate arson by slaves in Cape Town in the eighteenth century, and in 1803 much damage was caused in the village of Stellenbosch by a fire begun by slaves who hoped to obtain booty and then escape.[115] The authorities were so aware of these dangers that they warned one slave who had set fire accidentally to a field after cooking some fish in the open that he would be hanged if it happened again.[116] A decree of 1741 imposed penalties on slaves or masters who caused field fires.[117] Acts of arson were clearly more pre-meditated than the kind of spontaneous attacks described above, although they sometimes arose out of specific resentments against punishment or the way in which the slave had been treated. Such cases of desperate action were normally followed by attempted escape; in one case a slave arsonist who acted because of blows he had been given by his master was found hiding in nearby corn fields and cut the throat of one of his captors resisting arrest. He was sentenced to be half-strangled and then burnt to death; a grimly fitting punishment for the crime of arson.[118] Sometimes, however, there was no immediate cause of an arson attempt; one Madagascan slave who set fire to the roof of his master's farmhouse in 1720 gave the alarm and helped the other slaves to douse it, and only later confessed, in an ingenious explanation, that he had 'been led by the Devil'.[119] Another threatened to burn down his master's house in 1776 in a frenzy of rage, whilst in 1791 farm buildings were set on fire by a slave who had been falsely accused by his master of stealing clothing from other slaves.[120] *Drosters* could also use arson as a weapon against farmers who attempted to obstruct them and in one case a recaptured *droster* returned to the farm of his captor, who was not his master, and set the roof alight in the middle of the night.[121]

Poisoning was another method of slave resistance, open particularly to those who prepared the master's food. In 1775, a Madagascan slave who resented being ordered by his mistress to fetch vegetables from a neighbouring farm because he wanted to tend to his own onions, put a snake's head in the pot of stew cooking in the kitchen, and was only found out because the slave housemaid saw him there.[122] Normally rural slaves learnt the properties of plants and roots from the Khoikhoi. Again, opportunities were greater in Cape Town. In 1754, a slave obtained mercury from the Company hospital which he used to attempt to poison his owner and in 1800 another obtained poison from a slave in the Company Slave Lodge.[123]

According to Sparrman, the lack of female slaves in the colony was a major cause of slave violence.[124] One overt sign of disregard for the order mechanism of the slave system which was also a response to the frustrations of male slaves without female company, was the attempted rape of the mistress by her slave. There are comparatively few cases of this in the records, however. In 1744 one slave claimed that his master and family were all 'like apes' and that he could force his owner's wife to sleep with him if he wished, but it proved an idle boast.[125] The severe punishment of a torturous death and the strong taboos on such conduct made this action pointless in most cases for slaves. Most rapes by slaves were of slave or Khoikhoi women where the threat of severe reprisal or of detection was not so great.

There were also surprisingly few planned physical attacks on masters by their slaves. Cases of assault were usually when a *droster* was challenged or were spontaneous outbursts of anger or desperation of the kind already described. Presumably the coercive nature of the legal system and the virtual certainty of painful death if apprehended deterred many slaves from plotting such action. There were exceptions: in 1739 a Bougies slave working on the farm of his master's step-son attacked the wife and daughter of the family in a closed room with a knife, but was overpowered by the farmer and his other slaves, and broken alive on the wheel.[126] Another slave who stabbed his master in 1728 killed himself immediately afterwards.[127] In one notorious case, the wife of a Cape Town inhabitant plotted together with one of her slaves to murder her husband, but they only managed to persuade a *droster* to assist them by threatening to turn him over to the authorities if he refused.[128]

Not only were there relatively few planned murders or assaults by individual slaves on their masters, but there were also few organised plots by groups of slaves and no attempts in the eighteenth century at rebellion. The Cape colonists had more cause to fear rebellion from the Khoisan than from their slaves.[129] In the remoter districts slaves sometimes joined Khoisan raiders; Lichtenstein described one occasion when slaves were 'induced to become partakers' in an attack by Khoisan on their master's farm in the Roggeveld, but there appears to have been no plan for further attacks.[130] Groups of slaves from Hangklip made periodic raids on nearby farms, but their prime purpose was to obtain food, although the danger to the lives of the farmers was recognised by the authorities.[131] The main threat of collective slave action appears to have been whilst they were on board ship before reaching the Cape and mutinies on slaving vessels broke out several times during the period.[132] Once landed and distributed amongst their owners, the problems of organisation and the lack of a unified slave community inhibited the potential for revolt. The only major rebellion of slaves at the Cape which broke out in the Roggeveld in 1823 failed largely because of the inability of the rebels to prevent news of their action spreading before they could unite closely together.[133] There was no well-developed creole slave group such as that which provided the leadership of the Jamaican revolt of 1831, nor was there any ideological impact such as the concepts of the French Revolution which led to the revolts in Haiti and Curacao at the end of the eighteenth century.[134] Significantly, the 1808 Malmesbury 'revolt' was partially a response to rumours that abolition of the slave trade would lead to general emancipation, and that of 1823 similarly the outcome of rumours of emancipation and the general uncertainty of government policy towards slaves.[135] The momentum to establish freedom in order to preserve cultural identity or protect slave religious interests which played an important part in the Jamaican slave rebellions did not exist at the Cape.[136] The size of the average slave unit on the farms and in Cape Town was small. Lacking the potential for revolt, the slave response tended to be more individualistic: a reaction to specific pressures and frustrations, and attacks as a means of retaliation or escape from the slave society rather than an attempt to overthrow it. In 1670 the Company feared that slaves were giving information away to their enemies, the French, but there is no sign that this was a concerted effort to obtain the overthrow of their masters' society and government.[137]

There was one means of slave response to his condition which did not incur the risk of later punishment for his action or the dangers and fears of escape and possible recapture, and yet destroyed valuable property of the master: suicide. At the Cape, as in other slave societies, suicide was the most tragic form of slave response, reflecting the desperation of the slave condition.[138] Yet distinctions must be made in the nature and possible motivations of slave suicide. Some were bids to avoid the torture of certain painful death by the authorities when slaves were on the point of capture after committing crimes or running away. Often suicide was committed after attacking the master or when theft was discovered.[139] In 1794 a recaptured *droster* stabbed himself, although unsuccessfully, to avoid falling into the hands of his master's *knecht* for the inevitable reprisal which would follow.[140] In 1761 a sixteen-year-old slave boy committed suicide because he was afraid of being flogged.[141] Such acts were indicative of the extreme fear held by slaves of the punishments of both masters and the authorities after the failure of an escape bid or some other criminal offence.

More indicative of the desperation of some slaves were the cases of suicide which were planned as a means of escaping from the ordinary situation of the slave who was not being threatened by imminent punishment. Such cases occurred regularly throughout this period and were of great concern to the government and masters alike. The authorities were in part concerned that masters should not pass off the death of their slaves through maltreatment or murder as suicide, and therefore required that every suicide case be examined by the Landdrost or his representatives at the scene of the death. As in the case of death by accident, all slave suicides had to be immediately reported by owners.[142] They were also determined that slave suicides should not act as an example to other slaves in the area, and made gruesome examples of each case. The body was normally left to rot in a visible position – often hanging from a tree or on the execution ground in Cape Town. In 1786, the Landdrost of Swellendam proposed that the body of a slave woman who had drowned herself be fished out of the river and laid on a plank nearby until it decomposed, 'to frighten the other slaves and hopefully by this spectacle they will change their minds if any thoughts of also taking such actions may lie within them'.[143] The Stellenbosch Landdrost in 1741 wrote to the Council of Justice that a slave who had stabbed himself after killing his lover out of jealousy had died while he was at the farm, but that since there were no trees nearby nor a suitable beam from which to hang the body, they had found it necessary to 'take him from the farmyard and leave him lying in the field nearby'.[144] Punishment for unsuccessful suicides was also intended as a deterrent against attempts by others. The need to emphasise the fact to other slaves was shown in one case when a slave sent by his master to the authorities to be punished was returned to be chastised domestically in the view of the whole labour force of the farm.[145]

From the notes made by the visits of the Landdrosts to the farms in cases of slave suicide, some broad indications of the nature of the slave response can be obtained. They appear to have been evenly distributed between urban and rural slaves, with an average of about fifteen to twenty reported each year, a figure that contrasts notably with the low incidence of suicide amongst the burghers.[146] The lack of complete lists makes deductions about variations in the incidence of suicide over time of doubtful value, although it is significant that there was a high number of slave suicides recorded in the 1730s and 1740s, and again in the 1780s; both periods when labour demands on slaves were intensifying. More apparent is that overwhelmingly slaves who committed suicide were foreign-born males; those who undertook the heaviest work on the farms and had memories of a previous life outside the Cape. The normal method was by hanging, usually from a beam in the slave quarters or a farm building, or from a tree, although there were also some cases of death from self-inflicted wounds.[147]

The Council of Justice lists rarely give an indication of the background to each case and the possible motivation.The visiting inspectors were less interested in motives than in future prevention and establishing the cause of death, and used the legal formula, repeated in each report, that death came 'from the slave's own hand without the least cause'. Certainly some apparent suicides were deaths of slaves caused by masters or others who were anxious to conceal their guilt, although careful inspection was made of the body for signs of wounds or stripes. A more useful source are the criminal court records, where unsuccessful slave suicide cases were sometimes brought. A rare example of the articulation by a slave of his motives is provided by a case in Drakenstein in 1739, when a Malabar slave threatened his mistress and her child with a knife and then said he would kill himself since slavery had deprived him of all desire to live. He particularly resented not only the imposition of work, but also the lack of freedom to go where he wanted, to wear his own clothes and to have female company; all benefits which he had enjoyed in his own land. Since his master owned everything he had, including his life, he explained that he could only achieve freedom by escaping that life and thereby depriving his owner of his possession. After threatening to kill his master's family, he was finally overcome before he could stab himself. He got his wish of death, if not in the way he could have desired; he was broken alive on the wheel.[148]

Such an overt expression of the desire to escape the slave condition was matched by suicide cases where there were more specific grievances. Many were of either newly arrived slaves or those who had recently been sold or were afraid of sale; some after being separated from lovers by sale.[149] In 1786 a female slave threw each of her children into the river and then drowned herself after the accidental drowning of her slave husband.[150]

Suicide was the most evident expression of the misery in which Cape slaves could live. It was an individual expression of the refusal to attempt to survive within the confines of the slave system. As such it was an extreme manifestation of the general pattern of slave response; individual action caused by specific frustrations and recognition that punishments after escape or other acts of resistance were severe. There were limitations on collective slave rebellion, but the frequent points of tension and the relative isolation of many farmsteads led to a high level of individual resistance and bids for escape. The Cape slave was often caught between the circumstances of his deprivation which produced resistance, often instinctively, and the collective power of the master class and the authorities which defeated him in his attempts. Patterns of slave response thus highlight the violence and frequent brutality of Cape society.

10

Slavery and Cape society

The heavy dependence of major sectors of the Cape economy on slave labour during the VOC period meant that crucial features of its social structure were conditioned by slavery. This was especially evident in the western rural districts where the development of social stratification between slaveowners and their labourers provided a basic class division which coincided with racial differences to an extent unknown in other parts of the settlement. There was thus an evident regional difference in both economic and social structure and a much more rigid pattern in the arable slave regions than in Cape Town. In the latter, levels of manumission and inter-breeding were higher and the presence of skilled slaves, artisans, Free Blacks and colonists who were not slaveowners produced a more complex social pattern which did not lead to the same level of polarisation. On the pastoral frontier regions, the lesser dependence upon slavery and the existence of a variety of other labour relationships in a differing demographic environment also produced another kind of class structure.[1]

Much debate has centred around the extent to which the early colonial Cape was a racially structured society.[2] There was no direct link between the structure of South African slaveholding society and the later institutionalised racism that followed expansion inland and the process of industrialisation in the nineteenth and early twentieth centuries. Yet it is a mistake to deny the existence of a class stratification which coincided with racial divisions in key areas of the colony during the VOC period.[3] In a comparative context the rigidity of some sectors of Cape slave society was more acute than in many other colonial areas. The western Cape accepted the racial discrimination of industrial South Africa with a legacy of class and ethnic identity which it had received from the era of slavery and had maintained after emancipation. Slaveowners of the farming regions developed a level of group consciousness that assumed racial lines earlier than elsewhere. The corollary of this was the growth of a labouring class identity, made up of both slaves and Khoikhoi, which polarised rural society. By contrast, the urban and frontier environments did not produce such an acute division within society before the end of the eighteenth century, although the blurring of social categories in Cape Town was only partial.

The economic dependence on slavery led to an increasing stratification of Cape society; slaveholders in the arable areas, at least, became a clearly identifiable group with a common economic basis of production and a cohesion of status and 'life-style'. As in the Americas, a complete slave society in which status, wealth and cultural identity became identified with slave ownership gradually emerged. The exceptionally high incidence of slave ownership amongst arable farmers was one driving factor behind this, and meant that, unlike many New World slave societies, there was less social differentiation amongst farmers in the core arable region. This is not to deny that during the century there developed some social stratification within the arable farmer group. The mechanics of the arable economy of the Cape is a much neglected topic, but pioneering studies by Robert Ross and Pieter van Duin indicate that there was a 'rural elite' who monopolised local political power as well as wealth expressed in terms of slaveholding size, and who, by the time of the Patriot era, had developed clearly defined interests.[4] Yet although such distinctions may have been significant, they were not sufficient to break down the cohesion of the slaveowning class. Moreover, the system of partible inheritance and the high degree of inter-marriage between the main families meant that social stratification in the western Cape was less sharp than in many other colonial slave societies.[5]

One aspect of this identity was the attitude to labour. The widespread incidence of slaveholding in both arable and urban sectors of the economy meant that, as Armstrong has pointed out, 'everyone aspired to have slaves, and having them, not to work'.[6] In common with most slave societies, manual labour was treated with contempt by freemen, and thought to be only fitting for slaves. This outlook was evident as early as the 1717 debate; that such ideas were becoming more widespread by the middle of the century is clear from the famous comment of Van Imhoff in 1743 that, 'having imported slaves every common or ordinary European becomes a gentleman and prefers to be served rather than serve'.[7] By the end of the century, in 1797, Van Ryneveld, whilst believing that slavery was necessary to the rural economy, acknowledged that 'the facility of procuring slaves renders the inhabitants of this country lazy, haughty and brutal'.[8] His view was shared by Barrow who visited the Cape in the same year and commented that slavery had led to a general aversion to work by the colonists: 'even the lower class of people object to their children going out as servants, or being bound as apprentices to learn the useful trades, which in their contracted ideas, would be considered as condemning them to perform the work of slaves'.[9] By 1826, a young English immigrant wrote home to his parents that 'there is no hard work expected to be done by white people in Cape Town, for it is done by slaves'.[10]

The growth of such attitudes was closely associated with the increasingly widespread incidence of slaveholding. The master class thus came to define itself by its dissociation from labour fitting only for slaves. The distinction between those who owned land and labour, and those who provided it became especially acute in the arable south-west. There the master class included during the course of the century the white *knechts* who increasingly took the roles of overseers or farm managers, rather than manual labourers as some had been in the earlier days of the colony.[11] Many *knechts* later achieved the status of burghers after accumulating capital or marrying widows with land; the most notable example of his upward mobility being the career of Martin Melck, an ex-*knecht* who became the wealthiest farmer in Stellenbosch district.[12]

A common method of production was unifying the arable farming class, based upon the ownership of slaves. This unity was also evident in the cultural homogeneity of the burghers of the Cape Town hinterland by the end of the VOC period; despite their diverse European origins, Dutch, German, Scandinavian and French settlers used a common language and adopted similar attitudes towards politics, as the Patriot movement indicated. There were, of course, differences between them of wealth and access to local power but they were insufficient to break down the basic unity that had emerged during the course of the eighteenth century.[13]

This ethnic and cultural identity was recognised by the slaves, although only hints of their perception of the master class can be obtained from the available records. In 1743 a *knecht* found an escaped slave of his employer called Hannibal near the sheep pastures and brought him back to the house, but he broke loose, and with the help of the other slaves on the farm tied up the *knecht*, took the keys from his pocket and made off with ammunition, clothes and food. As they left, Hannibal said to the *knecht*, 'Now you can tend your cattle yourself, and now 'your people' (*jouw natie*) can come and set you free.'[14] The association of the *knecht* with the master class was not surprising since he was recapturing a *droster* for punishment and was presumably a slave overseer, but the identification by a slave of the *knechts* and masters as a single group or *natie* is significant. The following year, a slave on a Stellenbosch farm who arrived in late at night and asked the other slaves for food, told them that they were making too much noise: 'What are you doing, do you want to wake up 'the Dutch people' (*de duits volk*) so that they will punish me?'[15] The colonists and Company used the word *duits* to refer to themselves as a group, despite their diverse European origins. Again, a slave was identifying the master class as a group of common descent or nationality to which he himself did not belong; a distinction which, when combined with the association of *swart volk* and manual labour, emphasised the fundamental racial identity of rural Cape social division.

The process of social cohesion amongst the whites in the region was accompanied by an identity of interests amongst their labourers. Slaves in any society were never absorbed entirely into the cultural and class position of their masters, and especially not in European colonial societies.[16] At the Cape, although most slaves failed to develop a characteristic culture, their slave status excluded them from many aspects of the master society. What became critical to the response of the slave population and ultimately to the social structure of the slave regions was the degree of internal differentiation amongst them.[17] There was a great diversity of slave cultural origin and a lack of unified response which muted the potential for collective rebellion. Slaves gave each other away to masters when it was in their interests, although the prosecutor in a criminal case of 1737 commented that 'It is well known that one slave will seldom tell tales against another.'[18] Divisions of interest between field labourers and domestic slaves, or as the result of sexual jealousies have been noted. Nevertheless, there was less stratification of the Cape rural slave population by labour function than, for example, in the plantation societies of the Americas. Smaller-scale holdings, both of slaves and of land, as well as the likelihood of sale by the divisions of an estate, prevented the emergence of a high degree of specialisation of employment or a hierarchy of labour organisation of the kind which did emerge between skilled and unskilled slaves in Cape Town.

A relatively undifferentiated rural labour force led to greater unity of status and position in the economy amongst farm slaves than in many other colonial rural slave systems. Moreover, it significantly affected the position of the non-slave rural labourers, the Khoikhoi. During the course of the eighteenth century, as the Khoikhoi were reduced from a state of independence which they had maintained in the early days of the Company's rule in the western Cape to dependence upon farmers as permanent labourers, they became increasingly subject to the same kind of restrictions and treatment as slaves.[19] Although records of Khoikhoi labour are incomplete, there are indications that after the breakdown of the independent chiefdoms in the western Cape by the end of the seventeenth century, some Khoikhoi became permanent labourers, but that there was a greater influx in the later part of the eighteenth century as the Khoikhoi were forced away from land appropriated in the east. They thus came to work on the farms of the arable producers at a time when slavery was firmly entrenched, and became a part of the slave production system. This was the result of the economy of the region which provided for few alternatives but that of labour also performed by slaves. Dundas' comment in 1800 of the Khoikhoi and San in the pastoral regions that 'they had long lived in a state of slavery and under oppression', was equally true of the arable western districts.[20] Barrow claimed that although the treatment of slaves by rural masters was bad, it was 'infinitely better than that of the Hottentots who are in their employ'.[21] Cases of severe maltreatment of Khoikhoi matched those of slave abuse, and although Khoikhoi, being officially free labour, were entitled to wages, often given in kind, and were hired on a contract basis, these were often not paid and the contract ignored.[22] Cape farmers made little distinction between the personal status of their Khoikhoi and slave labourers, who lived and worked together.

The Company legal system did attempt to maintain the distinction between Khoikhoi and slaves, but it proved increasingly difficult to do so as the century progressed and both groups became involved in a similar structure of labour coercion. As Ross has pointed out, the Khoikhoi might have had nominal rights in the legal code but by the end of the Company period 'they could no longer exercise them'.[23] The Stellenbosch Heemraad complained in 1797 that allowing the Khoikhoi access to the courts would 'give them the idea that they are on an equal footing with the burghers', and in 1800 Khoikhoi who was accused of murdering his employer stated that he had been beaten with a cudgel and that the farmer 'had told him whilst he distributed the blows that he had permission from the General and the Fiscaal to kill a Hottentot without any risk, and that he had been of the opinion that there would be no justice done to him if he complained'.[24]

The circumstances of Khoikhoi absorption into the arable labour structure and the breakdown of their independence therefore meant that they were reduced in status and economic role to the level of the slaves. This tendency increased notably during the course of the eighteenth century.[25] At the same time, the arable farmers and their *knechts* were increasingly becoming a unified class by their economic position as employers and controllers of labour. The rural western Cape by the end of the eighteenth century was thus a two-class society with slaves and those of enslaved status in one group and producers and slaveowners in the other. This was a tendency of all slave societies in varying degrees, but it seems to have been particularly acute in the arable Cape. Economic circumstance and the structure of rural society determined a dichotomy which became increasingly marked during the course of the Company period. Of major significance was the fact that it was also marked by racial lines.

In other parts of the colony, such a division was less acute. In Cape Town, the existence of a higher proportion of non-slaveowning burghers as well as skilled artisans, Chinese merchants and Batavian political exiles blurred the distinction between a white social group monopolising control of exchange and production and a black labouring class of the kind that existed in the hinterland. Clearly the wealthiest inhabitants of the city were free burghers and slaveowners, whilst menial work was performed by slaves. Nevertheless, access to earnings enabled some slaves to obtain manumission, and there was a free black community in Cape Town, some of whom were also slave-owners.[26] The level of cross-breeding between slaves and others was higher than elsewhere, although largely in the Company Slave Lodge and other brothels of the town. There was less unity of interest between Company officials, wealthy burghers with investments in agriculture as well as property in Cape Town and petty commodity traders or hostel-keepers, than amongst the farmers of the arable region. As in all urban environments, despite its slave component, social fluidity was greater than in the countryside.

In the pastoral districts, and especially in the eastern part of the colony, slavery played a much less direct role in the determination of social structure. Other forms of patron–client relationships emerged between stock farmers and labourers, although the use of slaves in domestic work and on some pastoral farms for field labour did retain the structure of master–slave subservience outside the western regions and indenture and use of the *inboek* system were ideologically based on this principle of absolute control of labour.

142

These tendencies and relationships between slavery and the wider social formation may be examined more closely in relation to three mechanisms which had potential for breaking down, or at least blurring the distinction between slave and freemen: manumisson of slaves, the status of emancipated slaves and sexual contacts between the two groups. Because of the implications for the origins of racial prejudice, these aspects of the Cape slave system have received much attention in recent years. Whilst economic factors determined much of the social structure of the colony, it was also true that the policy of the VOC was responsible for determining the legal context of the ordering of that society in its policies of slave manumission, relations with the Khoikhoi and miscegenation.[27]

Although manumission records are not a reliable guide to the degree of severity of treatment in a slave society, since manumission may be used by a slaveowner as a means of absolving himself from the responsibility of feeding and clothing an older and economically unproductive slave, they do indicate the extent to which a 'free black' population can emerge within the structure of the slave society. Precise rates of manumission are of little value unless set in a comparative context; Cruse's much quoted figure of 893 slaves manumitted between 1715 and 1792 needs to be compared to the rates of manumission in other colonial slave societies.[28] Contrary to the opinion expressed in some works that manumission was readily available at the Cape, the analysis of records by Elphick and Shell has shown that levels of manumission were considerably lower than those of Brazil and Latin American slave societies and more akin to the North American plantation systems, confirming Thunberg's impression that 'slaves are very seldom enfranchised'.[29] Limitations were placed on the manumission of older and economically useless slaves by legislation which forced owners to pay a sum of money to the Diaconij to cover costs if the freed slave later applied for poor relief. De la Caille believed that it was this legislation that kept the rate of slave manumission in the colony as a whole so low.[30] At least one example is recorded of an urban slaveowner who was unable to pay 50 Rxds to the Diaconij, but who was the heir to an estate in which a slave had been emancipated by will. He was forced to make a special appeal to the Council of Policy to be excused from the obligation, but there is no indication that this was granted.[31]

The imposition of a duty on slave manumissions was only one of a series of legislative measures applied at the Cape which effectively lowered the level of emancipations. Restrictions were also placed on the freeing of heathen slaves, although the corollary of this was that Christian slaves were entitled to freedom; such an idea did emerge in the colony but was little applied in practice and in 1770 the decree that baptised slaves could not be sold fell short of the expectation of manumission for converts.[32] By the end of the seventeenth century, it was an accepted prerequisite of manumission that a slave should be baptised, speak good Dutch and have a guarantor who would pay the Poor Fund, which might provide relief if the freed slave became

143

destitute. All of these qualifications were unlikely for most slaves. As Thunberg stressed, the high cost of manumission made it only feasible for some urban slaves who had sources of income or support from the free black community.[33]

This indeed appears to have been the case. Although there are a few records of manumission of rural slaves, these were exceptional, and were mainly of favoured household slaves, many of them female, who were freed at their master's death.[34] As Elphick and Shell have shown, the overwhelming majority of manumitted slaves lived in Cape Town and less than 5% of the private slaveowners who freed their slaves lived outside the Cape district. Almost 25% of the owners of such slaves were themselves Free Blacks, all of whom lived in the city. Furthermore, analysis of the origins of freed slaves showed that during the whole of the eighteenth century, less than 2% were African, just over 50% were Cape-born and the remainder were Indian or Indonesian. It would appear that the best opportunity for manumission in a society where it was extremely limited, was for an Eastern slave with skills to purchase his own freedom or with a family who were Free Blacks and prepared to do so for him or her.[35] The increasing restrictions on manumission were akin to trends of greater control over access to freedom in some American colonial states at the time, whilst demand for sureties and the need for Council approval of manumission by will were similar to restrictions associated with the rigid slave societies of the British Caribbean and which also applied to the plantation society of Dutch Surinam.[36]

The best indication of the increasing polarisation of Cape rural society and the comparative fluidity of Cape Town in comparison to its hinterland is the number and status of Free Blacks in each area. The position of a Free Black community in any slave society is also indicative of the extent to which racial characteristics, as distinct from slave status, determined the structuring of society. The Dutch East Indies was an example of a colonial society in which half-castes or *mestizos* could be assimilated into the ruling group, and they acted as middlemen in colonial Makasar in much the same way as in the Latin American colonies during the VOC period. As the Cape was under the aegis of the Batavian authorities and its administrators usually had experience of the East Indies, it might be expected that a similar pattern would emerge there.[37]

This, however, assumes a common economic basis for both colonial regions which was conspicuously absent. Whilst the potential for livelihood by slaves or half-castes in Cape Town might have resembled that of the Indonesian ports, there was no parallel in the Dutch East Indies to the burgher farming community of the western Cape. The low level of manumission and the limited role of the free black community in the countryside was the product of its economic structure. The need for capital, land and the support of a family kin network effectively precluded arable farming by Free Blacks as the eighteenth century progressed. The usual explanation given for the absence of a free black rural population and the low manumission rate is the lack of intermediary roles in the economy which they could fill; such positions were carried out either by whites or slaves.[38] As Hughes has pointed out, however, the concept of an 'interstitial position' is a vague one, and more precise reasons must be given.[39]

The low number of manumissions is not a complete explanation of the lack of a free black group since slaves freed in Cape Town could have moved into the rural region, and some Free Blacks were exiles from Batavia who had never been enslaved. Although the percentage of Free Blacks in the total burgher population never rose above 8% in the eighteenth century, it was considerably higher in the Cape district which included arable farming areas.[40] Moreover, the VOC directors in 1682 instructed Simon van der Stel and the Council of Policy that 'if you are of the opinion that they [slaves] would be more zealous if made free, you may make the experiment with one or two families; and leave nothing untried which is likely in any degree to tend to the advancement of agriculture'.[41] In the seventeenth century, some Free Blacks were given land in the Stellenbosch area on 'an equal footing' with burgher immigrants.[42]

Nevertheless, even at this early period, the number of Free Blacks recorded in the *opgaaf* rolls of the rural districts was extremely low. The number of Free Blacks who recorded some possession of livestock, wine or grain in the Cape district between 1692 and 1773 was less than five per annum, and many of these recorded only livestock holdings.[43] Arable production by free black males was extremely rare.

The impression obtained from the Cape district is thus of minimal opportunity for free black farmers. This assumes that Free Blacks who took up agriculture were identified as such in the census records. It seems that those who were not descendants of racially mixed families were always given the appellation *vrijswaart* in official documents and identified as such in the local community. Moreover, conclusions for the Cape are paralleled by Hattingh's study of the Free Blacks of Stellenbosch. This reveals a similar trend of a very small number of pastoral farmers, although there were several free black wine producers and grain farmers in the earlier decades of the eighteenth century and one who farmed into the 1730s.[44] One freed Company slave married a Drakenstein wine and grain farmer and their family was granted land which they maintained for a long period in that region.[45] They were, however, exceptions. By the middle of the eighteenth century, there were no identifiable free black arable farmers. Le Vaillant recorded in the early 1780s that two Free Blacks jointly owned an estate in the rural Cape, although this has been questioned.[46] If it was so, it was doubtless a cattle and sheep ranch.

Surviving inventories of free black rural estates indicate that their net value was low and that most were poorly provided with furniture and farming equipment. An exception was the estate left to Angela van Bengal by her burgher husband in 1698 which was valued at 6,495 Rxds, a good average for the period, and consisted of a plot of land in Table Valley as well as a farm in Drakenstein, four male and one female slaves, seventy-three cattle, 260 sheep, ox-wagons, ploughs and furniture.[47] The free black couple, Helena van de Kaap and Jan Pietersz., only had one *opstal*, sixty cattle, five horses and a slave, with a total value of 431 Rxds after debts had been paid, when their estate was assessed in 1741.[48] Records of other estates are lacking, but the census records indicate that many were even poorer. Rural Free Blacks seem to have been living near to bankruptcy, and their plight worsened as the eighteenth century advanced.[49]

This indicates that one of the major problems faced by the free black farmers was a lack of capital to enable them to consolidate their holdings. Hattingh's study of the taxes paid by the Stellenbosch Free Blacks and their access to credit indicates that they little differed in wealth or status from many white farmers.[50] Nevertheless, lacking the contacts with other families that many burghers possessed, or the possibility of inheritance by the breakup of family estates, the ex-slaves competed with other arable producers at a serious disadvantage. Most of the farms of average size and below were indebted to a number of other burghers during the first few decades of the eighteenth century; the free black estates usually had debts owing only to other Free Blacks, whose capital resources were considerably less. By the middle of the eighteenth century it was very difficult for a burgher with little capital to set up an arable farm unless he had inherited it. Certainly freed slaves had little chance of doing so, and were forced to go either to Cape Town or further inland. Mentzel records a case of a freed slave who went back to working as a shepherd for his former master.[51]

Most of the free black population of the colony lived in Cape Town. Precise numbers are difficult to determine, but it appears that they increased slowly throughout the eighteenth century, and by 1773 there were at least 350 in the city.[52] As Elphick and Shell have demonstrated approximately 15 to 20% of the free burgher population of Cape Town were Free Blacks.[53] It also appears that some were able to accumulate property, slaves and obtain access to credit which their counterparts in the rural districts lacked.[54] To a large extent this was the result of the greater opportunities in the exchange and petty commodity economy of the town for those who did not have control of land or capital.[55] Nevertheless, it remained true that the average value of free black estates in Cape Town was lower than those of other colonists.[56] Whilst many were engaged in artisan manufacture and retail trading, they did not gain access to positions of major wealth or prestige in the city.[57]

Other social factors were working against the emergence of an economically powerful free black community. Despite their freedom from slavery, Free Blacks were not granted burgher status. Whilst there may have been little distinction of legal status between Free Blacks and whites during the seventeenth century, clear differentiation emerged during the course of the eighteenth.[58] Some Free Blacks identified themselves with the protests of Adam Tas against the Company in 1705 and in 1752 Rijk Tulbagh wrote to the Landdrost of Stellenbosch concerning a special levy to be raised on the orders of the Batavian authorities that 'although they do not stem from

European blood, the Free Blacks and all other similar persons living here nevertheless enjoy all the privileges and rights of burghers'.[59] This was true to a limited extent; Free Blacks could, for example, buy, own and manumit slaves, and were entitled to the same protection by the law against attacks from them.[60] A slave in 1744 complained that a Free Black was allowed to sit at table and eat with white burghers whilst he was unable to do so, and clearly such aspects of daily living could distinguish emancipated slaves from those still in bondage.[61]

Nevertheless, the distinction made implicitly by Tulbagh that Free Blacks had 'no European blood' became gradually more important as the century progressed. Theoretically, Free Blacks could be enslaved again if they broke laws, although there is no record that this ever happened.[62] Often deeds to manumission specified that the freed slave would be obliged to be respectful and obedient to his former owner and his family.[63] Free Blacks were also excluded from the burgher militia. As early as 1722 it was decreed that Free Blacks and Chinese living in Cape Town should be formed into a separate militia, 'so that they might not remain idle and have the opportunity for disorderly behaviour'.[64] One burgher wrote in protest to the Council in 1790 that despite his loyal service as 'a true burgher' and his lawful marriage to a Free Black, his half-caste son had been refused admission to the burgher corps by its leading officers, and the social status of his children thus depended upon 'the whim of my fellow burghers'.[65] Other forms of discrimination against Free Blacks in the colony abounded; in 1765, limitations were placed on their dress, the Diaconij was instructed to pay poor relief to them, but to limit the amount strictly, and limits on the service of Free Blacks in Cape Town administrative bodies were in evidence.[66] One of the problems was that the Company did not recognise the legality of Moslem marriages, and many free black offspring were regarded as 'born out of wedlock'.[67]

Social attitudes were also evident in the sexual contacts between inhabitants of the colony. Miscegenation was an important aspect of any colonial slave society, and the Cape was no exception; the most detailed studies of Afrikaner family origins indicate that approximately 7% of Afrikaner blood today is 'non-white' and that this stems from the Company period.[68] The access of a master to his female slave's sexual favours meant that 'slavery and a high degree of racial mixture inevitably go together'.[69] What is significant to the ordering of social structure, however, is the degree to which this was accepted by the community, the possibility of inter-racial marriage and the status of the offspring of such sexual encounters outside marriage.

The VOC did not initially disapprove of marriage between whites and Free Blacks. It had in the seventeenth century devised schemes for the colonisation of Ceylon and the East Indies by encouraging mixed marriages, although these had proved to be a failure.[70] The lack of white women at the Cape was the obvious driving force behind early racial mixing, and this continued to be true of some areas of the Cape well into the eighteenth century.[71] In the first decades of the colonial settlement there were thus a number of marriages between white settlers and female emancipated slaves; Governor Simon van der Stel descended from such a union.[72] Fredrickson contrasts this 'permissive South African pattern' with the concern of many American colonial states to prevent any miscegenation, let alone marriage between the racial groups.[73] Certainly sexual contacts between whites and slaves outside marriage also abounded; the Company Slave Lodge was a renowned brothel for visiting sailors and soldiers at the garrison, and, as in most ports, prostitution levels were high.[74] The high incidence of miscegenation in Cape Town led visitors later in the eighteenth century to comment that most slaves were 'as fair as Europeans' and that only imports kept any dark colour amongst them.[75]

It was the prevalence of this 'debauchery' in the Slave Lodge that led to attempts by the Company in the 1680s to restrict inter-racial sexual contacts. In 1681, 'lewd dancing and cohabitation of Europeans and female slaves' was prohibited by decree, and in 1685, following the visit of the Commissioner van Rheede, marriages between whites and freed slaves were forbidden, although an exception was made for half-caste slaves.[76] Attempts to control slave concubinage had also been made in 1671, and punishments set out for the white fathers of slave children.[77] In 1681, a male slave was hung for having 'criminal conversation with his master's daughter, and about three years ago with another European female, both before and after her marriage, many times, thus adding to his offence the greater crime of adultery'.[78]

Although these restrictions are significant indicators of the policies of the Company administration, they had little impact on the level of miscegenation in the Cape as a whole where, as in all colonial societies, sexual contact between racial groups was not infrequent. What was significant, however, were regional variations in the form that such contacts took. Most examples of permanent liaisons or inter-marriage continued in Cape Town, but were almost unknown in the rural Cape.[79] On the other hand, the farmers who owned female slaves had the opportunity for casual and illicit sexual contact.

The precise level of such miscegenation can never be known. Indications from visitors are that it was relatively common in a society where there were few women, and certainly many unmarried whites were involved in such activity. Mentzel commented that boys between the ages of sixteen and twenty-one 'more often than not commit some folly, and get entangled with a handsome slave-girl belonging to the household... the offence is venial in the public estimation. It does not hurt the boy's prospects; his escapade is a source of amusement and he is dubbed a young fellow who has shown the stuff he is made of.'[80] Some masters encouraged the co-habitation of their slaves with other whites since the offspring would be the owner's slaves.[81] Such sexual exploitation was not surprising, even after the marriage of a burgher. A white Company servant gave Sparrman a list (which he duly noted in his diary) 'of the constant order of precedence in love, which ought to be observed among the fair sex in Africa'; slaves listed in order by their place of origin were followed by 'the Hottentots, and last and worst of all the white Dutch women'.[82] Nevertheless, such escapades by married burghers were not always favoured by the community at large. One farmer in 1776 forced slaves and a *bastaard hottentot* to sleep with him, but was found out when his wife was away from the farm and other burghers found him in bed with one of them; witnesses were produced, and he was fined 100 Rxds.[83] In 1790 a Stellenbosch burgher, Andries Grundeling, woke a slave on another farm and offered to pay him to go to the farm of a female slave with whom he had made contact and call her to him; the slave was reluctant but went after some debate, but the barking of dogs roused the household before he could get near the girl. The owner found Grundeling lurking behind a hedge, and asked him 'if it was not scandalous behaviour for a burgher and if he was not ashamed to go round asking slaves at night in another man's house to fetch girls for him'.[84] The most notable case of all was that of David Malan Davidsz., a married burgher, who was found at night by a Stellenbosch farmer's widow in her slave quarters, hiding under the bed, and then ran off with one of her female slaves. Both Malan and the slave were reported missing, and over a year later had still not been traced.[85]

If liaisons between farmers and slave girls did not always meet with general approval, those between slave men and white women were still less acceptable. Both Sparrman and Thunberg record that cases of pregnancy arose out of such a situation; in one case, 'the father as a reward for his kindness, had been advanced from the condition of a slave to that of prisoner for life on Robben Island and the lady herself to that of wife to her father's bailiff'.[86] A Swellendam slave who caused the pregnancy of a burgher's daughter was sent by the Landdrost to the central Council of Justice in 1783.[87]

The existence of sexual contacts between slaves and freemen did have a considerable effect on the colony as a whole; Thunberg commented that it had a notable 'whitening' impact on the offspring.[88] Half-caste slaves held a privileged position in slave society, often fetching higher prices.[89] In 1766, a Batavian decree forbade the sale of half-caste slaves if the estate was solvent, and by the end of the century Van Ryneveld stated that such slaves should be manumitted, although there was considerable diversity of practice in the matter.[90] Thunberg records a case of a master who had two such slaves, one of whom was baptised and manumitted, the other kept in slavery.[91] The implication is that conversion was the critical factor and this was uncommon.

It appears therefore that, although there was considerable sexual contact between the racial groups of the western Cape, they did not break down the basic divide between white masters and black labourers; masters exploited their slaves sexually but this had little impact on the structure of the society in which they lived and the offspring of such unions were assimilated into the slave class. This was especially acute in the arable western districts where slavery was most widespread and followed the model of the North American slave colonies rather than the Dutch East Indies or the plantation society of the East African coast, where half-caste children were not enslaved.[92]

Even in the East Indies, however, where the social structure was considerably more fluid than that of the arable Cape, there was much colour prejudice and a contempt for Eurasian offspring.[93] It is thus hardly surprising that racial distinctions were emerging in the Cape. Sparrman noted in the early 1770s that 'a great many of the whites have so much pride, as to hinder, as far as lies in their power, the blacks or their offspring from mixing with their blood'.[94] They objected to the presence of half-castes in the church at *nagmaal* (Communion) and excluded slaves.[95] There was a cleavage based on racial lines within the social structure of the colony and this was reflected in the low level of manumissions, the limited role of Free Blacks and the illegitimacy of miscegenation. In all of these features, the arable western Cape, where slaves were most concentrated, was more rigid than elsewhere in the colony.

Plantation systems tends to lead to a greater class distinction between master and slave than other slave structures, and although the arable Cape was a small-scale farming economy, the polarisation of classes there was also evident.[96] That this divide was also racial – white farmers and *knechts* contrasted to coloured slaves and Khoikhoi – meant that the class structure became identified with the racial categories. The belief that manual labour was unsuitable for whites was accompanied by the concept that it was all that was fitting for slaves and people of colour. The debate over the origins of slavery and racism in the North American colonies has indicated that whilst preconceived racial concepts were brought from Europe, it was the reality of the economic structure that caused slavery of another race and that reinforced existing concepts to produce a more virulent racism.[97] There is less difficulty in assessing the causes of slavery at the Cape; the necessity of providing a labour force for the early burghers and the failure of other schemes led to the use of a system already known to the VOC in Indonesia.[98] Yet racial distinctions were implicit from the start. The essential belief of members of the Council of Policy in 1717 that manual labour was 'more fitting' for slaves showed that by the beginning of the eighteenth century the rural production system was already divided along racial, as well as class lines.

Just as the early American colonists of New England were aware of the concept of racial slavery from the West Indies, so too the Dutch in the early Cape were familiar with the institution, both from their involvement in the Atlantic slave trade and in Indonesia.[99] Certainly Van Riebeeck proposed alternatives to slaves; one being the introduction of Chinese nominally free labour, although, as Hughes has pointed out, the description of Chinese exiles and traders in Cape Town as *swarten* implies that the concept of 'blackness' was being used to cover anyone who was not white and had a subservient role in the economic structure, irrespective of their actual skin colour.[100] Justifications of slavery in Holland on the grounds that Europeans were naturally superior to other races, and the concept of the 'children of Ham' who were slaves, were openly expressed in the course of the eighteenth century. Although Legassick is concerned to demonstrate that racial distinction were less important than class divisions, he significantly cites the first mention of the 'curse of Ham' concept at the Cape as given by the Drakenstein Church Council in 1703, in an appeal for the conversion of the Khoikhoi, 'so that the children of Ham would no longer be the servants of [or?] bondsmen'.[101]

This is not to deny the pre-eminence of class factors in the structuring of the Cape slave system, or the growth of racism as an outcome, rather than a specific cause of the establishment of slavery.[102] Racial attitudes at the Cape developed within the context of the colonial social structure, and particularly that of a slave system.[103] The very existence of legal distinctions between slave and freeman obviated the need for overt expression of racist social divisions and controls. In the colony as a whole, as Elphick and Giliomee have argued, concepts of racial divisions of society largely arose as a response to the confusion created by the initial lack of a firm boundary line.[104] What is clear, however, in the debate centred around the role of the frontier in the formation of racial attitudes, is that overt social distinctions which coincided with race existed in the arable, slaveholding region of the colony earlier than in either Cape Town or the pastoral 'frontier' zone, even if this did not produce the virulent racism of the later nineteenth century.[105] The undoubted hardening of official attitudes against manumission, miscegenation and the squeezing out of the free black farmers which took place during the course of the eighteenth century, reflected the realities of the social structure in the arable regions. As MacCrone pointed out, the increase in numbers of slaves in the region and the fears of slave resistance by the farmers led to harsher restrictions, and even by the start of the eighteenth century, slavery was clearly established as 'no longer merely a form of cheap labour but as an institution'.[106]

It thus seems clear that the greater rigidity of eighteenth-century Cape society was the result of slavery and the polarisation of society in the western areas. By the end of the VOC period, the development of a heightened colour consciousness was spreading beyond the arable region and was at least partially evident in Cape Town; as Giliomee stated, 'by 1820 a racial order was firmly established'.[107] Whilst the early Cape settlement may have lacked the rigidity of social structure of some North American colonies, examination of the slaveholding south-west indicates that this region approximated more closely to the North American pattern of racial discrimination by the eighteenth century than the Latin American systems. The distinction between whole colonial societies is, however, suspect; Davis has stressed the similarity of the slave systems of some regions of Latin and North America.[108] Regional differences were as significant, and this was certainly true of the Cape, where the arable western districts developed a more rigid social structure which coincided with race.

The VOC period saw an intensification of the use of the slave production system throughout the south-western arable area. Agriculture became closely linked with the availability, cost and use of slave labour. Moreover, the existence of a slave community led to a structure of control for slaveowners, which gave the arable producers clearly developed class-consciousness and power. In many respects, therefore, the rural slave production system created a class of slaveowners which resembled that of the southern States more closely than the non-arable producers of the Dutch East Indies or the absentee landowners of the West Indies, although Cape slaveowners lacked the same control of the political ordering of their society. Nevertheless, in the western districts, by the eighteenth century, a two-caste system had emerged, in which Free Blacks had no economic or social place and class roles were synonymous with racial categories. In Cape Town slavery was used for services rather than production and social divisions were more blurred, although there is evidence of increasing polarisation by the early nineteenth century.[109]

The period leading to emancipation and the restructuring of labour after it are both topics that require future research.[110] It seems clear, however, that the post-emancipation era, when the legal distinctions of slave and freeman were abolished, saw the further entrenchment of racial divisions between 'Coloured' labourers and white employers. Social stratification formed by the slave production system was thus perpetuated. The organisation of agriculture and the labour market remained closely tied to structures developed in the slave-based economy. The legacy of slavery in the VOC period was thus to have a significant impact on the western Cape as it moved into the industrial phase of South African history.

Notes

1. THE STUDY OF CAPE SLAVERY

1 Stampp 1952, p. 614.
2 Elkins 1975; Genovese 1975; Blassingame 1979; Fogel and Engerman 1974; Genovese 1966 and 1970. A summary of some of the most significant developments is Davis 1974.
3 Davis 1966; Genovese 1969.
4 Cooper 1977.
5 Patterson 1982.
6 Meillassoux 1975; Miers and Kopytoff 1977; Lovejoy 1983.
7 Fredrickson 1981. For critiques of some of the early South African material, Elphick 1983; Giliomee 1983.
8 Elphick and Giliomee 1979; Marks and Atmore 1980 contains two chapters of relevance to the Dutch Cape and slavery, Legassick 1980 and Newton-King 1980.
9 Ross 1975, 1977 and 1983d; Guelke and Shell 1983; Guelke 1983.
10 Van Duin and Ross 1984; Ross 1983b.
11 Ross 1979c, 1981 and 1983b.
12 De Kock 1950; Edwards 1942.
13 Greenstein 1973.
14 MacCrone 1937; Freund 1976; Legassick 1980.
15 Armstrong 1979.
16 Elphick and Shell 1979; Böeseken 1977; Hattingh 1979a; Ross 1983a.
17 Rayner 1981, 1983 and 1984; Shell 1983.
18 Worden 1982a.
19 Mentzel 1785, vol. I, p. 141.
20 Worden 1982b, pp. 43–4.

2. THE CREATION AND GROWTH OF A SLAVE SOCIETY

1 Instructions for the Commanders, 25 March 1651, Moodie 1838, vol. I, pp. 7–8.
2 Journal of Commander Riebeeck, 21 April 1652, Moodie 1838, vol. I, p. 11; Riebeeck to Chamber XVII, 4 May 1653, Moodie 1838, vol. I, p. 33; Blommaert 1938, pp. 10–11.
3 Riebeeck to Chamber XVII, 28 April 1655, Moodie 1838, vol. I, p. 62.
4 Robertson 1945, p. 170; Böeseken 1977, pp. 10–13; Blommaert 1938, pp. 24–8.
5 Böeseken 1977, p. 19.
6 Böeseken 1977, p. 23.
7 CA LM 30, p. 23, Precis of Cape Archives Annual Returns.

8 Resolution of Council of Policy, 22 January 1680, De Wet 1957, vol. II, p. 309; Böeseken 1977, p. 40.
9 CA LM 30, p. 23, Precis of Cape Archives Annual Returns; Handlin 1950, pp. 199–203; this view is criticised by Degler 1959, pp. 49–54.
10 Guelke 1979, pp. 44–5.
11 Elphick 1977, p. 102; Fredrickson 1981, pp. 55–6; Greenstein 1973, pp. 28–9; Marks 1972, pp. 63–4; MacCrone 1937, p. 47.
12 Fredrickson 1981, pp. 18–19; Boxer 1965, pp. 116–17 and pp. 210–17; Arasaratnam 1976, pp. 17–28; Gaastra 1982, pp. 35–60.
13 Worden 1978, pp. 2–4.
14 De Wet 1981, p. 5.
15 MacCrone 1937, p. 27; Guelke 1974, pp. 53–4; Fredrickson 1981, pp. 63–4.
16 Fredrickson 1981, pp. 64–5; Wills 1976, pp. 179–83.
17 Blommaert 1938, pp. 10–11.
18 Jordan 1961, pp. 243–50.
19 Armstrong 1979, p. 77; Schutte 1979*b*, pp. 101–15.
20 Armstrong 1979, pp. 74–5; Sutherland 1978, pp. 2–7.
21 Earle 1978, pp. 51–65; Patterson 1977, p. 20.
22 Guelke 1979, pp. 44–54; Van Duin and Ross, 1984.
23 Total figures of slaves in the eighteenth century were obtained from the annual census returns preserved in the AR VOC 4045–4360 and I am grateful to Robert Ross and Pieter van Duin for giving me access to their collection of these. Seventeenth-century figures are taken from CA LM 30 Precis of Cape Archives Annual Returns and Armstrong 1979, p. 91. Under-representation of slaves towards the end of the VOC period was a problem and a decree was issued in 1776 to attempt to control it; Jeffreys and Naude 1944, vol. III, p. 96. On this and other problems of fraudulent census returns, Worden 1982*a*, pp. 56–8.
24 Armstrong 1979, p. 86.
25 Worden 1982*a*, pp. 30–1; AR VOC 4365, p. 32, Bijlagen tot de Commissarissen-generaal, 1792.
26 Mentzel 1785, vol. II, p. 126.
27 Ross 1975.
28 Craton 1975, p. 275; Patterson 1975, pp. 170–6; Cooper 1977, p. 56.
29 Hopkins 1978, p. 99.
30 Hopkins 1978, p. 101; Brunt 1958, p. 165.
31 Barrow 1801, vol. II, p. 362.
32 Guelke 1974, p.247; estimates of Khoikhoi and San population numbers in the seventeenth and eighteenth centuries is provided in Elphick 1977, p. 23, footnote 1.
33 CA J 233, Stellenbosch district census, 1806.
34 CA J 193, Stellenbosch and Drakenstein district census, 1739.
35 Wood 1975, pp. 131–4.
36 Stampp 1956, p. 30.
37 Some of these figures were calculated by computer at the Instituut vir Historiese Navorsing at the University of the Western Cape, Bellville. I am grateful to Professor J.L. Hattingh of the Instituut and mnr A. Haller of the Computer Centre for their aid.
38 CA 1/SWM 14/1, pp. 2–3, Landdrost of Swellendam to Tulbagh, undated CA C 652, Swellendam Dagregister, 13 December 1745; Forbes 1965, p. 68.
39 Van Zyl 1978, p. 12.
40 Ross 1980*a*, p. 8.
41 Du Toit and Giliomee 1983, pp. 32–3.
42 De Chavonnes 1918, p. 85.
43 De Chavonnes 1918, p. 121.

44 De Chavonnes 1918, p. 126.
45 De Chavonnes 1918, p. 121.
46 De Chavonnes 1918, pp. 104–5.
47 Van Ryneveld 1797, Article 6.
48 Ross 1983*d*; see also Guelke and Shell 1983.

3. SLAVE LABOUR AND THE CAPE ECONOMY

1 Van Duin and Ross, 1984.
2 Greene 1942, pp. 101–3; Berlin 1980.
3 CA C 171, pp. 197–200, Resolutions of Council of Policy, 19 April 1786; Guelke 1974, pp. 158–9 and 402–8; Thunberg 1795, vol. I, p. 123 attributed extensive farming to water shortages.
4 Hopkins 1978, pp. 8–11; Yeo 1952, pp. 458–9; De Kock 1924, pp. 36–7.
5 CA C 654, pp. 1–4, Stellenbosch Dagregister, 11 January 1751; CA C 655, pp. 304–7, Stellenbosch Dagregister, 23 January 1775.
6 Appendix to draft of letter written by Hendrik Swellengrebel Jr to C. de Gijselaar, 26 June 1783, Schutte 1982, p. 168.
7 For example, AR VOC 4183, pp. 936–8, Stellenbosch Krijgsraad to Governor Hendrik Swellengrebel, 1751.
8 SAL MSD 3, pp. 8–9, Almanach der Africaanse hoveniers en landbouwers & C., 1705?; H. Cloete to Hendrik Swellengrebel Jr, 15 March 1787, Schutte 1982, p. 229 claimed that manuring only took place every two years and that a few lands did not require any manuring.
9 Kolb 1731, vol. II, p. 67.
10 Van Ryneveld 1797, Article 6.
11 H. Cloete to Hendrik Swellengrebel Jr, 15 March 1787, Schutte 1982, pp. 233–4.
12 Van Ryneveld 1797, Article 6; SAL MSD 3, p. 4, Almanach der Africaanse hoveniers en landbouwers & C., 1705?.
13 Mentzel 1785, vol. III, p. 165.
14 Mentzel 1785, vol. III, pp. 90 and 165.
15 SAL MSD 3, p. 2, Almanach der Africaanse hoveniers en landbouwers & C., 1705?.
16 Appendix to draft of letter written by Hendrik Swellengrebel Jr to C. de Gijselaar, 26 June 1783, Schutte 1982, p. 165.
17 SAL MSD 3, pp. 19 and 21, Almanach der Africaanse hoveniers en landbouwers & C., 1705?.
18 SAL MSD 3, pp. 1 and 3, Almanach der Africaanse hoveniers en landbouwers & C., 1705?; CA 1/STB 3/11, unpaginated, Testimony of Prins van Bengal, 14 March 1768.
19 Mentzel 1785, vol. III, pp. 182–3; SAL MSD 3, p. 5, Almanach der Africaanse hoveniers en landbouwers, & C., 1705?
20 Thunberg 1795, vol. I, pp. 244–5; another description of the same process is given in Valentyn 1726, vol. I, p. 189.
21 CA CJ 795, p. 287. Criminal Sentences No. 31, p. 287, Ceres van Madagascar and April van Ceijlon, 23 March 1786; SAL MSD 3, pp. 5–6, Almanach der Africaanse hoveniers en landbouwers & C., 1705?.
22 Mentzel 1785, vol. III, pp. 184–5; SAL MSD 3, pp. 37–8, Almanach der Africaanse hoveniers en landbouwers & C., 1705?.
23 Dubow 1982, p. 46.
24 CA 1/STB 22/151, Register of slaves sold at public auctions in Stellenbosch district, 1820–2.
25 See below, p. 87.

26 Appendix to draft of letter written by Hendrik Swellengrebel Jr to C. de Grijselaar, 26 June 1783, Schutte 1982, p. 167.
27 Van Duin and Ross, 1984; Worden 1982*a* p. 58.
28 CA J. 224, Stellenbosch and Drakenstein census, 1797/8.
29 CA J 37, Cape district census, 1799/1800. On the accuracy of this census, Barrow 1801, vol. II, p. 341.
30 Van Ryneveld 1797, Article 4.
31 Mentzel 1785, vol. II, p. 128.
32 CA BRD 12, p. 202, Petition of Cape farmers to Burgerraad, 1744.
33 Barrow 1801, vol. II, pp. 399–400.
34 White 1965, pp. 105–6.
35 Earle 1978; Berlin 1980. In classical Italy this problem was met either by employing slaves in workshops on the larger estates or in the cultivation of other crops, such as wine or olives. Similar kinds of solutions existed on the larger Cape farmsteads, White 1965, pp. 103–4.
36 Mentzel 1785, vol. III, pp. 165–6.
37 CA CJ 2945, p. 120, Vendurolle of estate of Jan Necker, 18 May 1789; CA 1/STB 16/135, Survey of grain produced in Stellenbosch district, 1797/8.
38 Mentzel 1785, vol. III, p. 181; Jooste 1973, chapter 3.
39 CA C 184, p. 229, Memorial of Johannes Colijn to Council of Policy, 27 November 1789.
40 Barrow 1801, vol. II, pp. 396–7.
41 Ross 1980*c*, p. 491; Jooste 1973, chapter 7; Van Zyl 1974, pp. 37–46 and 171–90.
42 Buttner 1718, p. 90.
43 CA 1/STB 16/134, Opgaaf van vee en koring, 1783–94.
44 Patterson 1977, p. 20.
45 CA J 224, Stellenbosch and Drakenstein census, 1797/8. Numbers of each type of farmer are indicated in Worden 1982*a*, p. 67.
46 This compares with similar developments in classical Italy, Duncan-Jones 1974, p. 37; Yeo 1952, p. 453.
47 The years chosen were 1688, 1692, 1705, 1723, 1731, 1741, 1752, 1761, 1773 and 1783. Data obtained from computer file of census records, Instituut vir Historiese Navorsing.
48 Malherbe 1978, pp. 44–50.
49 $R^2 = 0.88$, Worden 1982*a*, pp. 86–90.
50 The under-representation of grain returns may be sufficient explanation for this difference, Worden 1982*a*, pp. 86–90.
51 Van Rensburg 1954, pp. 20–6.
52 Worden 1982*a*, pp. 86–90.
53 Rayner 1983.
54 Hancock 1958; the debate on the impetus behind the growth of the pastoral sector continues following the challenges of Guelke 1974 and 1979, pp. 41–74 to Neumark 1957. A notable recent contribution on the impact of the meat market to the economy of Graaff-Reinet is Newton-King 1980*b*.
55 CA J 224, Stellenbosch and Drakenstein census 1797/8; CA J 37 Cape district census, 1799/1800.
56 Ross 1983*c*, p. 2.
57 Ross 1983*d*, pp. 207–8. Figures used in the table in Ross 1983*d* include slave women and children.
58 Worden 1982*a*, pp. 87–9.
59 This has been attributed to the effects of the smallpox epidemic of 1713, Guelke 1974, pp. 292–3, although Ross disputes the impact of the outbreak on labour supplies, Ross 1977. See also below, pp. 61–3.

60 Van Duin and Ross, 1984. The 1740–1 and 1741–2 harvests were particularly good and caused the Company to lower the price paid for wheat, Guelke 1974, p. 265.
61 CA BRD 12, pp. 197–8, Petition of Cape farmers to Burgerraad, 1744.
62 CA C 652, pp. 6–7, Stellenbosch Dagregister, 18 January 1740; CA C 652, pp. 513–16, Stellenbosch Dagregister, 27 January 1744.
63 The highest level of correlation after the 1780s was for mixed farmers in the Cape district in 1799/1800 ($R^2 = 0.51$); correlations for other types of farmers and districts were notably lower, Worden 1982a, pp. 87–9.
64 CA 1/STB 10/6, unpaginated, Memorial of Stellenbosch and Drakenstein burghers to the Commissioner-General of the Indies, May 1793.
65 CA BO 90, p. 17, Memorial to the burgher Senate, 1798.
66 CA BO 4, p. 113, Burgher Senate to Macartney, 29 November 1797.
67 Newton-King 1980a, pp. 179–82.
68 For example, CA 1/STB 3/11, unpaginated, Testimony of Jan Pretorius, 25 January 1764. This was forbidden by Batavian statute and in 1752 and 1766 the decree was repeated and fines of 25 Rxds for each day or night a slave was kept were imposed. A period longer than two mealtimes was considered to be slave theft, Van der Chijs 1885, vol. I, p. 574 and vol. IX, p. 577.
69 CA BO 19, pp. 18–19, Memorial to the Burgher Senate, 1798.
70 Van Ryneveld 1831, vol. VIII, p. 203.
71 CA C 171, p. 159, Resolutions of the Council of Policy, 19 April 1786.
72 Dunn 1973, pp. 52–3; Elphick 1977, p. 232.
73 Mentzel 1785, vol. II, p. 126. The best account of the disintegration of Khoikhoi society in the western Cape is Elphick 1977 and 1979, pp. 3–40.
74 Malherbe 1978, pp. 41–9.
75 CA J 233, Stellenbosch census return, 1806.
76 CA C 184, Memorial of Hendrik Cloete presented to the Council of Policy, 27 November 1789.
77 Le Vaillant 1790b, vol. I, p. 98.
78 CA 1/STB 10/6, unpaginated, Memorial of Stellenbosch and Drakenstein burghers to the Commissioner-General of the Indies, May 1793.
79 See below, p. 58. *Bastaard hottentots* earned the same rates as slaves when hired by their masters.
80 CA 1/STB 18/196, list of Bosjemen Hottentotten; Venter 1934.
81 Giliomee 1981, p. 85.
82 Christopher 1976, pp. 30–6.
83 Figures for Company slaves are listed in Armstrong 1979, p. 86. In 1752 there were about 1,203 privately owned slaves and 506 Company slaves. The figures for Company slaves remained relatively constant throughout the eighteenth century, whilst those of burgher slaves grew steadily so that the proportion of Company slaves in the city fell after the middle of the century.
84 Mentzel 1785, vol. I, p. 116 and vol. II, p. 124.
85 The best account of slave occupations in Cape Town is Ross 1980a.
86 Mentzel 1785, vol. I, pp. 111–12 and 114.
87 Valentyn 1726, vol. I, p. 106.
88 This was a function of female Company slaves in Colombo, Knapp 1981, p. 97.
89 Ross 1980a, p. 2.
90 Ross 1980a, pp. 2–3; Mentzel 1785, vol. II, p. 124.
91 Mentzel 1785, vol. I, p. 116.
92 Thunberg 1795, vol. I, p. 103.

93 C. de Jong, *Reizen naar de Kaap de Goede Hoop*, vol. I, pp. 143–4, cited in Ross 1980*a*, p. 4.
94 Franken 1940, pp. 60–7.
95 AR VOC 4187, Cape district census returns, 1752.
96 Knapp 1981, p. 93.
97 Mentzel 1785, vol. I, p. 140.
98 Schutte 1982, p. 179.
99 Mentzel 1785, vol. II, pp. 89–90.
100 Thunberg 1795, vol. I, p. 102; Mentzel 1785, vol. II, pp. 90–1.
101 Ross 1980*a*, pp. 4–5; Mentzel 1785, vol. II, p. 91.
102 Mentzel 1785, vol. I, p. 90.
103 Thunberg 1785, vol. I, p. 99.
104 Ross 1980*a*, p. 5; Elphick and Shell 1979, p. 153.

4. SLAVE TRADING

1 Postma 1972, pp. 237–48; Schutte 1979, pp. 101–4; Emmer 1976.
2 Sutherland 1980*b*, p. 10; Sutherland 1978, pp. 3–5.
3 Mentzel 1785, vol. I, p. 169; Armstrong 1981, pp. 11–19; Armstrong 1979, pp. 76–84. Detailed Journals of separate slave voyages from the Cape during the eighteenth century are: AR VOC 10,811–10,815, Copie dagregister Madagascar, 1696–1753; CA C 660–663, Scheeps en andere Journalen, 1664–1778; CA C 666, Dag register van Commies Holtsappel nopens Madagarsche slavenhandel, 1773–4; SAL MSD 3, Journal der zeetogt van Cabo de Goede Hoop naar d'Eijlanden Ansuanij en Madagascar met een korte beschrijving derselver Landen door Hendrik Frappe, 1715. Another account is published in Godee-Molsbergen, 1916, vol. III, pp. 220–57. For a discussion of Cape sources on the slave trade, Muller 1979, pp. 29–30. Little is known of the origins of slaves sold to the Dutch in Madagascar; Campbell suggested that they were obtained as war captives and brought down to the coast for sale to Arabs or Europeans, Campbell, 1815, p. 384.
4 Coetsee 1948, pp. 231–69; CA C 120, pp. 135–6, Resolutions of the Council of Policy, 17 April 1742; CA C 154, pp. 147–50, Resolutions of the Council of Policy, 26 February 1776; CA C 166, pp. 313–18, Resolutions of the Council of Policy, 29 April 1784.
5 Armstrong 1979, p. 78. An example of high mortality is the voyage of the Schuijlenburg from Madagascar to the Cape in 1752–3 when thirty-eight slaves out of a total of 178 (21.3%) died, AR VOC 10,814, Copie Dagregister van de Schuijlenburg, 1752–3. One contemporary gave the explanation that Malagasy slaves had been starved by their previous owners and died after eating too greedily once on board ship, SAL MSD 3, Journaal der zeetogt van Cabo de Goede Hoop naar d'Eijlanden Ansuanij en Madagascar, met een korte beschrijving derselver Landen door Hendrik Frappe, 1715. Such mortality rates are similar to the averages for the much longer trans-Atlantic slave trade and the Portuguese Mozambique to Rio run, Curtin 1969, pp. 276–86; Postma 1979, pp. 239–60.
   A notable slave mutiny took place on board the Meermin in 1765, CA C 144, pp. 125–73, Resolutions of the Council of Policy, 28 February 1766. Others are recorded in the journals, such as that on De Drie Heuvelen in 1754, AR VOC 10,815, Copie dagregister van De Drie Heuvelen, 1753.
6 Van Ryneveld 1797, Article 1.
7 On the failure of the free trade movement at the Cape, Boucher 1980*a*, pp. 14–17; CA BRD 12, pp. 132–3, Burgerraad to Governor Jan de la Fontaine, undated (early 1730s); CA BRD 13, p. 211, Heren XVII to Government of the Cape of Good Hope, 14 September 1731.
8 CA C 736, p. 31, Memorie gedaan aan vergadering van XVII door Kaapsche vryburgers, Article 19, 1783; Beyers 1967, p. 54; Boucher 1980*b*, p. 40.
9 Thunberg 1795, vol. I, p. 113.

10 CA GH 1/85, p. 41, Bigge's report on the state of slavery at the Cape, 1831.
11 Foreign shipping figures are listed in Beyers 1967, pp. 333–5.
12 Boucher 1974, pp. 8–12.
13 De Mist 1802, p. 252.
14 Beyers 1967, pp. 333–5. An estimated 5,700 slaves were transported by Portuguese traders from Mozambique to Brazil between 1791 and 1800, Anstey 1977, p. 261.
15 Mentzel 1785, vol. II, p. 125; CA C 185, pp. 336–42, Resolutions of the Council of Policy, 2 March 1790. The issue arose when a slave escaped from the colony on board ship and claimed his freedom after setting foot in Holland.
16 CA Miscellaneous 6, p. 28, Artikel-Brief van de VOC, LXIV, 4 September 1742, revised 11 October 1747.
17 These figures are based on the lists in Böeseken 1977, pp. 124–94.
18 Figures drawn from the surviving slave *transporten*, CA CJ 3074–3127. Number of such sales over ten were normally reached in the 1750s and 1760s, but the random nature of preservation of these records makes any conclusions highly speculative.
19 Bruijn and Van Eyck van Heslinga 1980, pp. 128–34 and 163.
20 Bruijn 1980, pp. 251–65.
21 CA C 168 (old number), p. 477, Appendix to Resolutions of the Council of Policy, 28 September 1767. This compares with the control by the Batavian authorities of slave imports from Makasar and Bali because of the fear of violence, Boxer 1965, p. 240.
22 CA C 179 (old number), p. 15, Appendix to Resolutions of the Council of Policy, 11 October 1776.
23 CA C 178 (old number), pp. 297–8, Appendix to Resolutions of the Council of Policy, 13 June 1977; CA C 216, pp. 20–1, Resolutions of the Council of Policy, 16 April 1793; CA C 174, pp. 103–5, Resolutions of the Council of Policy, 17 January 1787.
24 Bruijn and Van Eyck van Heslinga 1980, pp. 128–34 and 163; Ross 1980c, p. 487.
25 CA C 185, pp. 194–7, Resolutions of the Council of Policy, 9 February 1790.
26 CA C 171, pp. 173–4, Resolutions of the Council of Policy, 19 April 1786.
27 AR VOC 4314, p. 260, Brieven overgekomen, eerste deel, 1786. I am grateful to Robert Ross for this reference.
28 CA C 169, pp. 176–80, Resolutions of the Council of Policy, 11 October 1785.
29 CA C 170, p. 137, Resolutions of the Council of Policy, 6 January 1786.
30 Strict controls were exerted over slaves landed by French and Portuguese ships in 1791 and 1792 to prevent them from being sold clandestinely in Cape Town, CA C 198, pp. 149–54, Resolutions of the Council of Policy, 18 November 1791; CA C 210 (old number), pp. 245–7, Appendix to Resolutions of the Council of Policy 18 December 1792.
31 AR VOC 4362, unpaginated, Bijlagen tot de commissarissen-generaal, 1793, artikel 14 en 17.
32 AR VOC 4357, unpaginated, Resolutions, list of import duties paid on slaves, July to August 1792.
33 Giliomee 1975, pp. 182–3. The total slave population of the Cape in 1790 was 14,374, AR VOC 4350, pp. 81–3. The Jamaican slave population in 1790 was approximately 250,000 and slave imports about 8,000, Craton 1975, p. 275; Higman 1976, p. 75.
34 Giliomee 1975, pp. 182–4; Worden 1982a, pp. 154–5.
35 CA 1/STB 10/5, unpaginated, Secretary of Council of Policy to Landdrost of Stellenbosch, 12 October 1785 and 18 November 1785.
36 Five powers of attorney survive from the later eighteenth century, CA 1/GR 17/30, Graaff-Reinet Slave Powers and Relative Powers of Attorney, 1781–1834.
37 Hattingh 1979a, pp. 40–78.
38 CA SO 15/2, Extract from the proceedings of the Committee of Enquiry into the Illicit Traffic of Slaves, 4 May 1808. In 1827, the Guardian of Slaves commented that slaves who had 'fallen into artful hands were sent into the country', CA SO 3/1, p. 9, Report of the Guardian

of Slaves, 30 June 1827. In 1785, the Company stressed the need to prevent 'clandestine' landings and sales of slaves brought to the colony by the Portuguese, CA C 169, pp. 176–80, Resolutions of the Council of Policy, 11 October 1785. For slave smuggling to have had any great significance, however, there would have needed to be well-established networks of contacts and supply routes, and such a system could not have long existed in the relatively well-administered area of Cape Town and its hinterland without coming to the attention of the authorities.

39 Bradlow and Cairns 1978, pp. 90–106.

40 Patterson 1975, pp. 168–9.

41 For example, the inventory of the estate of Jan Elser, a wealthy Cape Town butcher in 1799, indicates that twenty-one out of the forty adult male slaves were of African origin and eighteen from India and Indonesia, but all slaves with skills or trades were eastern or Cape-born, CA MOOC 7/1/44, 61, Testamenten, 27 March 1799.

42 Bradlow and Cairns 1978, p. 89.

43 For example, a Malabar slave, Sing Sonko, was sold in Batavia in September 1771 and again at the Cape in February 1772, CA C 798, unpaginated, Miscellaneous slave papers. Other examples of multiple sales in the East Indies and India before slaves reached the Cape are found in the liquidated estate papers of Clara Pietersen, CA MOOC 14/1/102, 28 and 33, 1805, pointed out to me by Mrs M. Cairns and CA Miscellaneous 49, Serrurier papers, file (n).

44 For example, sale of Negotie van Boegis, CA MOOC 10/6, Vendurollen, between Nos. 2 and 3, 19 April 1752; sale of Casje, CA MOOC 10/1, 93, 19 March 1717.

45 Mentzel 1785, vol. III, p. 98.

46 Worden 1982a, p. 163, although no complete records of such sales exist and these conclusions are based on the surviving notarial documents, CA CJ 3080–3114.

47 Hattingh 1979a, pp. 48–53, analysis figures taken from Böeseken 1977.

48 CA BO 90, p. 18, Petition to De Wet, President of the Burgerraad, undated.

49 Klein 1978, pp. 95–120; Sutch 1975, pp. 173–210.

50 Ross 1977, pp. 421–2.

51 Worden 1982a, pp. 167–8.

52 Mentzel 1785, vol, II, p. 130. Rayner 1984, footnote 45 notes that by the nineteenth century this practice was widely acknowledged.

53 AR VOC 4223, 5, Case of Philip du Plessis, January 1760.

54 Resolutions of the Council of Policy, 8 August 1780, Jeffreys 1927, vol. II, p. 61; CA CJ 788, 22, Case of Rachel van de Caab, 31 January 1754.

55 CA CJ 788, 23, Case of Jacobus Frederick Sven van Hamburg and Harmer Kaal van Tollenspiker, 1 August 1754.

56 CA 1/STB 3/11, unpaginated, Testimony of Philander van Batavia, 23 November 1767; Van der Chijs 1885, vol. I, p. 574. A declaration of the health of a slave was made by some vendors, for example, that made by Jacobus Smits, CA C 798, unpaginated, Miscellaneous slave papers, 27 November 1798.

57 CA CJ 3113, 7, p. 22, Deed of Sale of Valentijn van Macasser, 13 February 1778; CA 1/STB 3/11, unpaginated, Testimony of Hendrik Ehlers, April 1776.

58 Worden 1982a, pp. 172–4; Ross 1981; Botha 1962, vol. II, pp. 60–80. For a contemporary view of the problem of partible inheritance, Thompson 1827, vol. II, pp. 94–5.

59 According to Roman law, natural heirs could not be passed over in silence in wills and had to be specifically excluded, Jolowicz and Nicholas 1972, p. 124. At the Cape it appears that children and other heirs could not be disinherited by will of more than one-third of their due portion, Ross 1981, p. 3.

60 For example, CA 1/STB 18/34, unpaginated, Inventory of the estate of Daniel Russouw Pietersz., 29 July 1790.

61 CA MOOC 7/1/10, 2, Will of Jan Bastiaansz. and his wife Geertruijd du Toit, 24 June 1745.
62 CA MOOC 8/11, 30, Inventory of the estate of Hans Hermensz., 20 April 1762.
63 Thompson 1827, vol II, p. 87. A fuller description of public auctions is given by Mentzel 1785, vol. II, pp. 93–9.
64 Worden 1982*a*, pp. 177–9.
65 CA A 1790, James Williams to his sister Mary, 5 January 1797.
66 Newton-King 1980*b*, p. 10.

5. SLAVE DEMOGRAPHY

1 Botha 1962, vol. II, p. 171.
2 Mentzel 1785, vol. II, p. 125.
3 Van Ryneveld 1797, Article 5.
4 Ross 1975 stresses the rapid increase of the 'white' population.
5 Worden 1982*a*, p. 108. The number of adult female slaves born at the Cape exceeded those imported throughout the eighteenth century whilst the reverse was time for adult male slaves.
6 Figures taken from journals of slaving expeditions from the Cape to Madagascar, AR VOC 10, 811–10, 815, Copie dagregister Madagascar, 1696–1753. Such estimates correspond to a similar sexual distribution of slaves in the eighteenth-century trans-Atlantic trade, Sheridan 1972, p. 20.
7 Macartney papers, 350 (274), Notes by Tennant in response to questions of Macartney, 21 March 1798.
8 AR VOC 4187, Cape district census return, 1752.
9 Figures from the *opgaaf* computer project, Instituut vir Historiese Navorsing.
10 Mentzel 1785, vol. II, p. 90.
11 AR VOC 4211, pp. 222–5. Figures obtained from Van Duin and Ross.
12 Armstrong 1979, p. 95.
13 These were the ages defined in the census returns of 1800, which was the first year in which the dividing age between children and adult slaves was specified, CA J 225, Stellenbosch census return, 1800.
14 CA 1/STB 18/32–18/35, Inventarissen, 1722–1804.
15 Higman 1976, pp. 116–17; Eblen 1975, pp. 211–47.
16 *The South African Almanac and Directory for the year 1832*, p. 161.
17 Mentzel 1785, vol. II, p. 130.
18 Sparrman 1785, vol. I, p. 102.
19 Wright 1831, p. 15; Burchell 1822, pp. 33–4.
20 De Kock 1950, p. 114; Campbell 1815, p. 5. For example, CA MOOC 8/19, 48, Inventory of the estate of Maria de Leeuw, 16 April 1789, CA MOOC 10/14, 22, Vendurolle of estate of Anna Gertruijd Albertijn, 10 November 1783.
21 Stavorinus 1798, vol. II, pp. 62–3; CA 1/STB 3/11, unpaginated, Testimony of Silvia van Madagascar, 21 June 1768.
22 Thunberg 1795, vol. I, p. 114.
23 Reproduced in *Die Banier*, 2 June 1963, CA Newspaper cuttings, vol. XIV, p. 103.
24 Ross 1979*c*, pp. 427–9; CA CJ 786, 42, pp. 263–70, Case of Cupido van Mallabaar, 28 May 1739.
25 The debate on the *inboek* system is recorded in CA C 655, pp. 525–30, Stellenbosch Dagregister, 4 September 1775; CA 1/STB 18/195; List of Bastaard Hottentots.
26 CA 1/STB 3/8, unpaginated, Testimony of Jannetje, 9 November 1746; CA 1/STB 18/31, unpaginated, Inventory of the estate of widow of William Nel Isaacsz., 23 June 1784.
27 CA 1/STB 18/195, Kaatje recorded in the list of Bastaard Hottentots, 3 June 1776; CA CJ 797, 45, p. 435, Case of Felix van Boegis, 7 August 1798. For white fertility figures, Ross

1976, pp. 952–3; Stavorinus 1796, p. 173; Thunberg 1795, vol. II, p. 38.

28 Van Ryneveld 1797, Article 5.

29 This factor has been noted as significant in reducing slave fertility levels in colonial Peru, Cushner 1975, p. 194.

30 For example, one slave miscarried after being beaten for failing to bring eggs to her master's table, CA 1/STB 3/11, unpaginated, Testimony of Juliana van de Caab, 17 July 1769.

31 Percival 1804, pp. 80–1; CA 1/STB 3/12, unpaginated, Testimony of Anna, 10 January 1792. Similar incidents took place in the United States, Gutman 1977, pp. 80–2.

32 Decree of 7/23 December 1803, Jeffreys and Naude 1944, vol. VI, p. 98. For an example of a rural slave with venereal disease, see CA CJ 2492, pp. 204–5, Report on post-mortem of Valentijn van Madagascar, 3 July 1794.

33 Figures calculated from CA CJ 788–794, Criminal Sententien, 1750–78.

34 Governor Bax and Council of Policy to Chamber XVII, 18 May 1678, Moodie 1838, vol. I, p. 363.

35 CA 1/STB 1/88, unpaginated, Examination of Cinna, 29 August 1705.

36 For example, CA MOOC 8/7, 64, Inventory of the estate of Daniel van de Lith, 5–7 December 1753.

37 CA CO 3927, p. 438, Memorial of Johannes Hogenburg and Johanna Rosina to Governor Somerset, undated. I am grateful to Roger Beck for this reference.

38 Lists of deaths of Company slaves were given monthly in the Dagregisteren and the Resolutions of the Council of Policy after the 1760s; a summary is given in Armstrong 1979, p. 88.

39 For example, CA C 140, pp. 194–8, Resolutions of the Council of Policy, 23 March 1760; CA C 143, pp. 107–8, Resolutions of the Council of Policy, 22 January 1765; CA C 149, pp. 164–7, Resolutions of the Council of Policy, 16 April 1771; Resolutions of the Council of Policy, 30 March 1779, Jeffreys 1927, vol. I, pp. 156–7; CA C 169, pp. 176–80, Resolutions of the Council of Policy, 11 October 1785.

40 CA C 184, p. 196, Memorial of Hendrik Cloete to the Council of Policy, 27 November 1789; Fransen 1978, p. 8; CA J 37, Cape district census returns, 1800, entry 1098.

41 Barrow 1801, vol. II, p. 344.

42 Van Zyl 1978, p. 9; CA J 282, Stellenbosch census returns, 1826.

43 Barrow 1801, vol. I, p. 44.

44 Percival 1804, p. 282. Curtin 1968, p. 203 indicates the considerably lower mortality rates of British military personnel at the Cape than in the West Indies. Ross 1976, pp. 952–3, stresses the low mortality rates of 'whites' in the eighteenth-century Cape.

45 Craton 1971, pp. 15–16; Godee-Molsbergen 1912, p. 106; Moodie 1838, vol. I, p. 363; CA C 172, pp. 35–7, Resolutions of the Council of Policy, 14 June 1786.

46 CA 1/STB 3/12, unpaginated, Testimony of David van de Caab, 10 January 1792.

47 Barrow 1801, vol. I, p. 44; Van Ryneveld 1797, Article 4.

48 Percival 1804, pp. 282–3; CA A 681, p. 12, letter of Mrs Kindersley, November 1764.

49 CA C 154, pp. 41–3, Resolutions of the Council of Policy, 5 January 1776; PRO CO 49, 1 p. 47, Craig to Secretary of State, 27 December 1795; CA BO 90, pp. 7–8, Burgher Senate to Macartney, 29 January 1797; decree of 19 November 1803, Jeffreys and Naude 1944, vol. VI, p. 93. Successful use of vaccine had been made by 1805, Van Ryneveld 1831, vol. VIII, p. 200.

50 Mentzel 1785, vol. II, p. 127; Stavorinus 1796, pp. 175–6; Valentyn 1726, vol. I, pp. 216–18.

51 Ross 1977, pp. 420–2.

52 Ross 1977, pp. 421–2; Worden 1982a, p. 163.

53 CA C 145, pp. 148–9, Resolutions of the Council of Policy, 10 March 1767; CA CJ 2486, pp. 94–5, Landdrost of Stellenbosch to Council of Justice, 10 October 1767.

54 Müller 1973, p. 26. Traces of malaria were found in Cape Town in the 1830s, Judges 1977, p. 90; CA 1/STB 10/3, unpaginated, Governor to Landdrost of Stellenbosch, 24 August 1756.

162

55 There may also have been a drop in slave imports which combined with high mortality rates to produce a decline in the total number of slaves, Armstrong 1979, p. 93.
56 Böeseken 1944, p. 62.
57 CA C 652, pp. 513–16, Stellenbosch Dagregister, 27 January 1744; CA C 653, p. 147, Stellenbosch Dagregister, 21 November 1746.
58 Decree of 1 February 1747, Jeffreys and Naude 1944, vol II, pp. 223–4.
59 CA C 654, p. 36 verso, Stellenbosch Dagregister, 13 March 1752.
60 CA C 184, p. 231, Memorial of Johannes Colijn to the Council of Policy, 27 November 1789.
61 CA BO 90, p. 12, Burgher Senate to Macartney, 30 January 1798.
62 Barrow 1801, vol. I, pp. 44–5.
63 See below, pp. 143–4; Elphick and Shell 1979, pp. 135–55; Giliomee 1977, p. 13.

6. PRICES AND PROFITS

1 Janssens in Idenburg 1946, pp. 102–3.
2 Genovese 1966, especially pp. 13–39; the disadvantages of slavery were cited by Weber 1947, pp. 253–4.
3 The most notable example of such a study is Conrad and Meyer 1965, pp. 43–92. For the debate which followed, Conrad and Meyer 1965, pp. 93–114; Genovese 1966, pp. 43–69; Aitken 1971.
4 Weber 1947, pp. 253–4; Fogel and Engerman 1974, vol. I, pp. 59–60 and pp. 184–5 cite some of the earlier writers on American slavery.
5 For example, Thompson 1827, vol. II, p. 92; see above, p. 33.
6 Hindness and Hirst 1975, pp. 230–1.
7 Heren XVII to Simon van der Stel and Council, 22 June 1683, Moodie 1838, vol. I, p. 390.
8 Robertson 1945, p. 171.
9 This is the formula used by Aufhauser 1974 for the British Caribbean, based on the pioneering study of slave profits in the American South by Conrad and Meyer 1965, pp. 43–92. The alternative method used by Evans of basing annual return estimates on the net rent received by slaveowners who hired out their slaves throughout the year is less applicable to the Cape, where no full records of slave hiring survive, and in the rural areas it was limited in extent to occasional hiring at peak labour periods see pp. 25–6 and Aitken 1971, pp. 197–205.
10 Boucher 1980b, p. 39 and Ross 1983b comment on this gap in Cape historiography, which is soon to be filled by Van Duin and Ross 1984.
11 CA BRD 12, p. 202, Petition of Cape farmers to Burgerraad, 1744. A *mud* was a grain measure approximately equivalent to one hectolitre, Kruyskamp 1976, vol. I, p. 1,509.
12 CA MOOC 14/36/iii, Blankenberg papers, J.A. Sichterman folder. I am indebted to Robert Ross for this reference.
13 Van Ryneveld 1797, Article 4.
14 Barrow 1801, vol. II, pp. 399–400.
15 See above, p. 31.
16 AR VOC 4073, Cape district census return, 1714.
17 CA C 184, p. 229, Memorial of Johannes Colijn, Resolutions of the Council of Policy, 27 November 1789. A leaguer (Dutch *legger*) was equivalent to approximately 575 litres, Sparrman 1785, vol. I, p. 75, footnote 179.
18 Barrow 1801, vol. II, p. 396.
19 AR VOC 4147, Cape district census return, 1741.
20 See pp. 27–30.
21 Mentzel 1785, vol. I, p. 128.
22 See above, pp. 26–7.

23 Wright 1831, pp. 24–6; Van Rensburg 1935, pp. 47–54.
24 CA MOOC 14/36/iii, Blankenberg papers, J.A. Sichterman folder; H. Cloete to H. Swellengrebel, 15 March 1787, Schutte 1982, p. 235; Barrow 1801, vol. II, p. 396 and p. 400.
25 CA AC 6, p. D22, Minutes of Evidence taken before Council, 12 January 1827. I am grateful to Mary Rayner for this reference.
26 CA C 184, p. 230, Memorial of Johannes Colijn, Resolutions of the Council of Policy, 27 November 1789.
27 CA 1/STB 16/134, Survey of grain, 1797/8.
28 CA 1/STB 3/11, unpaginated, Testimony of Piet and Galant van Ceijlon, 1–2 July 1767.
29 CA 1/STB 3/10, unpaginated, Testimony of Joseph Borsz. van Kippinge, 6 August 1750.
30 Böeseken 1938, p. 66.
31 H. Cloete to H. Swellengrebel, 15 March 1787, Schutte 1982, p. 235.
32 Mentzel 1785, vol. III, pp. 178–9.
33 CA C 184, p. 231, Memorial of Johannes Colijn, Resolutions of the Council of Policy, 27 November 1789.
34 CA CJ 2870–2913, Knecht contracten, 1692–1790.
35 For example, CA MOOC 8/5, 139, unpaginated, Inventory of the estate of Conrad Frederick Hoffman, 31 August 1736 (debt of 30 April 1736); Thunberg 1795, vol. II, p. 126; Botha 1962, vol. II, p. 174.
36 CA MOOC 14/36/iii, Blankenberg papers, J.A. Sichterman folder.
37 Barrow 1801, vol. II, p. 400.
38 CA C 184, pp. 229–31, Memorial of Johannes Colijn, Resolutions of the Council of Policy, 27 November 1789.
39 CA BRD 13, pp. 272–8, Decree of Governor Swellengrebel, 19 May 1744; AR VOC 4362, 42, Bijlagen tot de commissarissen-generaal, 1793.
40 The high cost of transportation may have been a primary factor inhibiting agricultural development inland, Giliomee 1981, pp. 95–6.
41 Guelke 1974, p. 277; figures for 1780–1800 from CA MOOC 8/17–8/22, Estate inventories, and 1/STB 18/34–18/35, Stellenbosch estate inventories.
42 See for example, Fogel and Engerman 1974, vol. I. pp. 73–88.
43 In the 1750s, for example, almost all male slaves in estate records were valued at 100 Rxds although as Table 6.4 indicates, there was considerable variation in the market price obtained at auctions, and the median was between 156 Rxds and 192 Rxds.
44 De Kock 1950, pp. 45–6; AR VOC 4365, 390–1, Bijlagen tot de commissarissen-generaal, May 1793.
45 Worden 1982a, p. 203, footnote 46.
46 CA MOOC 10/14, 21, Vendurolle of estate of William van der Vijver, Sale of February van Bengal, 21 February 1783.
47 Sparrman 1785, vol. I, p. 103; Newton-King 1978, Appendix 2; CA A 45, Summary of Prices and the State of the Colony. Higher prices were also offered for skilled vine-dressers in classical Italy, Duncan-Jones 1974, p. 53.
48 H. Cloete to H. Swellengrebel, 15 March 1787, Schutte 1982, pp. 235–6.
49 CA A 457, A 12, C1, Cloete estate papers.
50 H. Swellengrebel, A few considerations about the Cape, 1783, Schutte 1982, p. 164.
51 Valentyn 1726, vol. I, p. 219.
52 For the complaints of burghers at such price increases, Böeseken 1944, p. 68.
53 Marais 1939, p. 163; Van Zyl 1978, pp. 22–3.
54 CA BO 90, p. 8, Burgher Senate to Macartney, 29 November 1797.
55 Guelke 1974, pp. 273–9; guilders have been converted to rixdollars.
56 CA MOOC 14/36/iii, Blankenberg papers, J. A. Sichterman folder; Barrow 1801, vol. II, pp. 396 and 399.

57 Yeo 1952, pp. 463–4; Duncan-Jones 1974, pp. 53–4.
58 CA MOOC 14/36/iii, Blankenberg papers, J. A. Sichterman folder; Barrow 1801, vol. II, pp. 396–400.
59 AR VOC 4362, 42, Bijlagen tot de commissarissen-generaal, 1793.
60 Aufhauser 1974, pp. 65–6; Conrad and Meyer 1965, pp. 60–1; Stampp 1956, pp. 409–10.
61 This was the usual rate paid on loans made to the Landdrostdy and for borrowed capital by individuals as recorded in the Dagregisteren and estate accounts. See also De la Caille 1751, p. 35.
62 For example, complaints of Stellenbosch farmers against the lowering of the Company wheat price, CA C 652, pp. 512–16, Stellenbosch Dagregister, 27 January 1744; complaint of Constantia wine farmers, CA C 166, pp. 209–10, Resolutions of the Council of Policy, 9 March 1784; CA 1/STB 10/5, unpaginated, Land van Waveren grain farmers to Governor Jacob de Graaff, 31 March 1787; CA C 210, pp. 216–17, Resolutions of the Council of Policy, 18 December 1792. Van Ryneveld 1804, pp. 45–51 comments on the problems of arable farmers in the 1780s and 1790s.
63 Giliomee 1981, p. 80.
64 Thunberg 1795, p. 233.
65 Engerman 1973, pp. 53–4.
66 Worden 1982a, pp. 165–6.
67 Hattingh 1979a; see above, pp. 42–4.
68 Van Ryneveld 1797, Article 5.
69 Sparrman 1785, vol. I, p. 102.
70 Worden 1982a, pp. 218–19.
71 For the effects of this, see the romanticised account of Wilson of a dying slave who told his master how he regretted the 'ruin' that his death would cause, CA VC 58, p. 29, Description of Cape Colony in 1806 by Lieutenant-Colonel Wilson.
72 Fogel and Engerman 1974, vol. I, p. 153.
73 Sheridan 1972, p. 34.
74 Mentzel 1785, vol. II, p. 90.
75 Burchell 1822, p. 34; Thunberg 1795, vol. I, p. 232.
76 CA C 164, pp. 390–1, Resolutions of the Council of Policy, 21 April 1783.
77 Figures drawn from CA C 650, Stellenbosch Dagregister, 1729–37. See also Armstrong 1979, pp. 100–1.
78 Mentzel 1785, vol. II, p. 90.
79 De Chavonnes 1918, pp. 97–8, pp. 100–1 and p. 116.
80 Van Ryneveld 1797, Article 4.
81 Van Ryneveld 1797, Articles 4 and 6.
82 Engerman 1973.
83 Guelke 1974, pp. 160, 198; De Mist 1802, p. 253; Elphick 1979, pp. 27–9.
84 Ross 1977.
85 See above, p. 35; Malherbe 1978, p. 25.
86 For example, Mentzel 1785, vol. II, p. 126.
87 Cairnes cited in Hindness and Hirst 1975, pp. 162–4, although this view is rejected by Hindness and Hirst themselves; Fogel and Engerman 1974, vol. I, pp. 196–7; Genovese 1966, pp. 85–105.
88 Barrow 1801, vol. I, p. 359.
89 On agricultural developments in the Netherlands see Slicher van Bath 1963, pp. 240–3; Slicher van Bath 1978, pp. 152–95; De Vries 1974, especially pp. 119–73.
90 Hindness and Hirst 1975, pp. 165–7; Yeo 1952, pp. 467–8.
91 Fogel and Engerman 1974, vol. I, pp. 204–5; Craton and Greenland 1978, pp. 139–42.
92 De Chavonnes 1918, pp. 105–6; De Kock 1924, pp. 15–16.

93 CA C 171, p. 159, Resolutions of the Council of Policy, 19 April 1786.
94 Giliomee 1981, pp. 93–7; Guelke 1974, pp. 271–3 and p. 319.
95 CA 1/STB 10/5, unpaginated, Council of Policy to Landdrost of Stellenbosch, 26 November 1787; CA BO 90, p. 5, Memorial to Governor Craig, 3 December 1796; the sale of a slave in return for cattle is noted in CA 1/GR 17/40, Graaff-Reinet Miscellaneous slave papers, May 1798.
96 CA C 653, p. 147, Stellenbosch Dagregister, 21 November 1746.
97 De Kock 1924, p. 22; Aitken 1971, pp. 172–3.

7. SLAVE LIFE AND LABOUR

1 Most notably Genovese 1975; Gutman 1977; Blassingame 1979.
2 Barrow 1801, vol. II, p. 109.
3 CA 1/STB 3/11, unpaginated, Testimony of Andries Nolte, 14 October 1759; AR VOC 4117, pp. 4–5, Case of Philander van de Cust Coromandel, 14 January 1731.
4 CA 1/STB 3/11, unpaginated, Testimony of Philida van Terra de Natal refers to an old slave woman who 'got up as usual at 4 a.m. to bake bread', 1 October 1776; CA 1/STB 3/12, unpaginated, Testimony of Tieleman Roos Jansz. who met a slave returning from working in the fields after dusk, 17 November 1792; CA CJ 795, 31, Case of Ceres van Madagascar and April van Ceijlon, who were working in the wine-cellar at 8 p.m., 23 March 1786; CA CJ 795, 38, Case of Augustus van de Caab *et al* who attacked a farmhouse 'between 10 p.m. and 11 p.m.' when everybody was asleep, 23 November 1786.
5 Proclamation of 18 March 1823, Theal 1897, vol. XV, p. 340.
6 For example, in Dutch Surinam the normal working day was of ten hours' duration, but during harvests could be over fifteen hours, Müller 1973, p. 26. During the 1970s the average number of hours worked by farm labourers in the Karroo has been estimated at over ten hours a day during the summer, Wilson Kooy and Hendrie, 1977, p. 104.
7 Mentzel 1785, vol. III, p. 205 and above, p. 23.
8 Barrow 1801, vol. I, p. 44; Thunberg 1795, vol. I, p. 233.
9 CA CJ 3175, p. 21, Declaration by Andreas Greeff, 20 August 1767.
10 For example, CA 1/STB 3/12, unpaginated, Testimony of Maart van Mozambique, 1 July 1790; Thunberg 1795, vol. II, p. 46; Buttner 1718, p. 68.
11 Fransen 1978, p. 29.
12 CA 1/STB 3/13, 14, Testimony of Matthias Hoffman, January 1794; Stavorinus 1798, vol. II, p. 62.
13 I am grateful to Robert Ross for the information that the records made at the time of abolition indicate that 30% of the slave population were 'field labourers' or 'inferior field labourers', 44% were domestics and many of the rest were children. Very few were craftsmen. These figures include Cape Town, where almost all slaves were classified as 'domestics'; in the rural areas the proportion of field labourers was very much higher than 30%; BPP 215 (1836–7), p. 361 and p. 353.
14 For example, AR VOC 4264, 1, Case of Thomas van Tutocorijn, December 1769; CA 1/STB 3/12, unpaginated, Testimony of Julij van Malabar, 2 March 1791.
15 CA C 146, pp. 257–8, Resolutions of the Council of Policy, 8 November 1768; CA BRD 24, Lyste van burgers en kompanjie – amptenare in Kaapse distrik aantonende hoeveel geld, slawe en waens elke persoon vir die voltooing van die Plein voor die Kasteel moes stel, July 1762 aan August 1763.
16 Handler and Lange 1978, pp. 72–5.
17 CA Press Cuttings, XIV, p. 103, 'Story of an ex-slave woman' in *Die Banier*, 2 June 1963.
18 Higman 1976, p. 194; Marais 1939, p. 164.
19 Mentzel 1785, vol. II, p. 90; Van Ryneveld 1797, Article 5.

20 For example, CA 1/STB 3/12, unpaginated, Testimony of Lakeij, 11 January 1790.

21 AR VOC 4223, 5, Testimony of Philip du Plessis, January 1760.

22 Handler and Lange 1978, pp. 74–5; this figure would include the disabled, aged, sick, pregnant and very young children.

23 For example, Higman 1976, pp. 187–211.

24 Ross 1979c, pp. 429–30.

25 CA 1/STB 3/12, unpaginated, Testimony of Titus van de Caab, 1 May 1790; CA 1/STB 3/12, unpaginated, Testimony of Piet Claas, 12 April 1793.

26 Blassingame 1979, p. 161.

27 AR VOC 4255, 16, Case of Frans van Madagascar, 30 June 1768.

28 SAL MSD 5, p. 16, Korte beschreijving van Cabo de goede hoop door Coenraad Frederik Hofman; Mentzel 1785, vol. I, pp. 164–5 and vol. II, p. 85.

29 CA CJ 2884–2898, Knecht contracts, 1733–63, and CA J 197, Stellenbosch and Drakenstein census, 1752.

30 CA J 197, Stellenbosch and Drakenstein census, 1752 and AR VOC 4187, Cape census, 1752.

31 Craton 1975, pp. 261–2; Blassingame 1979, pp. 172–7.

32 CA C 651, pp. 282–5, Stellenbosch Dagregister, 13 July 1739; CA C 785, pp. 231–9, Case of Philander van Cust Coromandel, 11 January 1731; CA 1/STB 3/8, unpaginated, Testimony of Fortuijn van Bengal, 18 November 1743.

33 CA 1/STB 3/9, unpaginated, Testimony of Pieter van Malabar, September 1745.

34 For example, CA CJ 785, 26, Case of Philander van de Cust Coromandel, January 1731; CA CJ 786, 41, Case of Slamat van Mandaar, 28 May 1739; CA CJ 788, Case of Sijmon van Conchin, 24 May 1753.

35 CA C 146, pp. 257–61, Resolutions of the Council of Policy, 8 November 1768; Moodie 1838, vol. III, p. 8; CA 1/STB 3/8, unpaginated, Testimony of Jacob Breitenbach, undated.

36 CA A 681, Letter of Mrs Kindersley, No. 17, March 1765.

37 CA CJ 784, pp. 225–30, Case of Andries van Ceijlon, 10 February 1724; CA 1/STB 3/12, unpaginated, Testimony of Cobus, 5 June 1793.

38 CA CJ 2487, pp. 100–1, Landdrost of Stellenbosch to Council of Justice, 16 July 1778.

39 Hugo 1970, pp. 13–18.

40 AR VOC 4264, 1, Case of Thomas van Tutocorijn, January 1770; Hugo 1970, p. 14.

41 Sparrman 1785, vol. I, p. 89.

42 Valentyn 1726, vol. I, p. 100.

43 De la Caille 1751, p. 31.

44 Decree of 16–17 June 1681, Jeffreys and Naude 1944, vol. I, pp. 174–5; Van Rensburg 1935, p. 48.

45 Sparrman 1785, vol. I, pp. 88–9; Damberger 1801, p. 37 and p. 39.

46 H. Cloete to H. Swellengrebel, 15 March 1787, Schutte 1982, p. 235, although he comments that such provision of food and drink for slaves did not take place on many farmsteads; Mentzel 1785, vol. I, p. 169 and vol. II, p. 129; Lichtenstein 1812, vol. I, pp. 29–30.

47 CA 1/STB 3/10, unpaginated, Testimony of Joseph Borsz. van Kippinge, July 1750.

48 CA 1/STB 3/8, unpaginated, Testimony of Cinna, 29 August 1705; CA CJ 785, 17, pp. 144–9, Case of Augustus van Batavia, 16 December 1728.

49 Sparrman 1785, vol. I, pp. 92–3.

50 CA 1/STB 3/12, unpaginated, Testimony of Piet de Jager, 10 May 1791; CA CJ 2491, pp. 57–8, Landdrost of Stellenbosch to Council of Justice, 25 May 1791.

51 Percival 1804, p. 292; Barrow 1801, vol. I, p. 44.

52 Sparrman 1785, vol. I, p. 92; Thunberg 1795, vol. I, p. 302.

53 AR VOC 4264, 8, Case of Cesar, September 1769; AR VOC 4012, p. 544, Report of sale of vegetables by slaves to the fleets in Table Bay; Armstrong 1979, pp. 45–6; Van Zyl 1978, pp. 15–16; PRO 49, 1, p. 93, a proposal was made in 1796 that Company slaves should be

given 'a small parcel of ground and a portion of time for its cultivation', Craig to Secretary of State, 26 October 1796.

54 CA C 120, p. 75, Resolutions of the Council of Policy, 6 February 1742; CA 1/STB 3/11, unpaginated, Testimony of Paul van Ternaten, 25 June 1767; AR VOC 4247, 13, Case of Baatjoe van Boegies, May 1766.

55 Shell 1978, pp. 6–10; Franken 1940, p. 65; Golovnin 1808, p. 60. I am grateful to Dr Edna Bradlow for the latter reference.

56 CA CJ 785, 41, Case of Varken and Juniper, 12 May 1731; CA CJ 2487, pp. 86–91, Landdrost of Stellenbosch to Council of Justice, 20 June 1778; CA 1/STB 3/11, unpaginated, Testimony of October van de Caap, 10 March 1775; Thunberg 1795, vol. I, p. 102 and p. 115.

57 Mentzel 1785, vol. I, p. 169.

58 CA C 184, p. 230, Resolutions of the Council of Policy, 27 November 1789; Mentzel 1785, vol. II, p. 80; CA 1/STB 3/12, unpaginated, Testimony of Piet de Jager, 10 May 1791.

59 CA CJ 786, 42, Case of Cupido van Mallabaar, 28 May 1739; CA CJ 2487, pp. 57–9, Case of Thomas van de Caab, 17–18 May 1777, Landdrost of Stellenbosch to Council of Justice.

60 Stavorinus 1798, vol. II, p. 62; the inventory of Melck's estate also includes a slave kitchen, CA MOOC 7/1/25, 39, 24–26 June 1776.

61 For example, CA MOOC 8/3, 30, Inventory of the estate of Anna Elisabeth Sneeuwind, 19 September 1725; CA MOOC 8/6, 26, Inventory of the estate of Maria van Hoeve, October 1739; CA 1/STB 18/31, unpaginated, Inventory of the estate of Anna Kouting, January 1745; CA 1/STB 18/32, unpaginated, Inventory of the estate of Jan Andries Dissel, 23 June 1731.

62 CA 1/STB 3/11, unpaginated, Testimony of Adam van de Caab, 18 March 1776; CA 1/STB 3/12, unpaginated, Testimony of Johann Stegmann, 28 November 1791.

63 CA 1/STB 3/11, unpaginated, Testimony of Adam van de Caab, February 1776; CA C 653, p. 42, Stellenbosch Dagregister, 19 August 1746; CA CJ 788, 21, Case of Neptune van Bengal, 27 September 1753.

64 CA 1/STB 3/11, unpaginated, Testimony of July van Bengal, 2 July 1774; CA 1/STB 3/12, unpaginated, Testimony of Sangoor van Macassar, June 1791.

65 Wade 1964, pp. 111–12.

66 Geyser 1982, pp. 31–5 and pp. 37–8.

67 CA 1/STB 3/11, unpaginated, Testimony of Jacob Pietersz., 1 February 1764; CA 1/STB 3/12, unpaginated, Testimony of Jeptha van Madagascar, 10 May 1791; Cairns 1977, p. 10; Sheridan 1975, pp. 290–307; Savitt 1978, pp. 15–17.

68 Thunberg 1795, vol. I, p. 302.

69 Armstrong 1979, p. 83; Bradlow and Cairns 1978, pp. 95–6.

70 CA 1/STB 3/12, unpaginated, Testimony of Jeptha van Madagascar, May 1791.

71 For example, CA CJ 789, 11, Case of Baatjoe van Mandhaar, 3 November 1757.

72 For example, Bosman 1962; Franken 1953; Scholtz 1980, pp. 29–41 is the most recent summary of the debate.

73 Franken 1953, pp. 130–1; Stoops 1979, p. 315.

74 Muller 1979, p. 27.

75 Franken 1953, pp. 41–79.

76 Cited in Valkhoff 1972, p. 64; on the use of 'Low-Portuguese' and Malay in the later eighteenth century and the process of change to Dutch, see Valkhoff 1966, pp. 146–91.

77 Boxer 1965, p. 224; Batavian decree of 5–8 July 1642, Van der Chijs 1885, vol. I, p. 575.

78 Memorandum of Van Riebeeck, 5 May 1662, Moodie 1838, vol. I, p. 251.

79 Sparrman 1785, vol. I, pp. 88–9; Thunberg 1795, vol. II, p. 46. See also Bradlow and Cairns 1978, pp. 84–5.

80 Burchell 1822, p. 39 and p. 77.

81 Sparrman 1785, vol. I, p. 73; CA CJ 785, 33, Case of Foerij and Damon, 11 December 1732; CA 1/STB 3/9, unpaginated, Testimony of Philip Cordiers, 30 September 1741; CA 1/STB 3/11, unpaginated, Testimony of Gerrit Smit, 8 May 1775.

82 CA 1/STB 3/11, unpaginated, Testimony of October van de Caab, 10 March 1775.

83 CA CJ 2490, pp. 82–3, Landdrost of Stellenbosch to Council of Justice, 19 July 1789.

84 Mullin 1972, pp. 46–8.

85 Gutman 1977.

86 Wright 1831, pp. 15–16.

87 Burchell 1822, pp. 33–4.

88 Ross 1979c, pp. 425–6; CA CJ 2489, pp. 42–7 and pp. 59–64, Landdrost of Swellendam to Council of Justice and Jacob van Reenen to Landdrost of Swellendam, 12–27 December 1786.

89 See above, p. 58.

90 Stavorinus 1798, vol. II, pp. 62–3.

91 CA 1/STB 3/8, unpaginated, Testimony of Manika van Bengal, 8 January 1749.

92 CA 1/STB 3/11, unpaginated, Testimony of Dina van de Caab, 2 August 1774.

93 CA SO 3/20A, Article 51, Observation of the Protector of Slaves for the Report between June and December, 1830.

94 CA CJ 784, 21, Case of Anthonij van Goa, 27 March 1721; CA 1/STB 3/12, unpaginated, Testimony of Jan Roux, 31 January 1791.

95 Ross 1979c, pp. 427–8.

96 CA 1/STB 3/9, unpaginated, Testimony of Januarij van Rio de la Goa, 29 October 1744; Sparrman 1785, vol. I, p. 102.

97 Ross 1979c, pp. 431–2.

98 Gutman 1977, p. 185. It has been suggested for colonial America that the shift of slave-naming practice from the names of whites to those of Biblical and Classical characters reflects an association of ideas with Roman and Hebrew bondsmen and a distinction of slaves from colonists, Handlin and Handlin 1950, p. 217. Names of months seem to have been a common South African usage; for example, they were used for Khoikhoi and Sotho labourers in Graaff-Reinet district in the 1860s, Dubow 1982, p. 46.

99 Raboteau 1978, especially pp. 96–210; Knight 1970, pp. 108–10; Idenburg 1946, pp. 84–5; Nachtigal 1893, pp. 86–100. One attempt in 1736 to set up a mission for the Khoikhoi only lasted for eight years and had little success, Schmidt 1980.

100 Batavian decree of 5–8 July 1642, Van der Chijs 1885, vol. I, p. 573; extract from the instructions for Simon van der Stel, 16 July 1685, Moodie 1838, vol. I, p. 397; Wright 1831, p. 4; Hattingh 1982.

101 List of slave baptisms in Dutch Reformed Church archives, K. A. Bylae 1832–91, in Instituut vir Historiese Navorsing I am grateful to dr Hans Heese for access to this information. See also Elphick and Shell 1979, pp. 120–1.

102 Nachtigal 1893, p. 81; Valentyn 1726, vol. II, p. 259.

103 Sparrman 1785, vol. I, p. 90.

104 CA SO 17/1, Notes collected from colonial placcaards etc., unpaginated, Order of the Government in India, 10 April 1770; a Batavian decree of 20 June 1766 forbade the sale of Christian slaves, Van der Chijs 1885, vol. IX, p. 580; Elphick and Shell 1979, pp. 120–3; Godee-Molsbergen 1912, pp. 110–12.

105 De la Caille 1751, p. 35.

106 Vos 1911, pp. 137–8; Marais 1939, p. 168; Van Rensburg 1935, pp. 28–30.

107 Wright 1831, p. 4.

108 Davids 1980, pp. 31–4; Bradlow 1981; Ross 1983a, pp. 20–1; Rochlin 1956; Kähler 1975.

109 Shell 1974; Bradlow 1981, pp. 12–13.

110 Davids 1980, p. xxi; Davids 1981, p. 182.

111 Shell 1974, pp. 42–3; Davids 1980, p. 42; Wright 1831, p. 4.
112 Ross 1983*a*, pp. 20–1; Rayner 1984, p. 31.
113 Resolutions of the Council of Policy, 31 August 1779, Jeffreys 1927, vol. I, pp. 92–3; Du Toit 1937, pp. 252–3; Thunberg 1795, vol. I, pp. 109–10; Geyser 1982, pp. 53–5.
114 Marais 1939, pp. 171–2.
115 Muller 1979, p. 27.
116 Lichtenstein 1812, vol. I, pp. 33–4; Botha 1973, p. 37.
117 Wright 1831, p. 9; CA 1/STB 3/11, unpaginated, Testimony of Johan Christian Spring in 't Veld, October 1761.
118 Burchell 1822, p. 31.
119 Decree of 29 April/1 May 1766, Jeffreys and Naude 1944, vol. III, p. 64; Franken 1978, p. 92.
120 Resolutions of the Council of Policy, CA C 172, pp. 289–90, 9 August 1786; CA C 180, pp. 190–3, 21 November 1788.
121 Decree of 21–2 January 1692, Jeffreys and Naude 1944, vol. I, p. 267; CA CJ 795, 25, Case of Spaldje, 22 September 1785; Mentzel 1785, vol. II, p. 86.
122 CA 1/STB 3/9, unpaginated, Testimony of Piet, 24 September 1745.
123 CA CJ 784, 29, Case of Andries van Ceijlon, 10 February 1724; CA CJ 786, 68, Case of Jan van Terra de Natal *et al*, 21 March 1743; CA CJ 797, 37, Case of Klaas, 29 March 1798.
124 CA CJ 788, 3, Case of Fortuijn van Bengal, 5 February 1750.
125 Arndt 1928, pp. 5–10; CA 1/STB 3/12, Testimony of Rosetta van de Caab, June 1791; CA CJ 795, 25, Case of Spaldje, 22 September 1785.
126 CA 1/STB 3/12, unpaginated, Testimony of Jacobus Groenewald, 16 May 1791.
127 AR VOC 4223, 5, Case of Manuel van Maratte, January 1760; CA CJ 797, 30, pp. 231–43, Case of Januarij van Bengal, 22 June 1797.
128 Patterson 1967, pp. 230–1.
129 Patterson 1982, p. 100.

8. SLAVE DISCIPLINE AND COMPANY LAW

1 Somerville 1803, p. 405.
2 De Mist 1802, p. 252.
3 A collection of *bewyse uit verskeie bronne vir die goeie behandeling van die slawe deur die Suid-Afrikaanse burgers* appears in Stockenstrom 1934, pp. 61–6. Examples of this view in secondary works are, Grosse-Verhaus 1976, pp. 960–2; Deherain 1909, pp. 242–3; De Kock 1950, pp. 217–18.
4 Froude cited in Stochenstrom 1934, p. 65, No. 21.
5 Barrow 1801, vol. II, p. 109; Percival 1804, p. 292.
6 Mentzel 1785, vol. II, p. 129.
7 Boxer 1965, p. 295.
8 For example, Theal cited in Stockenstrom 1934, p. 65, No. 19.
9 For example, Cloete cited in Stockenstrom 1934, p. 64, No. 17.
10 The notion of defining slaves as property alone has recently been challenged by Patterson's study of comparative slavery, but it may be retained as part of a wider definition which includes the exercise of power within the Cape master system, Patterson 1982, pp. 21–7.
11 For example, CA CJ 3113, No. 7, Sale of Valentijn van Macassar, 13 February 1778; CA 1/STB 3/11, unpaginated, Testimony of Hendrik Ehlers, 4 April 1776; De Kock 1950, p. 44.
12 For example, CA MOOC 8/1, 34, Inventory of the estate of Anna Veldhausen, 29 March 1698.
13 Van Ryneveld 1797, Article 3.
14 AR VOC 4264, 25, Case of Johannes Kuuhn, October 1770.

15 For example, CA CJ 795, 12, pp. 113–20, Case of Bacchus van Boegies, 22 April 1784 and CA 1/STB 3/11, unpaginated, Testimony of Filida van de Caab, 25 January 1775.
16 Sparrman 1785, vol. I, p. 274.
17 CA CJ 3603, p. 218, Testimony of David George Annosi, 10 March 1798; CA CJ 2490, pp. 177–8, Bletterman to Council of Justice, 2 April 1790.
18 Sparrman 1785, vol. I, p. 102.
19 Sparrman 1785, vol. I, p. 73 and p. 89.
20 AR VOC 4264, 1, Case of Thomas van Tutocorijn, January 1770.
21 Worden 1982b.
22 Ross 1983a, pp. 19–20.
23 CA AC 5, Burgher Senate to Council, 30 June 1826.
24 Percival 1804, pp. 284–5; Mentzel 1785, vol. I, p. 116.
25 Sparrman 1785, vol. I, p. 73; Thunberg 1795, vol. I, p. 246; CA 1/STB 3/12, unpaginated, Testimony of Maart van Mozambique, 1 July 1790.
26 CA C 650, pp. 774–5, Stellenbosch Dagregister, 6 August 1736; CA CJ 2491, pp. 112–14, Bletterman to Council of Justice, 6 September 1791; Burchell 1822, p. 34.
27 Wade 1964, pp. 180–1.
28 CA CJ 788, 24, Case of Jephta van de Caab, 15 August 1754.
29 Stampp 1956, pp. 144–8.
30 CA 1/STB 3/13, 11, unpaginated, Testimony of Dirk Hoffman, 24 January 1794.
31 CA 1/STB 3/12, unpaginated, Testimony of Tielemann Ross Jansz., 22 November 1792.
32 CA 1/STB 3/12, unpaginated, Testimony of Daniel Malan Davidsz., 22 June 1793.
33 CA 1/STB 3/11, unpaginated, Testimony of Andries Nolte, 14 October 1759.
34 CA 1/STB 3/11, unpaginated, Testimony of Elisabeth Grove and others in the case of Diederick Bleumer, September 1776; Ross 1979c, p. 429.
35 CA 1/STB 3/8, unpaginated, Testimony of Jacobus Meijburg, [1741?]; CA 1/STB 3/10, unpaginated, Testimonies of Jan Lategaan and Julij van Bengal, October 1749; CA 1/STB 3/12, unpaginated, Testimony of Jason van Bengal, November 1793.
36 Fogel and Engerman 1974, vol. I, p. 144; Stampp 1956, p. 164.
37 CA 1/STB 3/8, unpaginated, Testimony of Fortuijn van Balij, March 1748.
38 Hugo 1970, pp. 13–15; Vogt 1974, pp. 106–7 and pp. 112–13.
39 See above, p. 87.
40 Stampp 1956, pp. 171–2.
41 Marais 1939, pp. 173–6; Thunberg 1795, vol. I, p. 114; Ross 1983a, pp. 29–37.
42 CA 1/STB 3/11, unpaginated, Testimony of January van Bengal, June 1767.
43 Burchell 1822, pp. 86–7.
44 CA MOOC 8/9, 6, Inventory of the estate of Reijner Lafebre, 19–20 August 1755.
45 CA 1/STB 3/11, unpaginated, Testimony of Jan Lodewijk Pretorius, January 1764; CA CJ 3175, pp. 2–4, Testimony of Hendrik Gildenhuisen, 14 December 1765.
46 For example, CA CJ 785, 40, Case of Pieter van Sambouwa, 12 May 1735; CA CJ 786, 41, Case of Slamat van Mandaar, 28 May 1739; CA CJ 786, 45, Case of Augustus van Bengal, 16 July 1739.
47 CA 1/STB 3/12, unpaginated, Testimony of Daniel Malan Davidsz., 22 June 1793.
48 CA 1/STB 3/8, unpaginated, Testimony of Manika van Bengal, 9 January 1749.
49 CA 1/STB 3/10, unpaginated, Testimony of April van Malabar, December 1752.
50 CA CJ 3173, pp. 56–8, Report of Council of Justice on the suicide of October van Ambon, November 1760.
51 AR VOC 4255, 16, Case of Frans van Madagascar, June 1768; Van Deburg 1979, pp. 11–12.
52 Sparrman 1785, vol. I, p. 102; CA CJ 786, 69, Case of Aron van Malabar, 2 May 1743.
53 '*sijn volmagt laat die doen wat hij wil*', CA 1/STB 3/12, unpaginated, Testimony of Maart van Bengal, 11 October 1791.

171

54 CA 1/STB 3/11, unpaginated, Testimony of Johan Spring in t' veld, October 1761; Ross 1983a, pp. 29–37.

55 CA C 652, pp. 148–50, Stellenbosch Dagregister, 27 February 1741; CA 1/STB 10/6, unpaginated, Memorial of farmers to Landdrost of Stellenbosch, May 1793; decree of 25 June 1765, Jeffreys and Naude 1944, vol. III, pp. 59–60.

56 AR VOC 4264, 25, Case of Johannes Kuuhn, October 1770.

57 De Chavonnes 1918, pp. 137–8. For discussion of *knecht* contracts, see above, p. 89, De Kock 1950, p. 62; Mentzel 1785, vol. III, pp. 98–9.

58 De Chavonnes 1918, p. 126; Resolutions of the Council of Policy, 5 January 1682, Jeffreys and Naude 1944, vol. I, p. 183.

59 For example, CA 1/STB 10/1, p. 182, Assenburgh to Stellenbosch Heemraden, 11 February 1711; CA 1/STB 3/8, unpaginated, Testimony of Stellenbosch Heemraden on examination of corpse of Maart van Malabar, 2 May 1737.

60 CA CJ 2492, p. 213, Landdrost of Stellenbosch to Council of Justice, 30 August 1794.

61 AR VOC 4264, 4, Case of Jan Harmen Tome, January 1770.

62 CA 1/STB 3/9, unpaginated, Testimony of Christoffel Jansz., 13 May 1741; AR VOC 4146, 11, Case of Jan Leij, July 1741.

63 Stampp 1956, p. 185.

64 One example from many is CA 1/STB 3/12, unpaginated, Testimony of Abraham Christoffel Botma, April 1786. The threat of sale inland is indicated in CA CJ 795, 38, Case of Damon van Bougies *et al*, November 1786; CA 1/STB 3/8, unpaginated, Testimony of Manika van Bengal, 9 January 1749.

65 CA SO 3/1, unpaginated, Report of the Proceedings of the Registrar and Guardian of Slaves at the Cape of Good Hope during the half year ending 24 June 1827.

66 For example, CA CJ 3173, 137–9, Case of Anna Boekelenberg, 2 August 1763; Ross 1979a, pp. 8–9. This compares with the Deep South, Wade 1964, pp. 183–91. Similar threats were used in the rural districts, Worden 1982a, p. 296.

67 CA C 736, p. 29, Memorie gedaan maken en aan den wel edele groot achtbare heeren gecommitteerde bewindhebberen, der generale geoctroyeerde nederlandsche O.I. compagnie, 7 May 1779; Beyers 1967, p. 51; Schutte 1979a, especially pp. 192–205.

68 Craton 1975, pp. 260–1; Fogel and Engerman 1974, vol. I, pp. 128–9.

69 Ross 1980b, pp. 6–7.

70 Ross 1983d, pp. 196–7.

71 CA C 213, pp. 177–8, Resolutions of the Council of Policy, 12 February 1793; CA C 155, pp. 135–6, Resolutions of the Council of Policy, 18 March 1777; Resolutions of the Council of Policy, 21 March 1780, Jeffreys 1927, vol. II, pp. 33–5.

72 Thunberg 1795, vol. II, pp. 37–8.

73 Decree of 5–8 July 1642, Van der Chijs 1885, vol. I, p. 573.

74 Decree of 15 January 1681, Van der Chijs 1885, vol. IX, p. 575.

75 Decrees of 6 August 1658 and 10 July 1731, Jeffreys and Naude 1944, vol. I, pp. 36–7 and vol. II, pp. 149–50.

76 Venter 1940, pp. 36–8.

77 AR VOC 4365, Bijlagen 405–6, Verslag der commissarissen-generaal, 1793.

78 CA CJ 784, 11, Case of Antony van Malabar, 1 December 1718; CA CJ 2485, pp. 121–6, Landdrost of Swellendam to Council of Justice, 7–13 October 1750.

79 Decree of 3–5 September 1754, Article 1, Jeffreys and Naude 1944, vol. III, p. 2.

80 CA 1/STB 3/11, unpaginated, Testimony of Silvester van de Caab, February 1768; CA 1/STB 3/11, unpaginated, Testimony of Josias de Kock, May 1770.

81 CA CJ 75, pp. 160–4, Minutes of the Council of Justice, 1 August 1793.

82 CA 1/STB 3/12, unpaginated, Testimony of David van de Caab, 10 January 1792.

83 Resolusie van schepenen, 15 January 1681, Van der Chijs 1885, vol. IX, pp. 575–6; Van Ryneveld 1797, Article 3.

84 Decree of 10 July 1731, Jeffreys and Naude 1944, vol. II, p. 149.

85 CA C 220, pp. 367–8, Resolutions of the Council of Policy, 27 December 1793; decree of 27 December 1793/11 January 1794, Jeffreys and Naude 1944, vol. IV, p. 224.

86 Venter 1940, pp. 38–9; Van Ryneveld 1797, Article 3.

87 AR VOC 4135, 16, Case of Johannes Groenewald and Jan Verbeek, 25 April 1737.

88 CA CJ 2486, pp. 94–5, Landdrost of Stellenbosch to Council of Justice, 10 October 1767.

89 AR VOC 4223, 5, Testimony of Philip du Plessis, January 1760.

90 AR VOC 4247, 11, Case of Jan Adriaan de Necker, June 1766.

91 CA CJ 80, pp. 130–3, Minutes of the Council of Justice, 3 May 1798.

92 Barrow 1801, vol. II, pp. 338–9.

93 Le Vaillant 1790*b*, p. 102.

94 Resolutions of the Council of Policy, 23 June 1729, De Wet 1957, vol. VIII, pp. 41–2; CA CJ 333, pp. 265–84, Documents in the criminal cases of Jan Botma and Jan Steenkamp; CA CJ 11, pp. 48–50, Minutes of the Council of Justice, 25 Augutst 1729.

95 Thunberg 1795, vol. I, p. 115.

96 AR VOC 4264, 16, Case of Johannes Kuuhn, October 1770.

97 For example, Schipio van Bengal was sold in an auction of 10–11 April 1747 from the estate of his previous owner, Gerrit Olivier, 'following the decision of the Council of Justice of this Government dated 5 October 1737 that he should never again come under the authority of Jan Groenewald', CA MOOC 10/5, 76, Vendurolle of estate of Gerrit Olivier, 10–11 April 1747. Jan Groenewald had been convicted of murdering his slave ten years previously, AR VOC 4135, 16, Case of Jan Groenewald, 25 April 1737.

98 CA CJ 107, pp. 178–9, Copy of Minutes of Council of Justice (Criminal), 24 September 1767; CA CJ 108, pp. 168–9, Copy of Minutes of Council of Justice (Criminal), 8 September 1768; AR VOC 4247, 44, Case of Daniel Conrad Braun.

99 CA BO 49, p. 9, Landdrost of Stellenbosch to Craig, 11 September 1796; CA 1/STB 10/9, p. 121, Secretary to Landdrost of Stellenbosch, 12 September 1796; CA CJ 78, pp. 193–6, Minutes of the Council of Justice, 22 September 1796; CA CJ 78, p. 207, Minutes of the Council of Justice, 6 October 1796; CA CJ 79, pp. 115–17, Minutes of the Council of Justice, 20 April 1797; CA CJ 79, p. 133, Minutes of the Council of Justice, 24 April 1797.

100 CA CJ 791, 38, Case of Johan Kettenaar, 3 December 1767; CA CJ 799, 25, Case of Carel Hendrik Lewald, 24 September 1801.

101 CA CJ 2490, pp. 32–3, Landdrost of Stellenbosch to Council of Justice, 8 May 1789.

102 CA 1/STB 10/1, p. 184. Council of Policy to Landdrost of Stellenbosch, 21 February 1711; CA CJ 2487, pp. 183–4, Landdrost of Stellenbosch to Council of Justice, 19 December 1780.

103 AR VOC 4185, pp. 674–5, Jacobus Botha d'oude to Council of Justice, 25 February 1751.

104 Thunberg 1795, vol. I, p. 114.

105 Stampp 1956, pp. 198–9; Thunberg 1795, vol. II, p. 126; De Kock 1950, p. 186; Botha 1962, vol. II, p. 174.

106 For example, CA C 140, p. 244, Resolutions of the Council of Policy, 20 July 1762; CA C 144, p. 227, Resolutions of the Council of Policy, 18 March 1766; CA C 154, pp. 67–8, Resolutions of the Council of Policy, 6 February 1776.

107 Botha 1962, vol. II, pp. 101–5; Venter 1940, pp. 36–7; an example of such a case is CA C 650, p. 49, Stellenbosch Dagregister, 11 December 1729.

108 Hugo 1970, p. 7.

109 Botha 1962, vol. II, pp. 170–9; Van Ryneveld 1797, Article 3; Finley 1980, p. 98.

110 Decree of 3–5 September 1754, Jeffreys and Naude 1944, vol. III, pp. 2–6; Ross 1980*b*.

111 Van Ryneveld 1797, Article 3.

112 Wright 1831, pp. 10–14; Stampp 1956, p. 227.
113 Goveia 1969, pp. 114–18 and 120–2; Hall 1977, pp. 174–86.
114 Wright 1831, p. 22; Ross 1979*b*, p. 83.
115 Thunberg believed that 'slaves can give no evidence', which was not the case, although it indicates that the potential use of slave evidence was limited, Thunberg 1795, vol. I, p. 115.
116 AR VOC 4288 (unmarked case number), Case of Diederik Jacob Bleumer, 21 August 1777.
117 AR VOC 4146, 11, Case of Jan Leij, July 1740.
118 CA CJ 3603, pp. 365–6, Case of Geijlingh, August 1798.
119 CA 1/STB 3/11, unpaginated, Testimony of Silvester van de Caab, February 1768; CA CJ 2487, pp. 123–4 and pp. 128–32, Landdrost of Stellenbosch to Council of Justice, 21 February 1779.
120 Council of Justice to Craig, 14 January 1796, Theal 1897, vol. I, p. 304.
121 A summary of the punishments for specified crimes at the Cape was drawn up at the beginning of the nineteenth century, Bourke papers, Rhodes House, Oxford, MSS. Afr. t. 7/30. I am grateful to Mary Rayner for pointing out this reference to me.
122 Mentzel 1785, vol. II, p. 133; Thunberg 1795, vol. I, pp. 277–8; Barrow 1801, vol. I, pp. 41–2; Greenstein 1973, pp. 37–8.
123 Sparrman 1785, vol. I, p. 49; CA BO 222, p. 33, Sketches of the Political and Commercial History of the Cape of Good Hope; CA A 681, Letter 16, p. 4, Letter of Mrs Kindersley, February 1765; CA CJ 10, pp. 42–4, Minutes of Council of Justice, 22 July 1728; CA CJ 2569, p. 41, Council of Justice to Landdrost of Stellenbosch, 5 June 1738.
124 Weisser 1979, pp. 133–8.
125 PRO CO 49, 1, p. 67, Craig to Secretary of State, 28 April 1798.
126 Botha 1962, vol. II, pp. 131–2; Ross 1980*b*, pp. 13–14; Huusen 1976, pp. 123–4.
127 AR VOC 4151, pp. 57–62, Case of Jacob van Bengal, 14 October 1741.
128 AR VOC 4247, 44, Case of Daniel Conrad Braun.
129 AR VOC 4264, pp. 38–40, Case of Fortuijn van Bengal, 14 June 1770.
130 CA CJ 2492, pp. 201–3, Extract from Report of Council of Justice, 23 June 1794; CA BO 90, pp. 96–101, Andreas Scheuble to Sir George Yonge, 7 August 1801.

9. THE SLAVE RESPONSE

1 Elkins 1975; for the place of Elkins' ideas in American slave historiography, Davis 1974, pp. 4–5.
2 Stampp 1971, pp. 379–87; Genovese 1975, pp. 597–8.
3 Aptheker 1974.
4 Craton 1979, p. 125.
5 These factors were critical in supporting the internal response of slaves in America, Stampp 1971, pp. 382–3.
6 On broad models of slave response, see particularly Mullin 1972, pp. 34–8; Cooper 1979, pp. 118–20; Genovese 1979, pp. 11–12.
7 A fuller account of the nature of slave resistance at the Cape is Ross 1983*a*.
8 Van Ryneveld 1797, Article 5.
9 For comment on the effects of violence on the under-privileged in Cape Town, Hallett 1980, p. 127.
10 Mentzel 1785, vol. II, p. 129.
11 Stampp 1971, p. 386.
12 Sparrman 1785, vol. I, p. 102.
13 On the prevalence of slave violence at the Cape, and fear of it, see Armstrong 1979, p. 107; Hattingh 1979*b*, pp. 15–19; Leftwich 1976, vol. II, p. 42.

14 Decree of 17–19 August 1686, Jeffreys and Naude 1944, vol. I, pp. 219–20; general decree of 2 January 1687, Jeffreys and Naude 1944, vol. I, p. 230.

15 CA 1/STB 3/8, unpaginated, Testimony of Hendrik Krugel, Daniel Bokkelenberg, Nicolaas Pilletje and Daniel Malan, November to December 1742.

16 Cairns 1980; CA C 138, pp. 348–74, Resolutions of the Council of Policy, 15 July to 19 August 1760. These emergency measures were withdrawn after the murderers were caught.

17 CA C 654, p. 377, Swellendam Dagregister, [?] June 1758.

18 CA C 218, pp. 271–5, Resolutions of the Council of Policy, 24 September 1793; CA 1/STB 10/7, unpaginated, Landdrost of Swellendam to Council of Policy, 12 July [?] 1793.

19 Aptheker 1974, pp. 18–52; Stampp 1971, p. 370.

20 AR VOC 4264, 25, Case of Johannes Kuuhn, October 1770.

21 Somerville 1803, p. 405; Percival 1804, pp. 288–9; Burchell 1822, p. 32; Le Vaillant 1790*a*, pp. 43–5; Barrow 1801, vol. I, pp. 46–7 and vol. II, p. 108. The Batavian authorities also considered that slaves from the Celebese islands (Sulawesi) were all 'of a dangerous disposition' and should be carefully controlled, 18 May 1688, Van der Chijs 1885, vol. III, pp. 229–30.

22 62.96% of the 351 slaves recorded in legal records over the period 1672–1772 were of Indonesian origin, Bradlow and Cairns 1978, p. 99.

23 Burchell 1822, p. 33; Percival 1804, p. 287.

24 For example, Cooper 1977, p. 208; less acculturated central African slaves recently imported to the East African plantations led to high risk escape rates; in Jamaica planters considered the escape risk of African imports to be higher than locally born slaves, although this was sometimes unjustified; Higman 1976, pp. 178–9 and p. 211; Craton 1975, pp. 270–1. Similar patterns existed in other Dutch colonies such as New Netherlands and Surinam; McManus 1966, p. 5; Van Deursen 1975, p. 216.

25 Genovese 1979, p. 12.

26 For example, Drosters Kloof (near Worcester), Weglopers Heuvel (in the Picquetbergen) and Drosders Nek (near Caledon), Botha 1926, pp. 100–1.

27 Boucher 1974, p. 19. Examples of slaves escaping in ships from the Cape to Holland are AR VOC 4185, 673, Case of Jan van de Caab, February 1751 and AR VOC 4190, 18–19, Case of Jacob van de Caab, April 1752. One slave who escaped to Holland 'had the temerity' to enlist in the service of the VOC fifteen months after his escape, and his master reported to the Council of Justice that he had been seen on a Company ship which was harboured in False Bay. He was returned to the Council of Justice for punishment since the Council of Policy feared that 'other slaves will follow his example', CA C 120, pp. 173–6, Resolutions of the Council of Policy, 17 May 1742. A slave attempted to escape as a stowaway on an English ship in 1705, CA 1/STB 10/1, pp. 118–19, Willem van der Stel to Landdrost of Stellenbosch, 17 February 1705.

28 Sparrman 1785, vol. I, pp. 72–3; Mentzel 1785, vol. I, p. 90; Ross 1983*a*, pp. 54–72; Ross 1979*a*, pp. 6–7; CA VC 58, pp. 55–6, Wilson, Description of Cape Colony in 1806.

29 Mullin 1972, especially pp. 34–8.

30 Complete lists of escaped Company slaves are available for specific years, mainly in the 1760s, and a list drawn up in 1767 showed that twelve slaves had escaped since 1753 and not been recovered, although this does not include those who had attempted to escape and been recaptured. It is notable that all the *drosters* recorded were foreign-born slaves, five Madagascan slaves escaped together in 1757, and several died 'in the field' after their escape, presumably from hunger or exposure; CA C 145, pp. 293–6, Resolutions of the Council of Policy, 8 September 1767.

31 Moodie 1838, vol. I, p. 382.

32 For example, in 1751, ten newly landed slaves from the East Indies escaped, ran *amok*,

attacked Stellenbosch farmsteads, shooting one farmer, and then made for Hangklip, CA CJ 2485, pp. 130–3, Landdrost of Stellenbosch to Rijk Tulbagh, 12 February 1751.

33 For example, a Bengali slave attempted to escape only after a Cape-born slave told him the way to 'the path that leads to the Caffers', CA CJ 786, 36 and AR VOC 4138, 25, Case of Cupido van Bengal, 23 October 1738.

34 Guelke 1974, pp. 72 and 251; Ross 1983a, pp. 38–53. There are more signs of such cooperation between Khoikhoi and slaves in the eighteenth century than in the seventeenth, perhaps a sign of the growing identity of interests as the Khoikhoi were reduced to servile labour in the western districts; Elphick 1979, pp. 30–3.

35 CA CJ 2487, pp. 100–1, Landdrost of Stellenbosch to Council of Justice, 16 July 1778. Other Khoikhoi were less well disposed towards slaves; one group of *drosters* making for Hangklip were given away to the authorities by a Khoikhoi who had pretended to join their group and assist them, CA CJ 795, 36, Case of October van Madagascar *et al*, 24 August 1786.

36 For example, CA 1/STB 3/8, unpaginated, Testimonies of slaves Phoenix, Dolphin, Augustus, Pedro and Cupido, all undated [1742?].

37 CA CJ 788, 11, Case of Robo van Bouton *et al*, 5 August 1751.

38 For example, CA CJ 785, 25, Case of Lena van de Caab *et al*, November 1730; CA CJ 785, 28, Case of Moses van Angola *et al*, 10 January 1732.

39 For example, AR VOC 4135, 6, Case of Aron van Madagascar, March 1737.

40 CA CJ 785, 17, Case of Augustus van Batavia, 16 December 1728.

41 CA CJ 786, 34, Case of Moses van Balij, 18 December 1738.

42 CA 1/STB 3/8, unpaginated, Testimony of Reijnier van Madagascar, 8–9 January 1749.

43 CA CJ 786, 33, Cases of January van Nagapatnam, Jourdaan van Bengal, Limoen van Macassar, Fortuijn van Mandaar and Amsterdam van Timor, 27 November 1738.

44 Mullin 1972, pp. 83–8.

45 For escape from the western Cape to Xhosa and Khoikhoi settlements, Ross 1983a, pp. 38–53 and 81–95. In New Amsterdam escape into neighbouring territory was relatively easy whilst *drosters* from Dutch Curaçao were offered protection by the Spanish crown in Venezuela, McManus 1966, p. 21; Römer 1976, pp. 183–4.

46 Despatch from Governor and Council to the Heren XVII, 27 March 1680, Moodie 1838, vol. I, p. 374.

47 Despatch from Governor and Council to the Heren XVII, 27 March 1680, Moodie 1838, vol. I, p. 374.

48 Decree of 18–27 September 1714, Jeffreys and Naude 1944, vol. II, pp. 38–9.

49 CA BRD 12, pp. 197–8, Petition of Cape farmers to Burgerraad, 1744.

50 For example, CA C 650, pp. 665–6, Stellenbosch Dagregister, 1 September 1735.

51 De Chavonnes 1918, p. 104.

52 CA SO 3/1, unpaginated, Report of the Proceedings of the Registrar and Guardian of Slaves at the Cape of Good Hope during the half year ending 24 June 1827.

53 Greenstein 1973, p. 32.

54 Percival 1804, p. 298. One slave stated after his capture that he had been living from food supplied by another slave who knew that he was hiding in the vicinity, CA 1/STB 3/11, unpaginated, Testimony of Gerrit Marits, 8 June 1775. Another was captured after he was reported by slave shepherds whom he had approached for flints and tobacco, CA 1/STB 3/11, unpaginated, Testimony of Charl Theron, 25 March 1768. Damberger found in his travels through the western Cape that he could obtain food from slaves 'in pastures and fields' without the knowledge of their owners, Damberger 1801, pp. 39–40.

55 CA 1/STB 3/12, unpaginated, Testimonies of Pieter Hugo, Johannes Hartog, Jan Hartman, and widow of Hendrik Hottenkamp, September 1793.

56 For example, CA CJ 785, 32, Case of Pagalet van de Cust Coromandel, 2 October 1732.

57 CA 1/STB 3/9, unpaginated, Testimony of Pieter van de Hever, 4 May 1744.

58 CA A 681, p. 13, Letter of Mrs Kindersley, November 1764.

59 Landdrost of Swellendam to Council of Policy, 7 April 1781, Jeffreys 1927, vol. III, p. 312.

60 This provides a contrast to the Zanzibari clove plantations, on which Cooper believes that the high risk of escape produced a developed sense of paternalism by masters towards their slaves, Cooper 1977, pp. 209–10.

61 CA CJ 2486, pp. 91–3, Landdrost of Swellendam to Council of Justice, 3 June 1767. Examples of slaves flogged to death after recapture are, CA 1/STB 3/8, unpaginated, Testimonies of Jan Spoeldam and Abraham van Boegis, 27 May 1737; CA 1/STB 3/8, unpaginated, Testimony of Jacobus Meijburg, [1741?]; CA 1/STB 3/11, unpaginated, Testimony of Silvia van de Caab, 25 June 1767; CA 1/STB 3/12, unpaginated, Testimony of Daniel Boosman, 23 April 1790; CA 1/STB 3/12, unpaginated, Testimony of Johannes van Nieuwkerken, 8 June 1793. In colonial North America, corporal punishment for escape was a means of distinguishing between slaves and indentured servants, although at the Cape VOC employees could be whipped for breaking their contracts; Jordan 1962, pp. 23–4; Towner 1962, p. 214.

62 Lists of escaped VOC servants are, AR VOC 4265, 5; AR VOC 4247, 2; AR VOC 4275, 1. A general pardon was issued in 1762, CA C 140, pp. 349–53, Resolutions of the Council of Policy, 16 November 1762. The escape of prisoners from Robben Island into the interior is indicated in CA 1/STB 10/5, unpaginated, Secretary of Council of Justice to Landdrost of Stellenbosch, 24 April 1787.

63 CA C 152, pp. 394–6, Resolutions of the Council of Policy, 6 December 1774, also printed in Moodie 1838, vol. II, p. 34 from which this translation is taken.

64 CA C 656, pp. 388–96, Stellenbosch Dagregister, 7 August 1780.

65 For example in the Deep South, Stampp 1956, p. 117.

66 CA CJ 788, 20, Case of October van Madagascar, 28 June 1753.

67 For example, CA 1/STB 3/9, unpaginated, Testimony of Bernhardus van Biljon, 3 July 1744 and CA 1/STB 3/9, unpaginated, Testimony of Lea van Rio de la Goa, 29 July 1744.

68 Attempts were made to use a pass system for slaves as early as 1709; decree of 5 February 1709, Jeffreys and Naude 1944, vol. II, pp. 10–11.

69 CA CJ 795, 38, Case of August van de Caab *et al*, 23 November 1786.

70 Hattingh 1979b, p. 10; Valentyn 1726, vol. I, p. 136.

71 CA 1/STB 10/1, pp. 4–13, Council of Policy to Landdrost of Stellenbosch, 31 July 1690; Hattingh 1979b, pp. 9–10; decree of 29 July to 23 August 1690, Jeffreys and Naude 1944, vol. I, pp. 258–9.

72 CA BKRD 1, pp. 142–3, Burger Krijgsraad, Notulen, 4 July 1740; CA C 654, pp. 129–30, Swellendam Dagregister, 5 May 1753; CA C 654, p. 225, Swellendam Dagregister, 24 October 1755; CA C 657, pp. 65–8, Stellenbosch Dagregister, 9 April 1782.

73 CA C 652, pp. 197–8, Stellenbosch Dagregister, 25 July 1741.

74 CA BRD 12, p. 138, Secretary to Jan Swart, 28 November 1736; CA BRD 12, p. 140, Secretary to Michiel Hendriksz., Michiel Nieman and Jurriaan Appel, 28 November 1736; CA BRD 12, p. 142, Secretary to Landdrost of Stellenbosch, undated; CA BRD 12, pp. 13–14, Report to Maurits Pasques de Chavonnes, undated.

75 CA C 653, pp. 508–9, Stellenbosch Dagregister, 2 July 1748.

76 CA C 650, pp. 734–5, Stellenbosch Dagregister, 12 March 1736.

77 CA C 652, p. 224, Stellenbosch Dagregister, 3 October 1741.

78 Valentyn 1726, vol. I, pp. 213–14; Ross 1983a, pp. 29–37.

79 CA C 650, pp. 190–3, Stellenbosch Dagregister, 9–12 September 1731.

80 CA CJ 2490, pp. 82–3, Landdrost of Stellenbosch to Council of Justice, 19 July 1789.

81 CA C 652, pp. 90–1, Stellenbosch Dagregister, 6 September 1740; CA C 653, pp. 433–5, Stellenbosch Dagregister, 30 January 1748.

82 Ross 1979a, p. 35.

83 Rewards for slave capture were set by Batavian decree and modified by local orders: decree of 1 January 1622, Van der Chijs 1885, vol. I, p. 92; CA BRD 12, pp. 12–15, Report to Maurits Pasques de Chavonnes, undated; decree of 7 August 1743, Jeffreys and Naude 1944, vol. II, p. 209; decree of 24–8 November 1794, Jeffreys and Naude 1944, vol. IV, pp. 255–6.

84 In 1743 a decree specified rewards of 3 Rxds for *drosters* caught 'this side of the Hottentot Holland Kloof and the Picquetbergen', 6 Rxds 'on this side of the Breede River and the Sand Oliphants River beyond the Picquetbergen' and 10 Rxds 'towards the north and the east beyond the Klip and Oliphants rivers', decree of 7 August 1743, Jeffreys and Naude 1944, vol. II, p. 209.

85 Decree of 22 November 1768, Van der Chijs 1885, vol. VIII, p. 551.

86 Decree of 15 February 1715, Article 71, Jeffreys and Naude 1944, vol. II, p. 54; general decree of 11 October 1740, Article 80, Jeffreys and Naude 1944, vol. II, p. 192; CA 1/STB 3/11, unpaginated, Testimony of Gerrit Marits, 8 June 1775; CA CJ 2491, pp. 112–14, Landdrost of Stellenbosch to Council of Justice, 6 September 1791.

87 Decree of 18 November 1672, Jeffreys and Naude 1944, vol. I, pp. 120–1; decree of 3–5 September 1754, Article 3, Jeffreys and Naude 1944, vol. III, p. 2; AR VOC 4135, 27, Case of Clara Tant, July 1737.

88 CA J 210, Notice dated 20 January 1714 bound with Stellenbosch census, 1777/8; CA 1/STB 10/1, pp. 274–5, Council of Policy to Landdrost of Stellenbosch, 11 January 1717.

89 CA 1/STB 3/8, unpaginated, Testimony of Michiel Pentz., 7 February 1747.

90 Moodie 1838, vol. II, p. 19 and pp. 72–3.

91 Decree of 13–16 October 1722, Jeffreys and Naude 1944, vol. II, pp. 95–7; Van Deursen 1975, p. 212; Cooper 1977, pp. 208–9.

92 For example, CA 1/STB 10/4, unpaginated, Council of Policy to Landdrost of Stellenbosch, 25 March 1779.

93 CA 1/STB 3/8, unpaginated, Testimony of Anthonij van Terra de Natal, 21 February 1748; CA 1/STB 3/10, unpaginated, Report of Veld-Corporaal Jacobus Gildenhuijsen, 12 November 1755; CA 1/STB 3/11, unpaginated, Testimony of Schalk Willemsz. Burgerd Schalksz., 21 February 1776; CA CJ 799, 1, Case of Daniel van Batavia *et al*, 10 April 1800.

94 CA CJ 789, 15, Case of Titus van Mocha, 8 June 1758.

95 AR VOC 4146, 11, Case of Jan Leij, July 1740.

96 For example, CA 1/STB 3/12, unpaginated, Testimony of Gabriel van Mallabar, 28 June 1793; CA CJ 2487, pp. 86–91, Reports of Landdrost of Stellenbosch and surgeon to Council of Justice, 22 June 1778.

97 The nature of the surviving evidence in judicial records tends to conceal such responses although there are signs of support, especially by domestic slaves and when owners were threatened by attacks from other slaves. For example, AR VOC 4185, 8, Case of Barkat van Boegies, April 1751; CA CJ 795, 12, Case of Bacchus van Boegies, April 1784.

98 For example, CA MOOC 8/7, 64, Inventory of the estate of Daniel van der Lith, 5–7 December 1753.

99 The obligation of slaves to obey their masters was one advantage of employing them rather than free labour, as was made clear during the 1717 Council of Policy debate, De Chavonnes 1918, p. 126.

100 CA 1/STB 3/12, unpaginated, Testimony of Adam van Mozambique, 17 March 1787.

101 CA 1/STB 3/11, unpaginated, Testimony of Filida van de Caab, 25 January 1775; CA 1/STB 3/11, unpaginated, Testimony of Elisabeth Grove, 26 September 1776.

102 CA CJ 795, 38, Case of August van de Caab *et al*, 23 November 1786.

103 Mullin 1972, pp. 62–4 and p. 78.

104 CA 1/STB 3/12, unpaginated, Testimony of Jephta van Madagascar, 10 May 1791.

105 AR VOC 4255, 16, Case of Frans van Madagascar, 30 June 1768.

106 CA 1/STB 3/8, unpaginated, Testimony of Christoffel Groenewald, [1740s]; CA 1/STB 3/11, unpaginated, Testimony of Piet, 1 July 1767.
107 CA 1/STB 3/11, unpaginated, Testimony of Andries Nolte, 14 October 1759.
108 AR VOC 4185, 8, Case of Barkat van Boegies, April 1751.
109 For example CA 1/STB 3/9, unpaginated, Testimony of Christoffel Jansz., 13 May 1741.
110 CA 1/STB 3/12, unpaginated, Testimony of Daniel Malan Davidsz., 22 June 1793; CA CJ 796, 25, Case of Caesar van Madagascar, 7 October 1793.
111 CA CJ 795, 49, Case of Baatjoe van Sambouwa, 1 December 1787; CA CJ 2489, p. 97, Landdrost of Stellenbosch to Council of Justice, 14 August 1787.
112 CA CJ 784, 15, Case of Thomas de Croes van Trancquebaar, 7 September 1719.
113 CA 1/STB 3/8, unpaginated, Testimony of Manika van Bengal, 9 January 1749; CA CJ 798, 7, Case of Jasmijn van Bourbon, 9 January 1800.
114 CA CJ 784, 17, Case of Jonas van Monado, 23 November 1719.
115 Mentzel 1785, vol. I, pp. 134–5; Ross 1983a, p. 54; Lichtenstein 1812, vol. II, p. 128.
116 CA 1/STB 3/8, unpaginated, Testimony of Julij van Bengal, 6 February 1741.
117 Decree of 19 January 1741, Jeffreys and Naude 1944, vol. II, pp. 196–7.
118 CA CJ 784, 1, Case of Aaron van Bengal, 8 April 1717.
119 CA CJ 784, 19, Case of Adolph van Madagascar, 18 July 1720.
120 CA 1/STB 3/11, unpaginated, Testimony of Maart van Bougies, March 1776; CA 1/STB 3/12, unpaginated, Testimony of Jephta van de Caab, May 1791.
121 CA 1/STB 3/8, unpaginated, Testimony of Pieter Laubser, 9 December 1741.
122 CA 1/STB 3/11, unpaginated, Testimony of Pieter de Villiers, 6 November 1775; CA 1/STB 3/11, unpaginated, Testimony of Carolina van Madagascar, 6 November 1775.
123 CA CJ 788, 22, Case of Rachel van de Caab, 31 January 1754; CA CJ 799, 10, Case of Coetoe van Madagascar and Tea van Sambouwa, 11 May 1801.
124 Sparrman 1785, vol. I, p. 103.
125 CA 1/STB 3/9, unpaginated, Testimony of Januarij van Rio de la Goa, 29 October 1744.
126 CA CJ 786, 44, Case of Hoemar van Boegies, 28 May 1739.
127 CA CJ 10, pp. 42–5, Council of Justice, Notulen (Criminal) 22 July 1728.
128 CA CJ 783, 3, Case of Maria Mouton, Titus van Bengal and Fortuijn van Angola, 30 August 1714.
129 The most serious rebellion to take place in the colony during the eighteenth century was that of the Khoikhoi in 1799–1803, Newton-King and Malherbe 1981.
130 Lichtenstein 1812, vol. I, pp. 124–6.
131 CA 1/STB 10/5, unpaginated, Council of Justice to Landdrost of Stellenbosch, 18 October 1786.
132 One of the most notable was that which took place aboard the Meermin in 1765; CA C 144, pp. 125–73, Resolutions of the Council of Policy, 28 February 1766. See also above, p. 42.
133 Ross 1983a, pp. 96–116.
134 Higman 1976, p. 227; Römer 1976, p. 186; Pollak-Eltz 1977, pp. 442 and 444; Genovese 1979, pp. 82–125.
135 CA A 378 (d), pp. 12–16, Cory, 'Short history of slavery at the Cape'; Lourens, 'The revolt of the Malmesbury slaves', source unknown, Cape Archives Press Cuttings, vol. XIX, p. 72; Ross 1983a, pp. 96–116; Mnguni 1952, p. 45; Freund 1979, p. 224.
136 Craton 1979, pp. 116–21; Craton 1982a, pp. 100–22.
137 AR VOC 4006, p. 80, Despatch of Heren XVII to Batavia, 25 September 1670.
138 Examples of the prevalence of suicide in other slave societies are, Roberts 1957, pp. 224–5; Stampp 1956, pp. 128–9; Russell 1946, pp. 429–30; Römer 1976, pp. 183–5.
139 For example, CA CJ 10, pp. 42–5, Council of Justice, Notulen (Criminal), 22 July 1728; CA CJ 785, 44, Case of Baatjoe van Bougies, 1 December 1735; CA CJ 3173, pp. 56–8, Report

on the death of October van Ambon, 27 November 1760; CA C 650, p. 816, Stellenbosch
Dagregister, 21 December 1736.

140 CA CJ 2492, p. 213, Landdrost of Stellenbosch to Council of Justice, 30 August 1794; CA CJ
2492, pp. 222–3, Landdrost of Stellenbosch to Council of Justice, 26 September 1794.

141 CA CJ 3173, pp. 79–81, Report on the death of Julij van Bengal, 31 March 1761.

142 CA C 147, pp. 301–2, Resolutions of the Council of Policy, 14 November 1769.

143 CA CJ 2489, pp. 42–3, Landdrost of Swellendam to Council of Justice, 28 December 1786.

144 CA CJ 2485, pp. 52–4, Landdrost of Stellenbosch to Council of Justice, 6 September 1741.

145 CA CJ 2489, pp. 161–2, Landdrost of Stellenbosch to Council of Justice, 27 November 1788.

146 Despite the claim of Adam Tas of a high burgher suicide rate in the 1700s, De Wet 1981,
pp. 178–9; CA CJ 3172–3175, Annotatie boeken en dokumente re verongelukkes en zelf-
moorden, 1705–92.

147 CA CJ 3172–3175, Annotatie boeken en dokumente re verongelukkes en zelf-moorden,
1705–92.

148 CA CJ 786, 42, Case of Cupido van Mallabaar, 28 May 1739.

149 For example, CA CJ 3173, pp. 21–3, Report on the death of Alexander van de Caab, 22
October 1757; CA CJ 3173, pp. 58–61, Report on the death of an unnamed slave belonging
to Jan Meijers, 4 December 1760. One estimate of slave suicides in North America concludes
that 60% of them took place immediately after sales, Russell 1946, pp. 429–30.

150 CA CJ 2489, pp. 42–7, Landdrost of Swellendam to Council of Justice, 28 October 1786; CA
CJ 2489, pp. 59–64, Council of Justice to Landdrost of Swellendam, 27 December 1786.

10. SLAVERY AND CAPE SOCIETY

1 Legassick notes of the eighteenth century that, 'if there was a trend in class relationships . . . it
was a trend away from master–slave towards chief–subject or patron–client on the frontier',
Legassick 1980, p. 68. The coercive but less rigid social order of the 'open' frontier during the
VOC period is discussed in Giliomee 1981, especially pp. 82–8.

2 For example, Freund 1976; Giliomee and Elphick 1979; Van Arkel, Quispel and Ross 1983.

3 One recent study of the late eighteenth-century Cape stresses that the colony had 'a class
society in which race mattered in the determination of status but was not all-important' and
in comparing it to the Deep South stated that, 'one cannot yet speak confidently of racial
castes, as one could for the South of the same era, because there was relatively little legalised
discrimination against free people of colour', Fredrickson 1981, pp. 84–5. For criticisms of
this view in relation to slavery and race at the Cape, Giliomee 1983, especially pp. 12–17;
Elphick 1983, pp. 508–12.

4 Ross 1983d, especially pp. 195–7.

5 Ross 1976, p. 955; Ross 1981, p. 9 and footnote 22.

6 Armstrong 1979, p. 98.

7 De Chavonnes 1918, p. 137; Patterson 1975, p. 189.

8 Van Ryneveld 1797, Article 6.

9 Barrow 1801, vol. I, p. 47.

10 William Crout to his parents, 26 July 1826, cited in Long 1947, pp. 88–91.

11 See above, p. 8.

12 Hoge 1933.

13 This contrasts with the cultural disunity of East African plantation owners and was more
akin to the pattern of New World slaveholding societies, Cooper 1977, p. 267.

14 CA 1/STB 3/8, unpaginated, Testimony of Hendrik Tessenaar, 6 October 1743. My
emphasis.

15 CA 1/STB 3/9, unpaginated, Testimony of Lea van Rio de la Goa, 29 July 1744. My
emphasis.

16 This a feature which occurred in some African slave societies, Cooper 1979, pp. 123–4; Klein 1978, p. 605.
17 American slave studies have demonstrated the inadequacy of the belief of many masters that slaves constituted an undifferentiated population, Sio 1967, p. 341.
18 Two examples of slaves betraying *drosters* are CA 1/STB 3/11, unpaginated, Testimonies of Charl Theron, Coridon van de Cust Coromandel and Manuel van Bougies, March 1768; AR VOC 4135, 6, Case of Aron van Madagascar, 28 March 1737.
19 Elphick 1977, pp. 175–81; Ross 1979*b*.
20 Cited in Newton-King 1981, p. 14. For comment on the coercion of Khoikhoi labourers in Graaff-Reinet district in the late eighteenth century, Newton-King 1980*b*, pp. 1–2.
21 Barrow 1801, vol. II, p. 109.
22 Worden 1982*a*, p. 376.
23 Ross 1979*b*, p. 87.
24 Fredrickson 1981, p. 149; CA CJ 798, 13, Case of Carel Hardenberg, 30 April 1800.
25 Worden 1982*a*, pp. 377–8.
26 Elphick and Shell 1979, p. 140; Hattingh 1983.
27 Giliomee and Elphick 1979, pp. 369–70.
28 Cruse 1947, p. 253.
29 Thunberg 1795, vol. I, p. 140. The main revisionist view is Elphick and Shell 1979, pp. 135–45. On the United States, McClelland and Zeckhauser 1982, p. 16.
30 De la Caille 1751, pp. 310–11.
31 CA C 218, pp. 63–71, Resolutions of the Council of Policy, 4 September 1793.
32 Mentzel 1785, vol. I, p. 117; Böeseken 1983, pp. 71–2; Fredrickson 1981, pp. 82–3.
33 Thunberg 1795, vol. I, p. 233.
34 Worden 1982*a*, pp. 383–4.
35 Cruse 1947, p. 253; Elphick and Shell 1979, pp. 135–45; Patterson 1975, pp. 180–2.
36 Tannenbaum 1947, pp. 68–71; Müller 1973, p. 27.
37 Fredrickson 1981, pp. 96–8; Sutherland 1980*b*, especially pp. 16–19.
38 Patterson 1975, pp. 200–1; Legassick 1980, pp. 55–6; Giliomee and Elphick 1979, p. 373.
39 Hughes 1979, p. 47.
40 Elphick and Shell 1979, pp. 148–9.
41 Despatch from Heren XVII to Simon van der Stel and Council of Policy, 8 June 1682, Moodie 1838, vol. I, pp. 387–8.
42 MacCrone 1937, pp. 71–2; Böeseken 1970, pp. 15–16; Guelke 1974, p. 5.
43 Worden 1982*a*, pp. 387–8.
44 Hattingh 1981*a*, pp. 12–66.
45 Cairns 1979, pp. 85–6 and pp. 96–7.
46 Le Vaillant 1790*a*, vol. II, p. 370; Forbes 1965, p. 120.
47 CA MOOC 8/1, 33, Inventory of estate of Armour Willemsz. Basson, 1698.
48 CA MOOC 8/6, 47, Inventory of estate of Helena van de Kaap and Vrijswart Jan Pietersz., 14 July 1741.
49 Elphick and Shell 1979, p. 150.
50 Hattingh 1981*a*, pp. 67–75.
51 Mentzel 1785, vol. II, p. 131.
52 AR VOC 4276, Cape district census returns, 1773. Precise figures cannot be determined exactly from the census but this appears to have been the average figure for this period.
53 Elphick and Shell 1979, p. 149, although no precise figures for urban Free Blacks can be drawn from the census returns.
54 An example of a wealthy free black estate is CA MOOC 8/6, 74, Inventory of the estate of Cornelius Jansz. van Bengalen, 14–15 June, 1744.
55 Elphick and Shell 1979, pp. 152–5.

56 CA MOOC 8/1–8/22, Inventories, 1685–1800.
57 Giliomee and Elphick 1979, pp. 372–3.
58 Böeseken 1970, pp. 15–16.
59 Tas 1705, p. 274; CA 1/STB 10/3, unpaginated, Notes of Governor Tulbagh to Landdrost and Heemraden of Stellenbosch, 6 June 1752.
60 For example, Case of 2 September 1680, Moodie 1838, p. 385.
61 CA 1/STB 3/9, unpaginated, Testimony of January van Rio de la Goa and Francois Retief, 29 October 1744.
62 Grosse-Venhaus 1976, p. 962.
63 Hattingh 1981*a*, p. 41.
64 Decree of 29 September 1722, Jeffreys and Naude 1944, vol. II, p. 93. I am grateful to Candy Malherbe for this reference.
65 CA C 190, pp. 311–20, Memorial of Jan Smook to Council of Policy, received 19 November 1790. A case of exclusion of half-castes in Swellendam in 1780 is mentioned in Guelke 1974, p. 377.
66 Decree of 12 November 1765, Jeffreys and Naude 1944, vol. III, p. 62; Marais 1943, pp. 62–4; Elphick and Shell 1979, p. 146.
67 Davids 1981, p. 181.
68 Heese 1971, pp. 17–20.
69 Fredrickson 1981, p. 95.
70 Boxer 1965, pp. 220–2.
71 Ross 1975, pp. 223–4 and p. 230.
72 De Kock 1950, pp. 116–17; Heese 1971, p. 19; Anon 1953, pp. 23–5.
73 Fredrickson 1981, pp. 99–124.
74 Mentzel 1785, vol. I, p. 116 and vol. II, p. 125; Valkhoff 1972, pp. 99–106; Ross 1980*a*, pp. 5–6.
75 Le Vaillant 1790*a*, pp. 100–1; CA VC 58, pp. 29–30 and p. 32, Wilson's Description of Cape Colony in 1806.
76 Decree of 26 November 1681, Jeffreys and Naude 1944, vol. I, pp. 179–80; Fredrickson 1981, pp. 112–13; Greenstein 1973, pp. 30–1; Patterson 1975, p. 177; Marais 1939, p. 10.
77 Böeseken 1938, pp. 69–71; Elphick and Shell 1979, p. 126.
78 Sentence of Cupido van Bengal, 3 February 1681, Moodie 1838, vol. I, p. 384; Böeseken 1970, pp. 14–15. Other restrictions on inter-racial sexual contact in the seventeenth century are discussed in Giliomee 1977, p. 17.
79 Mentzel 1785, vol. II, p. 130; Freund 1976, pp. 58–61; Elphick 1983, p. 511.
80 Mentzel 1785, vol. II, pp. 109–10.
81 Mentzel 1785, vol. II, p. 130.
82 Sparrman 1785, vol. I, p. 101.
83 CA 1/STB 3/11, unpaginated, Testimony of Elisabeth Grove *et al*, 26 September 1776; AR VOC 4288, Case of Diederick Bleumer, August 1777. Ross cites this case as 'unique' although points out that 'the absence of other such prosecutions would seem to suggest that Bleumer's behaviour was rarely followed by other white men', Ross 1979*c*, p. 429.
84 CA 1/STB 3/12, unpaginated, Testimonies of Maart van Mozambique and Gerhardus Croezer, 1 July 1790.
85 CA 1/STB 3/12, unpaginated, Testimonies of Anna Dorothea Otto, Jan de Vos and Isaak de Vlaming, 18–19 August 1788; CA CJ 2489, pp. 154–6, Landdrost of Stellenbosch to Council of Justice, 14 August 1788 and 17 August 1788; CA CJ 195, 56, Case of David Malan Davidsz., 5 March 1789; CA C 183, pp. 304–50, Resolutions of the Council of Policy, 19 October 1789.
86 Sparrman 1785, vol. I, p. 94; Thunberg 1795, vol. I, pp. 137–8. Valkhoff 1972, pp. 114–15.
87 CA CJ 2488, p. 136, Landdrost of Swellendam to Council of Justice, 10 May 1783.

88 Thunberg 1795, vol. I, p. 112.
89 CA BO 222, p. 33, Sketches of the commercial and political history of the Cape of Good Hope; Burchell 1822, p. 32; Percival 1804, p. 285.
90 Batavian decree of 20 March 1766, Van der Chijs 1885, vol. VIII, p. 109; Van Ryneveld 1795, Article 3.
91 Thunberg 1795, vol. II, p. 127.
92 Freund 1976, pp. 62–3; Sutherland 1980*b*, p. 11; Cooper 1977, pp. 195–9.
93 Boxer 1965, pp. 232–3 and p. 230.
94 Sparrman 1785, vol. I, p. 264; Giliomee and Elphick 1979, p. 381.
95 Sparrman 1785, vol. I, p. 264; Vos 1911, pp. 217–18; Mnguni 1952, pp. 39–41.
96 Cooper 1979, p. 122.
97 Noel 1972; Cooper 1979, pp. 121–2; Sio 1967, p. 340.
98 Fredrickson 1979, pp. 74–5.
99 Jordan 1961, pp. 243–50.
100 Hughes 1979, p. 47.
101 Legassick 1980, p. 54; Schutte 1979*a*.
102 For which views see especially Legassick 1980, especially pp. 48–52; Freund 1976, p. 55.
103 A useful study of the Cape political economy and the role of social stratification within it is Leftwich 1976, especially chapter 3.
104 Giliomee and Elphick 1979, pp. 383–4.
105 Legassick 1980, p. 56; Davenport 1977, p. 24; Gray 1975, p. 450; Atmore and Marks 1980, pp. 6–8. The latest argument for the intensification and spread of racial divisions of labour in nineteenth-century South Africa places greater emphasis on the post-emancipation rural Cape than on the industrial sectors of the Rand, Van Arkel, Quispel and Ross 1983, pp. 62–70.
106 MacCrone 1937, pp. 78–9.
107 Giliomee 1977, p. 35.
108 Davis 1966, pp. 223–61.
109 Judges 1977, especially part 3; Bradlow 1983.
110 Ross 1983*b*, p. 15, comments on this gap in South African historiography and both Robert Ross and myself are beginning to examine post-emancipation labour relations in the rural Cape. John Marincowitz is currently working on rural labour and resistance in the Cape during this period for a PhD thesis (University of London).

Bibliography

A. MANUSCRIPT SOURCES

1 Cape (Government) Archives, Cape Town (CA)

1/1 Raad van Politie (Council of Policy) 1652–1795 (C)
C 24–C 231   Resolutien, 1700–95
C 232–C 235   Register op resolutien
C 239   Uittreksels uit resolutien, 1687–1795
C 120–C 222*   Bijlagen tot de resolutien, 1716–95
C 424–C 490*   Inkomende brieven, 1699–1795
C 506–C 582*   Uitgaande brieven, 1699–1795
C 635*   Dagregister van Kasteel, 1766–8
C 650–C 657*   Dagregisteren, Stellenbosch en Drakenstein, Swellendam, 1729–84
C 666*   Dagregister van Commies Holtsapfel nopens Madagarsche slaven handel, 1773–4
C 716*   Placaaten en Statuen van India, 1642
C 717*   Instructien uit Holland en India ontvangen, 1655–1765
C 736*   Memorie gedaan aan vergadering van XVII door Kaapsche vryburgers, 1782
C 798*   Gemengde stukke betreffende slawe, 1687–1780
*Some of the Council of Policy volumes were rebound and renumbered during the course of my research. The references in this work are to numbers in use at the Archives in December 1983; those marked with an asterisk are in the old series for volumes which are being rebound or are still to be sent for binding; the Resolutien, Register op Resolutien and Uittreksels uit Resolutien are the new numbers of volumes which have been rebound

1/2 Raad van Justitie (Council of Justice) 1652–1843 (CJ)
CJ 4–CJ 82   Original rolls and minutes (criminal only), 1701–1800
CJ 103–CJ 122   Copy criminal rolls and minutes, 1761–85
CJ 278–CJ 279   Index to criminal sententien, 1717–79
CJ 304–CJ 480   Documents in criminal cases, 1701–1800
CJ 661–CJ 732   Draft papers in criminal cases, 1711–1800
CJ 781–CJ 798   Criminal Sententien (sentences), 1697–1800
CJ 2485–CJ 2493   Incoming letters, 1729–1802
CJ 2562–CJ 2568   Copies of sentences of persons banished from Batavia, Ceylon and elsewhere
CJ 2569–CJ 2580   Outgoing letters, 1720–1800
CJ 2597–CJ 2648   Wills and codicils prepared in office of the Council of Justice, 1691–1793

CJ 2649–CJ 2685 Wills and codicils prepared in office of the Council of Policy, 1686–1793
CJ 2870–CJ 2913 Contracts, 1692–1790
CJ 2914–CJ 2948 Vendue rolls (Vendurollen), 1697–1794
CJ 2949–CJ 2951 Miscellaneous estate papers, 1724–1800
CJ 3074–CJ 3127 Miscellaneous notarial documents (including slave transfers)
CJ 3135 Index to wills and codicils, 1702–99
CJ 3172 Secretary's note book of inquests held on the bodies of drowned persons, 1705–56
CJ 3173 Note books of inquests held on the bodies of drowned, injured and other persons who died in accidents, 1757–66
CJ 3174 Note books of inquests held on the bodies of drowned persons, 1766–1791
CJ 3175 Documents referring to persons killed in accidents and suicides, 1765–92
CJ 3197 Manner of proceedings in criminal cases at the Cape of Good Hope, 1819
CJ 3600–CJ 3603 Miscellaneous draft minutes, records of proceedings and annexures of Council of Justice and Commissioners, 1784–1790

1/3 Master of the Supreme Court, Section Deceased Estates 1670–1834 (MOOC)
MOOC 6/1–MOOC 6/2 Death registers, 1758–1822
MOOC 6/5 Death register, *ab intestato*, slaves, 1823–1833
MOOC 7/1/1–MOOC 7/1/45 Wills, general series, 1689–1800
MOOC 7/2/1–MOOC 7/2/3 Index to wills, 1689–1834
MOOC 8/1–MOOC 8/22 Inventories (Inventarissen), 1685–1800
MOOC 8/76 Index to inventories
MOOC 10/1–MOOC 10/18 Vendue rolls (Vendurollen), 1691–1800
MOOC 13/1/1–MOOC 13/1/22 Liquidation accounts and summaries
MOOC 14/1–MOOC 14/91 Accounts and papers of liquidated estates, 1700–1800
MOOC 14/212–MOOC 14/215 Fragmentary estate papers, 1674–1799

1/5 Opgaaf rollen (Census rolls) 1692–1845 (J)
J 37–J 41 Kaapse distrik, 1800–07
J 107–J 127 Graaff-Reinet, 1787–1806
J 183–J 233 Stellenbosch en Drakenstein, 1692–1806
J 316–J 320 Swellendam c. 1752–1806
J 433 Kaapse distrik, c. 1752, Kaapstad, 1800
J 444 'Return of the sale of slaves by public auction in the Colony of the Cape of Good Hope', 1823–30

1/10 First British Occupation 1795–1803 (BO)
BO 1–BO 6 Letters from the Burgher Senate, December 1795 to March 1799
BO 18–BO 21 Letters received by Government from Fiscal, October 1795 to October 1802
BO 41 Letters received from Corn Board, June 1800 to November 1801
BO 42 Consumption of corn, January 1801 to October 1806
BO 43 Account of wheat, March to November 1801
BO 47–BO 60 Letters from Stellenbosch, October 1795 to December 1802
BO 90–BO 91 Documents referring to the importation of slaves, December 1796 to February 1803
BO 130–BO 131 Applications for emancipation of slaves, October 1795 to July 1800
BO 222–BO 223 Sketches of the commercial and political history of the Cape of Good Hope, c. 1796.
BO 233 Papers referring to produce: (2) report to Burgher Senate regarding state of wheat in Cape district, June 1797

Bibliography

1/15 Government House 1806–1910 (GH)
GH 1/85   General despatches from Secretary of State, August 1831
GH 23/1   General despatches to Secretary of State, 18 March 1806 to 18 May 1808

1/19 Attorney-General 1812–1923 (AG)
AG 56–AG 61   Placcaatboek, vols. 5–10, 1686–1802
AG 65–AG 67   Extract resolutions, Council of Policy, 1661–1781
AG 71   (ii) Miscellaneous loose and fragmentary documents, 1796–1817

1/21 Slave office 1816–1828 (SO)
SO 3/1   Reports of the Protector of Slaves, 1826–27
SO 3/20A   Confidential reports, Protector of Slaves, 1829–34
SO 3/26   Court cases, 1804–34
SO 7/34   Collected lists and returns of slaves
SO 15/1   Resolutions and extract resolutions by the Court of Justice and the Commission for the Adminstration of Justice for the Outlying Districts in Slave Matters, 1777–1834
SO 15/2   Extracts from various documents, 1717–1834
SO 15/3   Certificates and extracts, 1790–1838
SO 16/2   Agreements, contracts and statements, 1764–1836
SO 17/1   Notes collected from the colonial placcards etc. since 1652 upon the subject of slavery, and Indian statutes 1652–1818
SO 18/1   Miscellaneous slave papers, 1789–1848

1/39 Burger Krijgsraad (Burgher Military Council) 1718–1795 (BKR)
BKR 1–BKR 3   Notules van vergaderings van die Burgerkrygsraad, 1718–95

1/45 Clerk of the Advisory Council 1825–34 (AC)
AC 5–AC 6   Appendices to the minutes of Council, 4 May 1825 to 16 July 1827

2/2 Stellenbosch argief 1682–1910 (1/STB)
1/STB 1/1–1/STB 1/23   Notule van Landdros en Heemrade, 1691–1800
1/STB 1/132–STB 1/134   Rapporte van gekommitterde heemrade, 1746–1807
1/STB 3/8–1/STB 3/15   Krimineel verklarings, pleidooie en interrogatorien, 1702–1804
1/STB 8/1   Schouwactens, 1731–99
1/STB 10/1–1/STB 10/8   Inkomende briewe van Goewerneur en Politieke Raad, 1686–1795
1/STB 10/9–1/STB 10/10   Inkomende briewe van Goewerment en Amptenare, 1795–1801
1/STB 10/150   Inkomende briewe van Veldkornette en private persone, 1787–1801
1/STB 10/16–1/STB 10/17   Inkomende briewe van Raad van Justitie, 1785–95
1/STB 12/67   Taksasielyste, 1741–95
1/STB 16/126   Opsomming van opgawes, 1741–1809
1/STB 16/134   Opgaaf van vee, 1783–94
1/STB 16/135   Opgaaf van vee (ook van koring), 1696–1830
1/STB 16/136   Staat van koring gemaal, 1702
1/STB 18/2–1/STB 18/21   Testamente, 1698–1803
1/STB 18/30–1/STB 18/34   Inventarisse, 1687–1804
1/STB 18/41–1/STB 18/49   Kontrakte, 1701–1809
1/STB 18/195–1/STB 18/197   Lyste van ingeboekte Baster Hottentotte, 1776–1829
1/STB 19/167   Opgaaf van gewonne graan en lyste van gars, koring, kaf en strooi wat die landbouers aan die Goewerment moes lewer, 1799–1804
1/STB 19/169   Uittreksels uit die generale opgaaf rolle, die Statute van Indië omtrent slawe en diverse dokumente, 1719–1853

1/STB 20/1–1/STB 20/8 Uitgaande briewe van Landdros en Heemrade, 1687–1804
1/STB 22/127–1/STB 22/128 Transporte van slawe, 1793–1804
1/STB 22/151 Register van slawe per openbare veiling verkoop, 1816–27

2/3 Swellendam argief 1746–1926 (1/SWM)
1/SWM 1/1–1/SWM 1/3 Notule van Landdros en Heemrade, 1747–1798
1/SWM 3/10–1/SWM 3/17 Kriminele sake: algemene verklarings, 1746–95
1/SWM 10/1–1/SWM 10/2 Dagregisters, 1755–87
1/SWM 11/1–1/SWM 11/4 Inkomende briewe van Goewerneur en Politieke Raad, 1743–91
1/SWM 11/5–1/SWM 11/6 Inkomende briewe van Goewerneur en Sekretaris, 1795–1801
1/SWM 11/23 Inkomende briewe van Justitie, 1787, 1797
1/SWM 12/67 Opgaaf, 1793
1/SWM 14/1 Uitgaande briewe van Landdros en Heemrade, 1745–1767

2/4 Graaff-Reinet argief 1786–1914 (1/GR)
1/GR 15/71 Contracts of service, returns, miscellaneous papers, Bushmen and Native apprentices, 1792–1848
1/GR 17/30–1/GR 17/31 Transfer of slaves, 1781–1834
1/GR 17/40 Miscellaneous slave papers, 1789–1836

3/1 Burgerraad (Burgher Council) 1695–1803 (BRD)
BRD 1–BRD 8 Notule, 6 September aan 17 December 1799
BRD 12–BRD 14 Inkomende briewe, September 1707 aan Februarie 1802
BRD 24 Lyste van burgers en Kompanjie-amptenare in Kaapse distrik aantonende hoeveel geld, slawe en waens elke persoon vir die voltooiing van die Plein voor die Kasteel moes stel, July 1762 aan April 1763; Lys van burgers in Kaapse distrik aantonende die bydraes wat hulle moes lewer vir die bou van 'n nuwe pad tussen Kaapstad en Rondebosch, September 1773
BRD 25 Opgawes van burgers en Kompanjie-amptenare met lyste van Weduwees, Kaapse distrik, 1787–95
BRD 28 Quotisasie-rolle, 1799

6/8 and 6/8a Microfilms (Z)
ZA 4/1/1–ZA 4/1/9 First Nederburg collection, 'Uit Engeland overgekomen stukken', 1791–5
ZK 1/3–ZK 1/39 Resolutien, Raad van Politie, 1697–1795
ZK 1/41–ZK 1/68 Bijlagen tot de resolutien, 1716–95

8/1 Verbatim copy (VC)
VC 36 Reports of commissioners, 1657–1764
VC 58 Documents copied by Dr G. McC. Theal in the Public Records Office, London and the British Museum: (10) Description of the Cape Colony by Lt.-Col. Robert Wilson, of the 20th Light Dragoons, 1806

8/2 Leibbrandt MSS (LM)
LM 30 Precis of the Cape Archives, Annual Returns, 1668–1792
LM 31 Index to Annexures to Minutes of the Council of Policy, 1716–82
LM 32 Precis of VC 36, Instructions to Commissioners, 1657–1764
LM 59 Index to Testamenten
LM 60 Resolutions of Council of Policy, 1742–60
LM III–LM Vc Marginalia, Resolutien van Raad van Politie
LM XXXVIII South African Archivalia at the Rijksarchief at The Hague

Bibliography

8/5 Miscellaneous documents (M)

M 1 Statuten van India
M 6 Plakaten, instructien en artikelbrief, O.I. Co., 1657–1813
M 7 Statuten van India (Swellendam archives c. 1745)
M 49 Serrurier papers: file (n) transfer deeds of slaves
M 142 Laws relating to Hottentots, Bastaards and Freeblacks at the Cape of Good Hope, c. 1826

Accessions (A)

A 45 Summary of prices and the state of the colony by Bird
A 148 Papers related to the Cape of Good Hope, from the Royal Colonial Institute, 1797–8
A 378 (d) 'A Short history of slavery at the Cape' by G.E. Cory
A 455 Henry Dundas collection of papers
A 457 Cloete family papers
A 681 Letters of Mrs Kindersley
A 1414 J.N. von Dessin notebooks
A 1790 Letters of James Williams

2 South African Library, Cape Town, Manuscripts Collection (SAL)

Dessinian Collection (MSD)

MSD 1 Almanach der Africaanse hoveniers en landbouwers & C. [1705?, attributed to Governor William van der Stel]
MSD 3 Journaal der zeetogt [van Cabo de Goede Hoop] naar d'Eijlanden Ansuanij en Madagascar, met een korte beschrijving derselver Landen, door Hendrik Frappé [1715]
MSD 5 Korte beschreijving van Cabo de Goede Hoop door Coenraad Frederik Hofman [173–?]

3 University of the Witwatersrand, Johannesburg, Archives

Macartney Papers (Calendar No. 5)

55 Translation of papers of the Portuguese ship Joachim, 1796
65 Dundas to Macartney, 21 January 1797
76 Dundas to Craig, 18 February 1797
77 Huskison to Macartney, 18 February 1797
296 Dundas to Macartney, 26 January 1798
346 Alexander Tennant to Macartney, 20 March 1798
347 Notes compiled by Macartney relevant to Tennant's letter
350 Notes by Tennant, 21 March 1798
362 Tennant to Macartney, 9 April 1798
375 Christian to Macartney, 29 April 1798

4 Algemene Rijksarchief, The Hague (AR)

Eerste afdeling: Koloniaal archief

VOC I, 155 *Overgekomen brieven en pagieren van Kaap de Goede Hoop aan de Heeren XVII en Kamer Amsterdam*
VOC 4045–VOC 4360 Gewone-en secrete stukken, uit de Kaap de Goede Hoop, Mauritius (Perzië en Suratte) in Nederland aangekomen, 1700–94
VOC 4361–VOC 4366 Verslagen van commissarissen over Kaap de Goede Hoop, met bijlagen, 1793

VOC 4448–VOC 4454 Inhoudslijsten van de overgekomen brieven en papieren uit Indië en de Kaap aan de Heeren XVII en de Kamer Amsterdam, 1690–1796
VOC I, 160 *Originele en copie missiven aan Kamer Zeeland van Kaap de Goede Hoop*
VOC 10,811–VOC 10,815 Copie dagregister, gehouden tijdens een tocht van de Goede Hoop naar Madagascar wegens de slavenhandel, 1696–1753

5 Public Records Office, London (PRO)

Colonial Office: Cape of Good Hope (CO)

CO 49, 1–2 Precis of letters to the Secretary of State, 1795–1806
CO 49, 9 Letters from the Secretary of State: despatches, 1795–1806
CO 53, 45 Revenue accounts, 1799–1800
CO 53, 48–58 Reports of Protector of Slaves, 1826–34

6 Rhodes House, Oxford

Bourke Papers

MSS Afr. t. 7/30 Summary of Dutch law applied at the Cape of Good Hope, undated

B. NEWSPAPER ARTICLES

Cape (Government) Archives, Cape Town, Press Cuttings Collection

vol. 5, p. 53 'Natal survivor of slave days', *Cape Argus*, 25 May 1935
vol. 8, p. 76 'Cape slaves lived in misery and degradation', *Cape Argus*, 30 August, 1958
vol. 14, p. 103 'Slavery in the old Cape colony: story of an ex-slave woman as told in 1910', *Die Banier*, 2 June 1963
vol. 18, p. 284 'Mooi verhaal van slawe-liefde opgediep', *Die Burger*, 26 October 1967
vol. 19, p. 72 L.D. Lourens, 'The revolt of the Malmesbury slaves', *Cape Times*, undated
vol. 19, p. 195 L.D. Lourens, 'What the black circuit found,' *Cape Times*, 22 June 1968

C. PUBLISHED SOURCES

Dates used in the footnotes for contemporary published sources which have been reproduced in modern editions refer to the original date of publication. References in all such cases are to the edition specified in the bibliography.

Aitken, H.G.J. (ed.) 1971. *Did Slavery pay? Readings in the economics of black slavery in the United States*. Boston.
Anon. 1806. *Gleanings in Africa*. London.
    1953. The origin and incidence of miscegenation at the Cape during the Dutch East India Company's regime, 1652–1795. *Race Relations Journal*, 20: 23–7.
Anstey, R. 1975. *The Atlantic slave trade and British abolition, 1760–1810*. London.
    1977. The slave trade of the continental powers. *Economic History Review*, 30: 259–68.
Aptheker, H. 1974. *American Negro slave revolts*. 2nd edn. New York.
Armstrong, J.C. 1979. The slaves, 1652–1795. In R. Elphick and H. Giliomee (eds.), *The shaping of South African society, 1652–1820*, pp. 75–115. Cape Town and London.
    1981. 'Madagascar and the slave trade in the seventeenth century'. Unpublished paper, Colloque d'Histoire Malagache. Université de Madagascar. April 1981.
Arasaratnam, S. 1976. De VOC in Ceylon en Coromandel in de 17de en 18de eeuw. In M.A.P. Meilink-Roelofsz (ed.), *De VOC in Azië*, pp. 14–63. Bussum.

Bibliography

Arndt, E.H.D. 1928. *Banking and currency development in South Africa, 1652–1927.* Cape Town.

Aufhauser, R.K. 1974. Profitability of slavery in the British Caribbean. *Journal of Inter-Disciplinary History,* 5: 45–67.

Barrow, J. 1801. *An account of travels into the interior of Southern Africa in the years 1797 and 1798* (2 vols.) London.

Berlin, I. 1980. Time, space and the evolution of Afro-American society on British mainland North America. *American Historical Review,* 85: 44–78.

Beyers, C. 1967. *Die Kaapse patriotte.* 2nd edn. Cape Town.

Blassingame, J.W. 1979. *The slave community: plantation life in the antebellum South.* 2nd edn. New York.

Blommaert, W. 1938. Het invoeren van de slavernij aan de Kaap. *Argiefjaarboek vir Suid-Afrikaanse Geskiedenis,* 1: 1–29.

Böeseken, A.J. 1938. *Nederlandsche commissarissen aan de Kaap, 1657–1700.* The Hague.

1944. Die Nederlandse kommissarisse en die 18de eeuse samelewing aan die Kaap. *Argiefjaarboek vir Suid-Afrikaanse Geskiedenis:* 1–253.

1970. Die verhouding tussen Blank en Nie-Blank in Suid-Afrika aan die hand van die vroegste dokumente. *South African Historical Journal,* 2: 3–18.

1977. *Slaves and free blacks at the Cape, 1658–1700.* Cape Town.

Böeseken, A.J. (ed.) 1966. *Suid-Afrikaanse Argiefstukke: Belangrike Kaapse dokumente. Deel 1: Memoriën en Instructien, 1657–1699.* Cape Town.

Bosman, D.B. 1962. *Oor die ontastaan van Afrikaans.* Reprint. Amsterdam.

Botha, C.G. 1926. *Place names in the Cape Province.* Cape Town and Johannesburg.

1962. *Collected works* (3 vols.) Cape Town.

1973. *Social life and customs during the eighteenth century.* Cape Town.

Boucher, M. 1974. The Cape and foreign shipping, 1714–23. *South African Historical Journal,* 6: 3–29.

1980a. Dutch commerce and Cape trade in the mid-18th century. *Kleio,* 12: 14–17. Pretoria.

1980b. The early Cape in new perspective: review article. *Kleio,* 12: 37–42. Pretoria.

Boxer, C.R. 1965. *The Dutch seaborne empire, 1600–1800.* London.

Bradlow, E. 1983. Emancipation and race perceptions at the Cape. *South African Historical Journal,* 15: 10–33.

Bradlow, F.R. 1981. Islam at the Cape of Good Hope. *South African Historical Journal,* 13: 12–19.

Bradlow, F.R. and Cairns, M. 1978. *The early Cape Muslims: a study of their mosques, genealogy and origins.* Cape Town.

Bruijn, J.R. 1980. Between Batavia and the Cape: shipping patterns of the Dutch East India Company. *Journal of Southeast Asian Studies,* 11: 251–65.

Bruijn, J.R. and Van Eyck van Heslinga, E.S. (eds.) 1980. *Muiterij: oproer en bevechting op schepen van de VOC.* Haarlem.

Brunt, P.A. 1958. Review of Westermann, Tudor and Vogt. *Journal of Roman Studies,* 48: 164–70.

Burchell, W.J. 1822. *Travels in the interior of Southern Africa.* London.

Buttner, J.D. 1718. *Accounts of the Cape, brief description of Natal, journal extracts on the East Indies.* G.S. Nienaber and R. Raven-Hart (eds.) Cape Town, 1970.

Cairns, M. 1977. Matthias Krugel: his life and family at the Cape, 1703 to 1731. *Familia,* 14: 5–18. Cape Town.

1979. Armosyn Claasz of the Cape and her family. *Familia,* 16: 84–99. Cape Town.

1980. The Smuts family murders – 14.4.1760. *CABO,* 2: 13–16. Cape Town.

Campbell, J. 1815. *Travels in South Africa, undertaken at the request of the Missionary Society.* London.

Christopher, A.J. 1976. *Southern Africa: studies in historical geography.* Folkestone.

190

Coetsee, C.G. 1948. Die Kompanjie se besetting van Delagoabaai. *Argiefjaarboek vir Suid-Afrikaanse Geskiedenis*, 2.

Conrad, A.H. and Meyer, J.R. 1965. *Studies in econometric history*. London.

Cooper, F. 1977. *Plantation slavery on the east coast of Africa*. New Haven and London.

1979. The problem of slavery in African studies. *Journal of African History*, 20: 103–25.

Craton, M. 1971. Jamaican slave mortality: fresh light from Worthy Park, Longville and the Tharp estates. *Journal of Caribbean History*, 3: 1–27.

1975. Jamaican slavery. In S.L. Engerman and E.D. Genovese (eds.), *Race and slavery in the western hemisphere: quantitative studies*, pp. 249–84. Princeton.

1979. Proto-peasant revolts?: the late slave rebellions in the British West Indies, 1816–1832. *Past and Present*, 85: 99–125.

1982a. Slave culture, resistance and the achievement of emancipation in the British West Indies, 1783–1838. In J. Walvin (ed.), *Slavery and British society, 1776–1846*, pp. 100–22. London.

1982b. *Testing the chains: resistance to slavery in the British West Indies*. Ithaca.

Craton, M. and Greenland, G. 1978. *Searching for the invisible man: slaves and plantation life in Jamaica*. Cambridge, Massachusetts and London.

Cruse, H.P. 1947. *Die opheffing van die kleurling-bevolking*. Stellenbosch.

Curtin, P.D. 1968. Epidemiology and the slave trade. *Political Science Quarterly*, 83: 190–216.

1969. *The Atlantic slave trade*. Madison, Wisconsin.

Cushner, N.P. 1975. Slave mortality and reproduction on Jesuit haciendas in colonial Peru. *Hispanic American Historical Review*, 55: 177–99.

Damberger, C.F. 1801. *Travels in the interior of Africa, from the Cape of Good Hope to Morocco, from the years 1781 to 1797*. London.

Davenport, T.R.H. 1977. *South Africa: a modern history*. London.

David, P.A., Gutman, H.G., Sutch, R., Temin, P. and Wright, G. 1976. *Reckoning with slavery: a critical study in the quantitative history of American Negro slavery*. New York.

Davids, A. 1980. *The mosques of Bo-Kaap*. Athlone, Cape.

1981. Politics and the Muslims of Cape Town: a historical survey. *Studies in the history of Cape Town*, 4, pp. 174–220. (University of Cape Town Department of History in association with the Centre for African Studies.)

Davis, D.B. 1966. *The problem of slavery in western culture*. Ithaca and London.

1974. Slavery and the post-World War II historians. *Daedalus*, 103: 1–16.

De Chavonnes. 1918. *Reports of De Chavonnes and his council and of Van Imhoff, on the Cape*. Van Riebeeck Society, 1st series, vol. I, Cape Town.

Degler, C.N. 1959–60. Slavery and the genesis of American race prejudice. *Comparative studies in society and history*, 2: 49–66 and 488–95.

Deherain, H. 1909. *Le Cap du Bonne-Esperance au XVII* siècle*. Paris

De Kiewiet, C.W. 1941. *A history of South Africa: social and economic*. Oxford.

De Kock, M.H. 1924. *Ecnonomic history of South Africa*. Cape Town and Johannesburg.

De Kock, V. 1950. *Those in bondage: an account of the life of the slave at the Cape in the days of the Dutch East India Company*. Port Washington, New York and London.

De la Caille, N.L. 1751. *Travels at the Cape, 1751–3: an annotated translation of Journal historique du voyage fait au Cap de Bonne-Esperance into which has been interpolated relevant passages from Mémoires de l'Academie Royale des Sciences*. Trans. and ed. R. Raven-Hart. Cape Town and Rotterdam, 1976.

De Mist, J.A. 1802. *Memorandum containing recommendations for the form and administration of government at the Cape of Good Hope, 1802*. Van Riebeeck Society, vol. 3. Cape Town, 1920.

De Villiers, C.C. and Pama, C. 1966. *Geslagsregisters van die ou Kaapse families/Genealogies of old South African families* (3 vols.) Cape Town and Amsterdam.

De Vries, J. 1974. *The Dutch rural economy in the Golden Age, 1500–1700*. New Haven.

Bibliography

De Wet, G.C. (ed.) 1957. *Suid-Afrikaanse Argiefstukke: Kaap, Resolusies van die Politieke Raad, 1651–1734* (8 vols.) Parow, Cape and Pretoria, 1957–75.

1981. *Die vryliede en vryswartes in die Kaapse nedersetting, 1657–1707.* Cape Town.

Diederiks, H.A. 1976. Strafrecht en strafrechtspraktijk tijdens de Republiek in het bezonder in de achttiende eeuw. *Holland,* 8: 99–107.

Domar, E.D. 1970. The causes of slavery or serfdom: a hypothesis. *Journal of Economic History,* 30: 18–32.

Dominicus, F.C. 1919. *Het huiselik en maatschappelik leven van de Zuid-Afrikaner in de eerste helft der 18de eeuw.* The Hague.

Drescher, S. 1977. *Econocide: British slavery in the era of abolition.* Pittsburgh.

Dubow, S. 1982. *Land, labour and merchant capital: the experience of Graaff Reinet district in the pre-industrial rural economy of the Cape, 1852–1872.* University of Cape Town, Centre for African Studies, Communications No. 6.

Duncan-Jones, R. 1974. *The economy of the Roman empire: quantitative studies.* Cambridge.

Dunn, R.S. 1973. *Sugar and slaves: the rise of the planter class in the English West Indies, 1624–1713.* London.

Du Plessis, A.J. 1933. Die geskiedenis van die graan-kultuur in Suid Afrika, 1652–1752. *Annale van die Universiteit van Stellenbosch,* 11, reeks B, afl. 1.

Du Toit, A. and Giliomee, H. 1983. *Afrikaner political thought: analysis and documents, vol. I, 1780–1850.* Cape Town and Berkeley.

Du Toit, P.S. 1937. *Onderwys aan die Kaap onder kompanjie, 1652–1795: 'n kultuur-historiese studie.* Cape Town and Johannesburg.

Earle, C.V. 1978. A staple interpretation of slavery and free labor. *Geographical Review,* 68: 51–65.

Eblen, J.E. 1975. On the natural increase of slave populations: the example of the Cuban black population, 1775–1900. In S.L. Engerman and E.D. Genovese (eds.), *Race and slavery in the western hemisphere: quantitative studies,* pp. 217–48. Princeton.

Edwards, I.E. 1942. *Towards emancipation: a study in South African slavery.* Cardiff.

Elkins, S.M. 1975. *Slavery, a problem in American institutional and intellectual life.* 3rd edn. Chicago.

Elphick, R. 1977. *Kraal and castle: Khoikhoi and the founding of white South Africa.* New Haven.

1979. The Khoisan to c. 1770. In R. Elphick and H. Giliomee (eds.), *The shaping of South African society, 1652–1820,* pp. 3–40. Cape Town and London.

1983. A comparative history of white supremacy. *Journal of Interdisciplinary History,* 13: 503–13.

Elphick, R. and Giliomee, H. (eds.) 1979. *The shaping of South African society, 1652–1820.* Cape Town and London.

Elphick, R. and Shell, R. 1979. Intergroup relations: Khoikhoi, settlers, slaves and free blacks, 1652–1795. In R. Elphick and H. Giliomee (eds.). *The shaping of South African society, 1652–1820,* pp. 116–72. Cape Town and London.

Emmer, P.C. 1976. De geschiedenis van de atlantische slavenhandel en het Nederlandse aandeel daarin. *Kleio,* 17: 922–31. Leiden.

Engerman, S.L. 1973. Some considerations relating to property rights in man. *Journal of Economic History,* 33: 43–65.

Filliot, J.M. 1974. *La traité des esclaves vers les mascareignes au XVIIIe siècle.* Memoires orstrom No. 72. Paris.

Finley, M.I 1960. *Slavery in classical antiquity: views and controversies.* Cambridge.

1968. Slavery. *International Encyclopaedia of the Social Sciences,* 14: 307–13. New York.

1973. *The ancient economy.* London.

1980. *Ancient slavery and modern ideology.* London.

Fogel, W. and Engerman, S.L. 1974. *Time on the cross: the economics of American Negro slavery*

(2 vols.) London.

Forbes, V.S. (ed.) 1965. *Pioneer travellers of South Africa.* Cape Town.

Franken, J.L.M. 1927. Die taal van die slawekinders en fornikasie met slavinne. *Tydskrif vir Wetenskap en Kuns,* 6: 21–40.

1940. 'n Kaapse huishoue in die 18de: eeu uit von Dessin se briefboek en memoriaal. *Argiefjaarboek vir Suid-Afrikaanse Geskiedenis,* pp. 1–87.

1953. *Taalhistoriese bydraes.* Amsterdam and Cape Town.

1978. Die Hugenote aan die Kaap. *Argiefjaarboek vir Suid-Afrikaanse Geskiedenis.*

Fransen, H. 1978. *Groot Constantia: its history and a description of its architecture and collection.* 3rd edn. South African Cultural History Museum. Cape Town.

Fredrickson, G.M. 1981. *White supremacy: a comparative study in American and South African history.* New York and Oxford.

Freehling, W.W. 1972. The founding fathers and slavery. *American Historical Review,* 77: 81–93.

Freund, W.M. 1976. Race in the social structure of South Africa, 1652–1836. *Race and class,* 18: 53–67.

1979. The Cape under the transitional governments. In R. Elphick and H. Giliomee (eds.), *The shaping of South African society, 1652–1820,* pp. 211–42. Cape Town and London.

Gaastra, F.S. 1982. *De geschiedenis van de VOC.* Bussum.

Genovese, E.D. 1966. *The political economy of slavery: studies in the economy and society of the slave South.* London.

1969. The treatment of slaves in different countries: problems in the applications of the comparative method. In L. Foner and E.D. Genovese (eds.), *Slavery in the New World: a reader in comparative history,* pp. 202–10. Englewood Cliffs.

1970. *The world the slaveholders made: two essays in interpretation.* London.

1975. *Roll, Jordan, roll: the world the slaves made.* London.

1979. *From rebellion to revolution: Afro-American slave revolts in the making of the modern world.* Baton Rouge, Louisiana and London.

Geyer, A.L. 1923. *Das wirtschaftliche System der niederländischen ostindischen Kompanie am Kap der Guten Hoffnung, 1785–1795.* Munich and Berlin.

Geyser, O. 1982. *The history of the old Supreme Court building.* Johannesburg.

Giliomee, H. 1975. *Die Kaap tydens die eerste Britse bewind.* Cape Town and Pretoria.

1977. 'Race and class in early South Africa'. Unpublished lecture, University of Cape Town. May 1977.

1981. Processes in the development of the South African frontier. In H. Lamar and L. Thompson (eds.), *The frontier in history: North America and Southern Africa compared,* pp. 76–119. New Haven and London.

1983. White supremacy: a comparative perspective. *Standpunte,* 36: 8–30.

Giliomee, H. and Elphick, R. 1979. The structure of European domination at the Cape, 1652–1820. In R. Elphick and H. Giliomee (eds.), *The shaping of South African society, 1652–1820,* pp. 359–90. Cape Town and London.

Godee-Molsbergen, E.C. 1912–13. Hottentotten, slaven en blanken in compagniestijd in Zuid-Afrika. *Handelingen en medelingen van de maatschappij der Nederlandsche letterkunde te Leiden:* 102–18.

Godee-Molsbergen, E.C. (ed.) 1916. *Reizen in Zuid-Afrika in de hollandse tijd.* Linschoten Vereeniging, vols. 11, 12, 20 and 16. The Hague, 1916–32.

Golovnin, V.M. 1808. *Detained in Simon's Bay: the story of the detention of the Imperial Russian sloop Diana from April 1808 to May 1809.* Edited by O.H. Spohr. Cape Town, 1964.

Goveia, E.V. 1969. The West Indian slave laws of the eighteenth century. In L. Foner and E.D. Genovese (eds.), *Slavery in the New World: a reader in comparative history,* pp. 113–37. Englewood Cliffs.

Gray, R. (ed.) 1975. *The Cambridge History of Africa,* 4, c. 1600–c. 1790. Cambridge.

Bibliography

Gray, R. and Wood, B. 1976. The transition from indentured to involuntary servitude in colonial Georgia. *Explorations in economic history*, 13: 353–70.

Greene, L.J. 1942. *The Negro in colonial New Enland, 1620–1776*. New York.

Greenstein, L.J. 1973. Slave and citizen: the South African case. *Race*, 15: 25–46.

Grosse-Venhaus, G.K. 1976. Slavernij in Zuid-Afrika: een overzicht. *Kleio*, 17: 957–66. Leiden.

Guelke, L. 1974. 'The early European settlement of South Africa'. PhD thesis, University of Toronto.

    1979. The white settlers, 1652–1780. In R. Elphick and H. Giliomee (eds.), *The shaping of South African society, 1652–1820*, pp. 41–74. Cape Town and London.

    1983. A computer approach to mapping the opgaaf: the population of the Cape in 1731. *South African Journal of Photogrammetry, Remote Sensing and Cartography*, 13: 227–37.

Guelke, L. and Shell, R. 1983. An early colonial landed gentry: land and wealth in the Cape colony, 1682–1731. *Journal of Historical Geography*, 9: 265–86.

Gutman, H.G. 1977. *The black family in slavery and freedom, 1750–1925*. New York.

Hall, N. 1977. Slave laws of the Danish Virgin Islands in the later eighteenth century. In V. Rubin and A. Tuden (eds.), *Comparative perspectives on slavery in New World plantation societies*, pp. 174–86. New York.

Hallett, R. 1980. Violence and social life in Cape Town in the 1900s. *Studies in History of Cape Town*, 1, pp. 126–76. (University of Cape Town Department of History in association with the Centre for African Studies.)

Hancock, W.K. 1958. Trek. *Economic History Review*, 10: 331–9.

Handler, J.S. and Lange, F.W. 1978. *Plantation slavery in Barbados: an archaeological and historical investigation*. Cambridge, Massachusetts and London.

Handlin, O. and Handlin, M.F. 1950. Origins of the southern labor system. *William and Mary Quarterly*, 3rd series, 7: 199–222.

Harris, R.C. and Guelke, L. 1977. Land and society in early Canada and South Africa. *Journal of Historical Geography*, 3: 135–53.

Hattersley, A.F. 1936. Slavery at the Cape, 1652–1838. *Cambridge History of the British Empire*, 8, pp. 262–73. Cambridge.

    1973. *An illustrated social history of South Africa*. 2nd edn. Cape Town.

Hattingh, J.L. 1979a. 'n Ontleiding van sekere aspekte van slawerny aan die Kaap in die sewentiende eeu'. *Kronos*, 1: 34–78. Bellville, Cape.

    1979b. 'Slawe en Vryswartes in die Stellenbosse distrik, 1679–1795'. Unpublished paper. Streekskonferensie van die Suid-Afrikaanse Historiese Vereniging, Stellenbosch, October 1979.

    1981a. *Die eerste vryswartes van Stellenbosch, 1679–1720*. Bellville, Cape.

    1981b. Slawevrystellings aan die Kaap, 1700–1720. *Kronos*, 4: 24–37. Bellville, Cape.

    1982. Beleid en praktyk: die doop van slawekinders en die sluit van gemengde verhoudings aan die Kaap voor 1720. *Kronos*, 5: 25–42. Bellville, Cape.

    1983. 'Die grondbesit van Vryswartes in die Tafelvallei, 1652–1720'. Unpublished paper. Symposium on the History of Surveying and Land Tenure in the Cape, 1652–1812. Stellenbosch. July 1983.

Heese, H.F. 1979. Identiteitsprobleme gedurende die 17de eeu. *Kronos*, 1: 27–33. Bellville, Cape.

    1981. Slawegesinne in die Kaap, 1665–1795. *Kronos*, 4: 38–48. Bellville, Cape.

Heese, J.A. 1971. *Die herkoms van die Afrikaner, 1657–1867*. Cape Town.

Hengherr, E. 1953. 'Emancipation – and after: Cape slavery and issues arising from it, 1830–43'. MA thesis, University of Cape Town.

Higman, B.W. 1976. *Slave population and economy in Jamaica, 1807–1834*. Cambridge.

Hindness, B. and Hirst, P.Q. 1975. *Pre-capitalist modes of production*. London.

Hoge, J. 1933. Martin Melck. *Tydskrif vir Wetenskap en Kuns*, 12: 198–209.

    1938. Rassenmischung im Südafrika in 17. und 18. Jahrhundert. *Zeitschrift für Rassenkunde*, 8:

138–51. (Trans. in M.F. Valkhoff, *New light on Afrikaans and 'Malayo-Portuguese'*, pp. 99–118.)

Hopkins, K. 1978. *Conquerors and slaves: sociological studies in Roman history, Volume 1.* Cambridge.

Hughes, K. 1979. On the shaping of South African society. *Social dynamics,* 5: 39–50.

Hugo, A.M. 1970. *The Cape vernacular.* University of Cape Town, Inaugural Lecture. Cape Town.

Huussen, A.H. 1976. De rechtspraak in strafzaken voor het Hof van Holland in het eerste kwart van de achttiende eeuw. *Holland,* 8: 116–139.

Idenburg, P.J. 1946. *De Kaap de Goede Hoop gedurende de laatste jaren van het Nederlandsch bewind.* Leiden.

Jeffreys, K.M. (ed.) 1927. *Kaapse archiefstukken lopende over de jaren 1779–1783* (6 vols.) Cape Town and Pretoria, 1927–38.

Jeffreys, K.M. and Naude, S.D. (eds.) 1944. *Kaapse argiefstukke: Kaapse plakkaatboek, 1652–1806* (6 vols.) Cape Town and Parow, 1944–51.

Johnston, H.H. 1910. *The Negro in the new world.* London. Reprinted New York and London, 1969.

Jolowicz, H.F. and Nicholas, B. 1972. *Historical introduction to the study of Roman law.* 3rd. edn. Cambridge.

Jooste, G.J. 1973. 'Die geskiedenis van wynbou en wynhandel in die Kaapkolonie, 1753–1795'. MA thesis, University of Stellenbosch.

Jordan, W.D. 1961. The influence of the West Indies on the origins of New England slavery. *William and Mary Quarterly,* 3rd series, 18: 243–50.

1962. Modern tensions and the origins of American slavery. *Journal of Southern History,* 28: 18–30.

Judges, S. 1977. 'Poverty, living conditions and social relations – aspects of life in Cape Town in the 1930s'. MA thesis, University of Cape Town.

Kähler, H. 1975. Der Islam bei den Kap-Malaien. *Handbuch der Orientalistik,* Dritte Abteilung, Zweiter Band, Abschnitt 1. Leiden and Cologne.

Klein, H.S. 1978. *The middle passage: comparative studies in the Atlantic slave trade.* Princeton.

Klein, M.A. 1978. The study of slavery in Africa. *Journal of African History,* 19: 599–609.

Knapp, G. 1981. Europeans, Mestizos and slaves: the population of Colombo at the end of the seventeenth century. *Itinerario,* 5: 84–101. Leiden.

Knight, F.W. 1970. *Slave society in Cuba during the nineteenth century.* Madison, Milwaukee and London.

Kolb, P. 1731. *The present state of the Cape of Good Hope. Done into English by Mr Medley, London, 1731* (2 vols.) Reprinted, London, 1968.

Kruyskamp, C. 1976. *Grootwoordenboek der Nederlandse taal.* 10th edn. (2 vols.) The Hague.

Kunst, A.J.M. 1975. De handel in slaven en de slavernij op de Nederlandse Antillen. *Kristòf,* 2: 162–78. Curacao.

Lambrechts, H., Smit, G.J.J. and Van Schoor, M.C.E. 1975. *History for standard 5.* Elsies River, Cape.

Lane, A. (ed.) 1971. *The debate over slavery: Stanley Elkins and his critics.* Urbana and London.

Leftwich, A. 1976. 'Colonialism and the constitution of Cape society under the Dutch East India Company'. (2 vols.) DPhil thesis, University of York.

Legassick, M. 1980. The frontier tradition in South African historiography. In S. Marks and A. Atmore (eds.), *Economy and society in preindustrial South Africa,* pp. 44–79. London.

Le Vaillant, F. 1790a. *Voyage dans l'intérieur de l'Afrique par le Cap de Bonne-Esperance dans les années 1780–5* (2 vols.) Paris and London.

1790b. *Travels from the Cape of Good Hope into the interior parts of Africa.* London.

Lichtenstein, H. 1812. *Travels in southern Africa in the years 1803–1806.* First published 1812.

Bibliography

Van Riebeeck Society (2 vols.) vols. 10 and 11. Cape Town, 1928.

Long, U. 1947. *Index to authors of unofficial, privately-owned manuscripts relating to the history of South Africa, 1812–1920.* London.

Lovejoy, P.E. 1983. *Transformation in slavery: a history of slavery in Africa.* Cambridge.

McClelland, P.D. and Zeckhauser, R.J. 1982. *Demographic dimensions of the New Republic: American interregional migration, vital statistics and manumissions, 1800–1860.* Cambridge.

MacCrone, I.D. 1937. *Race attitudes in South Africa: historical experimental and psychological studies.* Johannesburg.

McManus, E.J. 1966. *A history of Negro slavery in New York.* New York.

Macmillan, W.M. 1927. *The Cape colour question: a historical survey.* London.

Malherbe, V.C. 1978. 'Diversification and mobility of Khoikhoi labour in the eastern districts of Cape Colony prior to the labour law of 1 November 1809'. MA thesis, University of Cape Town.

Marais, J.S. 1939. *The Cape coloured people, 1652–1937.* Johannesburg.

Marais, M.M. 1943. Armesorg aan die Kaap onder die kompagnie, 1652–1795. *Argiefjaarboek vir Suid-Afrikaanse Geskiedenis*: 1–71.

Marks, S. 1972. Khoisan resistance to the Dutch in the 17th. and 18th. centuries. *Journal of African History*, 13: 55–80.

Marks, S. and Atmore, A. (eds.) 1980. *Economy and society in pre-industrial South Africa.* London.

Martins, H. 1946. Slave-spore. *Die Brandwag*, 5 July 1946, pp. 12–13.

Meillassoux, C. 1975. *L'esclavage an Afrique précoloniale.* Paris.

Mellafe, R. 1975. *Negro slavery in Latin America.* Berkeley and Los Angeles.

Mentzel, O.F. 1785. *A complete and authentic geographical and topographical description of the famous and (all things considered) remarkable African Cape of Good Hope.* First published in 2 vols., 1785 and 1787. Van Riebeeck Society (3 vols.) vols. 4, 6 and 25. Cape Town, 1925 and 1944.

Miers, S. and Kopytoff, I. (eds.) 1977. *Slavery in Africa: historical and anthropological perspectives.* Madison, Wisconsin.

Mintz, S.W. 1974. *Slavery, colonialism and racism.* New York.

Mnguni (pseud.) 1952. *300 years.* Cape Town.

Moodie, D. (ed.) 1838. *The record or a series of official papers relative to the condition and treatment of the native tribes of South Africa.* Cape Town, 1838–41, reprint Amsterdam and Cape Town, 1960.

Müller, A.L. 1982. The impact of slavery on the economic development of South Africa. *Kronos*, 5: 1–24. Bellville, Cape.

Müller, M. 1973. Tien jaren Surinaamse guerilla en slavenopstanden, 1750–1759. *Tijdschrift voor Geschiedenis*, 86: 21–50.

Muller, C.F.J. (ed.) 1969. *500 years: a history of South Africa.* Pretoria and Cape Town.

1979. The South African archives as an important source for the history of the Indian Ocean, 1652–1795. *SA Argiefblad/SA Archives Journal*, 21: 20–41.

Mullin, G.W. 1972. *Flight and rebellion: slave resistance in eighteenth century Virginia.* New York.

Nachtigal, A. 1893. *De oudere zending in Zuid-Afrika.* Amsterdam.

Neumark, S.D. 1957. *Economic influences on the South African frontier, 1652–1836.* Stanford, California.

Newton-King, S. 1978. 'Background to the Khoikhoi rebellion of 1799–1803'. Unpublished paper. University of London, Institute of Commonwealth Studies, Societies of Southern Africa in the Nineteenth and Twentieth Centuries Postgraduate Seminar. November 1978.

1980a. The labour market of the Cape colony, 1807–28. In S. Marks and A. Atmore (eds.), *Economy and society in pre-industrial South Africa*, pp. 171–207. London.

1980b. 'Some thoughts about the political economy of Graaff-Reinet'. Unpublished paper.

University of Cape Town, Centre for African Studies, Africa Seminar. November 1980.

Newton-King, S. and Malherbe, V.C. 1981. *The Khoikhoi rebellion in the eastern Cape, 1799–1803*. University of Cape Town, Centre for African Studies, Communications No. 5.

Nieboer, H.J. 1910. *Slavery as an industrial system: ethnological researches*. 2nd edn. The Hague.

Noel, D.L. (ed.) 1972. *The origins of American slavery and racism*. Columbus, Ohio.

Patterson, O. 1967. *The sociology of slavery: an analysis of the origins, development and structure of Negro slave society in Jamaica*. London.

1977. The structural origins of slavery: a critique of the Nieboer-Domar hypothesis from a comparative perspective. In V. Rubin and A. Tuden (eds.), *Comparative perspectives on slavery in New World plantation societies*, pp. 12–34. New York.

1982. *Slavery and social death; a comparative study*. Cambridge, Massachusetts and London.

Patterson, S. 1975. Some speculations on the status and role of the free people of colour in the western Cape. In M. Fortes and S. Patterson (eds.), *Studies in African social anthropology*, pp. 159–205. London.

Percival, R. 1804. *An account of the Cape of Good Hope*. London.

Pitman, F.W. 1926. Slavery on the British West India plantations in the eighteenth century. *Journal of Negro History*, 11: 584–668.

Pollak-Eltz, A. 1977. Slave revolts in Venezuela. In V. Rubin and A. Tuden (eds.), *Comparative perspectives on slavery in New World plantation societies*, pp. 439–45. New York.

Postma, J. 1972. The dimension of the Dutch slave trade from western Africa. *Journal of African History*, 13: 237–48.

1979. Mortality in the Dutch slave trade, 1675–1795. In H.A. Gemery and J.S. Hogendorn (eds.), *The uncommon market: essays in the economic history of the Atlantic slave trade*, pp. 239–60. New York and London.

Raboteau, A.J. 1978. *Slave religion: the 'invisible institution' in the antebellum South*. New York.

Rayner, M. 1981. 'Slaves, slave owners and the British state: the Cape colony, 1806–34'. Unpublished paper. University of London, Institute of Commonwealth Studies, Societies of Southern Africa in the Nineteenth and Twentieth Centuries Postgraduate Seminar. January 1981.

1983. 'British economic hegemony and the development of the Cape colonial wine trade, 1806–1824'. Draft chapter of forthcoming PhD thesis. 'From slaves to servants: the impact of British antislavery policies upon class relations in the winegrowing districts of the Cape colony, 1806–1838'. Duke University.

1984. '"Laborers in the vineyard". Work and resistance to servitude during the years of the wine-farming boom in Cape Colony, 1806–1824'. Unpublished paper. Third History Workshop, University of the Witwatersrand, February 1984.

Roberts, G.W. 1957. *The population of Jamaica*. Cambridge.

Robertson, H.M. 1945. The economic development of the Cape under Van Riebeeck. *South African Journal of Economics*, 13: 1–17, 75–90, 170–84, 246–62.

Rochlin, S.A. 1956. Origins of Islam in the eastern Cape. *Africana Notes and News*, 12: 21–5.

Römer, R.A. 1976. Het slavenverzet. *Kristòf*, 3: 181–9. Curacao.

Ross, R. 1975. The 'white' population of South Africa in the eighteenth century. *Population Studies*, 29: 210–22.

1976. Gezin en koloniale geschiedenis. *Kleio*, 17: 950–56. Leiden.

1977. Smallpox at the Cape of Good Hope. *African Historical Demography*, Centre of African Studies, University of Edinburgh.

1979a. 'Cape Town: synthesis in the dialectic of continents'. Unpublished paper.

1979b. The changing legal position of the Khoisan in the Cape colony, 1625–1795. *African Perspectives*, 1979/2: 67–87.

1979c. Oppression, sexuality and slavery at the Cape of Good Hope. *Historical Reflections/Reflections Historiques*, 6: 421–33.

197

Bibliography

1980a. The occupation of slaves in eighteenth century Cape Town. *Studies in the history of Cape Town*, 2, pp. 1–14. (University of Cape Town Department of History in association with the Centre for African Studies.)

1980b. The rule of law at the Cape of Good Hope in the eighteenth century. *Journal of Imperial and Commonwealth History*, 9: 5–16.

1980c. De VOC in Zuid-Afrika, 1652–1795. *Algemene geschiedenis der Nederlanden*, 9, pp. 484–94. Haarlem.

1981. 'The Roman Dutch law of inheritance, landed property and the Afrikaner family structure'. Unpublished paper. Conference on the History of the Family in Africa, London. September 1981.

1982. Pre-industrial and industrial racial stratification in South Africa. In R. Ross (ed.), *Racism and colonialism: essays on ideology and social structure*, pp. 79–91. The Hague.

1983a. *Cape of Torments: slavery and resistance in South Africa*. London.

1983b. The first two centuries of colonial agriculture in the Cape colony: a historiographical review. *Social Dynamics* 9, 1: 30–49.

1983c. 'The relative importance of exports and the internal market for the agriculture of the Cape colony, 1770–1833'. Unpublished paper. Symposium on the Quantification and Structure of the Import and Export and Long Distance Trade of Africa in the 19th Century. Bonn, January 1983.

1983d. The rise of the Cape gentry. *Journal of Southern African Studies*, 9: 193–217.

Russell, M.J. 1946. American slave discontent in records of the high courts. *Journal of Negro History*, 31: 411–34.

Saunders, C.C., Webb, C. de B. and West, M. (eds.) 1979. *Perspectives on the Southern African past*. University of Cape Town, Centre for African Studies, Occasional Papers, No. 2.

Savitt, T.L. 1978. *Medicine and slavery: the diseases and health care of blacks in antebellum Virginia*. Urbana.

Schmidt, G. 1980. Von Capo und Hottentotten. *Kronos*, 2: 17–25.

Scholtz, J. du P. 1980. *Wording en ontwikkeling van Afrikaans*. Cape Town.

Schutte, G.J. 1979a. Company and colonists at the Cape. In R. Elphick and H. Giliomee (eds.), *The shaping of South African society 1652–1820*, pp. 173–210. Cape Town and London.

1979b. Zedelijke verplichting en gezonde staatkunde. Denken en doen rondom de slavernij in Nederland en koloniën eind 18ᵉ eeuw. *Documentatieblad Werkgroep 18ᵉ Eeuw*: 101–15.

Schutte, G.J. (ed.) 1982. H. Swellengrebel, *Briefwisseling oor Kaapse sake, 1778–1792*. Van Riebeeck Society 2nd series, vol. XIII. Cape Town.

Shell, R.C-H. 1974. 'Establishment and spread of Islam at the Cape, 1652–1838'. BA Honours dissertation, University of Cape Town.

1978. *De Meillon's people of colour: some notes on their dress and occupations*. Johannesburg.

1983. 'From rites to rebellion: Islamic conversion at the Cape, 1808 to 1815'. Unpublished paper. Conference on the History of Cape Town. Cape Town. July 1983.

Sheridan, R.B. 1972. Africa and the Atlantic slave trade. *American Historical Review*, 77: 15–35.

1975. Mortality and medical treatment of slaves in the British West Indies. In S.L. Engerman and E.D. Genovese (eds.), *Race and slavery in the western hemisphere: quantitative studies*, pp. 285–310. Princeton.

Sio, A.A. 1964. Interpretations of slavery: the slave status in the Americas. *Comparative Studies in Society and History*, 7: 289–308.

1967. Society, slavery and the slave. *Social and Economic Studies*, 16: 330–44.

Slicher van Bath, B.H. 1963. *The agrarian history of western Europe, 500–1850*. London.

1978. *Bijdragen tot de agrarische geschiedenis*. Utrecht and Antwerp.

Somerville, W. 1803. Cape of Good Hope, pp. 399–405 of an unknown encyclopaedia, ca. 1803/4? (African Studies Division, Jagger Library, University of Cape Town.)

Sparman, A. 1785. *A voyage to the Cape of Good Hope towards the Antarctic Polar Circle round the World and to the Country of the Hottentots and Caffres from the year 1772 to 1776.* Van Riebeeck Society (2 vols.) 2nd series, vols. 6 and 7. Cape Town, 1975 and 1977.

Spilhaus, M.W. 1949. *The first South Africans and the laws which governed them, to which is appended the diary of Adam Tas.* Cape Town and Johannesburg.

1966. *South Africa in the making, 1652–1806.* Cape Town, Wynberg and Johannesburg.

Stampp, K.M. 1952. The historian and southern Negro slavery. *American Historical Review,* 57: 613–24.

1956. *The peculiar institution: slavery in the antebellum South.* New York.

1971. Rebels and Sambos: the search for the Negro's personality in slavery. *Journal of Southern History,* 37: 367–92.

Stavorinus, J.S. 1796. *Beitrage zur nahern Kenntniss einiger Ostindischen Besikungen der vereinigten Niederlanden.* Rostock and Leipzig.

1798. *Voyages to the East Indies* (3 vols.) Trans. Samuel Wilcocke. London.

Stockenstrom, E. 1934. *Vrystelling van die slawe.* Stellenbosch.

Stoops, Y. 1979. The Afrikaner and his language. *Studies in African Linguistics,* 10: 313–16.

Sutch, R. 1975. The breeding of slaves for sale and the westward expansion of slavery, 1850–1860. In S.L. Engerman and E.D. Genovese (eds.), *Race and slavery in the western hemisphere: quantitative studies,* pp. 173–210. Princeton.

Sutherland, H. 1978. 'Slavery and the slave trade in Indonesia, with special reference to Sulawesi: sources, problems and perspectives'. Unpublished paper.

1980*a.* The historiography of slavery in Indonesia'. Unpublished paper. Seminar Overzeese Geschiedenis, Universiteit van Leiden. October 1980.

1980*b.* 'Mestizos as middlemen? Ethinicity and access in colonial Makasar'. Unpublished paper.

Tannenbaum, F. 1947. *Slave and citizen: the Negro in the Americas.* New York.

Tas, A. 1705. *Diary of Adam Tas, 1705–6.* Van Riebeeck Society, 2nd series, vol. 1. Cape Town, 1970.

Theal, G.M. 1888. *History of South Africa (1692–1795).* London.

(ed.) 1897. *Records of the Cape colony from February 1793 to April 1831* (35 vols.) London, 1897–1905.

Thompson, G. 1827. *Travels and adventures in southern Africa.* Van Riebeeck Society (2 vols.) vols. 48–9. Cape Town, 1968.

Thunberg, C.P. 1795. *Travels in Europe, Asia and Africa, made between the years 1770 and 1779.* 2nd edn. (4 vols.) London.

Toplin, R.B. 1974. *Slavery and race relations in Latin America.* Westport, Connecticut.

Towner, L.W. 1962. 'A foundness for freedom': servant protest in Puritan society. *William and Mary Quarterly,* 3rd series, 19: 201–19.

Trapido, S. 1975. Aspects in the transition from slavery to serfdom: the South African Republic, 1842–1902. *The societies of southern Africa in the 19th. centuries,* 6: 24–31. (University of London, Institute of Commonwealth Studies.)

Twombly, R.C. and Moore, R.H. 1967. Black Puritan: the Negro in seventeenth century Massachusetts. *William and Mary Quarterly,* 3rd series, 24: 224–42.

Valentyn, F. 1726. *Description of the Cape of Good Hope with the matters concerning it* (2 vols) Amsterdam. Van Riebeeck Society (2 vols.) 2nd series, vols. 2 and 4. Cape Town, 1971 and 1973.

Valkhoff, M.F. 1966. *Studies in Portuguese and Creole with special reference to South Africa.* Johannesburg.

1972. *New light on Afrikaans and 'Malayo-Portuguese'.* Louvain.

Van Arkel, D., Quispel, G.C. and Ross, R.J. 1983. *'De wijngaard des Heeren?': een onderzoek naar de wortels van 'die blanke baasskap' in Zuid-Afrika.* Cahiers Sociale Geschiedenis, vol. IV. Leiden.

Bibliography

Van Deburg, W.L. 1979. *The slave drivers: black agricultural labor supervisors in the antebellum South.* Westport.

Van der Chijs, J.A. (ed.) 1885–1900. *Nederlandsch-Indisch Plakkaatboek, 1602–1811* (17 vols.) Batavia and The Hague.

Van Deursen, A.Th. 1975. De Surinaamse negerslaaf in de negentiende eeu. *Tijdschrift voor Geschiedenis,* 88: 210–23.

Van Duin, P. and Ross, R. 1984. *The economy of the Cape colony in the eighteenth century.* Leiden.

Van Rensburg, A.J. 1935. 'Die toestand van die slawe aan die Kaap, 1806–1834'. MA thesis, University of Cape Town.

Van Rensburg, J.I.J. 1954. Die geskiedenis van die wingerd-kultuur in Suid-Afrika, 1652–1752. *Argiefjaarboek vir Suid-Afrikaanse Geskiedenis,* 2.

Van Ryneveld, W.S. 1797. *Replies to the questions on the importation etc. of slaves into the colony; proposed by His Excellency the Earl of Macartney, Etc., Etc., dated 29 November 1797.* (Original copies in Gubbins collection, University of the Witwatersrand, Johannesburg and Cape (Government) Archives, Accessions 455, Henry Dundas papers, file 107. Printed copy, undated, no place of publication, in African Studies Division, Jagger Library, University of Cape Town.)

1804. *Aanmerkingen over de verbetering van het vee aan de Kaap de Goede Hoop.* Van Riebeeck Society, vol. 23, Cape Town, 1942.

1831. Beschouwing over de veeteelt, landbouw, handel en finantie van de kolonie de Kaap de Goede Hoop, in 1805. *Nederduitsch Zuid-Afrikaanse Tijdschrift,* 8: (1831) 31–45, 112–26, 196–206, 287–301, 374–84, 445–53; 9: (1832) 100–7, 193–203, 279–90, 366–90; 10: (1833) 13–33, 105–16, 220–4, 297–304.

Van Zyl, D.J. 1974. *Kaapse wyn en brandewyn, 1795–1860.* Cape Town and Pretoria.

1978. Die slaaf in die ekonomiese lewe van die westelike distrikte van die Kaapkolonie, 1795–1834. *South African Historical Journal,* 10: 3–25.

Venter, P.J. 1934. Die inboekstelsel: 'n uitvloeisel van slawerny in die ou dae. *Die Huisgenoot,* 1 June 1934, pp. 25–6, 59–61.

1940. Landdros en heemrade (1682–1827). *Argiefjaarboek vir Suid-Afrikaanse Geskiedenis,* 2.

Vogt, J. 1974. *Ancient slavery and the ideal of man.* Oxford.

Vos, M.C. 1911. *Merkwaerdig verhaal aangaande het leven en de lot gevallen.* 4th edn. Cape Town.

Wade, R.C. 1964. *Slavery in the cities: the South, 1820–1860.* Oxford.

Wahl, C.V.E. 1950. 'Die administrasie van die Kaap onder goewerneur van Plettenberg'. MA thesis, University of Cape Town.

Weber, M. 1947. *The theory of social and economic organisation.* London.

Weisser, M.R. 1979. *Crime and punishment in early modern Europe.* Hassocks, Sussex.

Westermann, W.L. 1955. *The slave systems of Greek and Roman antiquity.* Philadelphia.

Wills, J.E. 1976. De VOC en de Chinezen in Taiwan, China en Batavia in de 17de en 18de eeuw. In M.A.P. Meilink-Roelofsz (ed.), *De VOC in Azië,* pp. 157–92. Bussum.

Wilson, F., Kooy, A. and Hendrie, D. (eds.) 1977. *Farm labour in South Africa.* Cape Town.

Wilson, M. and Thompson, L. (eds.) 1969. *The Oxford History of South Africa,* 1. Oxford.

Wood, P.H. 1975. 'More like a Negro country': demographic patterns in colonial South Carolina, 1700–1740. In S.L. Engerman and E.D. Genovese (eds.), *Race and slavery in the western hemisphere: quantitative studies,* pp. 131–72. Princeton.

Worden, N.A. 1978. 'Slavery and society at the Cape of Good Hope: an account of preliminary research'. Unpublished paper. University of London, Institute of Commonwealth Studies, African History Seminar. March 1978.

1981. The distribution of slaves in the western Cape during the eighteenth century *University of Cape Town, Centre for African Studies, Africa Seminar: Collected Papers,* 2: 1–23.

1982*a*. 'Rural slavery in the western districts of Cape colony during the eighteenth century'. PhD thesis, University of Cambridge.

1982*b*. Violence, crime and slavery on Cape farmsteads in the eighteenth century. *Kronos*, 5: 43–60. Bellville, Cape.

Wright, H.M. 1977. *The burden of the present: liberal-radical controversy over Southern African history*. Cape Town and London.

Wright, W. 1831. *Slavery at the Cape of Good Hope*. London.

Yeo, C.A. 1952. The economics of Roman and American slavery. *Finanzarchiv*, NF, 13: 444–85.

Index

For EU product safety concerns, contact us at Calle de José Abascal, 56–1°,
28003 Madrid, Spain or eugpsr@cambridge.org.

www.ingramcontent.com/pod-product-compliance
Ingram Content Group UK Ltd.
Pitfield, Milton Keynes, MK11 3LW, UK
UKHW010044140625
459647UK00012BA/1601